Praise for

THE CITY IS UP FOR GRABS

"This is a gripping, vividly detailed account of a uniquely chaotic and democratic time in a city almost always ruled by machine politicians. A product of Chicago's neighborhoods, Greg Pratt broke major stories that helped fuel Lori Lightfoot's sudden and unlikely rise to power. And no journalist revealed more of the 'senseless acts of self-harm' that hastened Lightfoot's rapid political unraveling."

—**Dan Mihalopoulos**, political reporter, WBEZ Chicago

"Deep and rich—an enormously enlightening history of Chicago's four-year kakistocracy. Gregory Pratt takes us with him on the trail, inside Mayor Lori Lightfoot's meetings, and around the city she'd promised to reform. Real politics, no fluff."

—**David Weigel**, politics reporter at Semafor and
author of *The Show That Never Ends*

"From rising crime to a deadly pandemic to deep financial stress, US cities have faced enormous challenges in recent years. Chicago, one of the nation's great cities, has been particularly vulnerable. Rich with detail, Greg Pratt's fine book exposes the unraveling of a mayor as her city falls into crisis. This is political reporting at its best."

—**Bruce Dold**, former publisher and editor, *Chicago Tribune*

"Political observers everywhere have wondered how and why Lori Lightfoot rose to power, then lost her way. Gregory Royal Pratt's incisive insights and dogged reporting on this one-term mayor give you all the answers. Pratt's comprehensive and potent analysis will serve as the enduring record of the Lightfoot era in Chicago."

—**Laura Washington**, contributing columnist,
Chicago Tribune, and political analyst, ABC7 Chicago

"*The City Is Up for Grabs* provides an intriguing and detailed accounting of an important time of transition in Chicago government and politics. Pratt takes readers on a journey through the twists and turns of a historic mayoral election, a global pandemic, and a time of intense disagreement over the future of the city. The book props open the door to the proverbial 'smoke-filled room' and provides an up-close glimpse of the people and moments who shaped this chapter of Chicago's history."

—**Becky Vevea**, Chalkbeat Chicago bureau chief and
former City Hall reporter for WBEZ

THE CITY IS UP FOR GRABS

HOW CHICAGO MAYOR LORI LIGHTFOOT LED AND LOST A CITY IN CRISIS

GREGORY ROYAL PRATT

CHICAGO
REVIEW
PRESS

Copyright © 2024 by Gregory Royal Pratt
All rights reserved
Published by Chicago Review Press Incorporated
814 North Franklin Street
Chicago, Illinois 60610
ISBN 978-1-64160-599-1

Library of Congress Control Number: 2023950462

Typesetting: Jonathan Hahn

Printed in the United States of America
5 4 3 2 1

To my mother, Alicia Chavez

CONTENTS

Prologue: Checkers vii

1   The Breach 1

2   "Sixteen Shots and a Cover Up" 15

3   Slaying Goliath 25

4   Pirate Booty 37

5   Butcher Paper 47

6   Bring in the Light 59

7   "I Support Bozo" 67

8   "Trained Seals" 75

9   Early Successes 83

10 Accountability Mondays 93

11 "All Is Not Forgotten" 103

12 La La Land 111

13 "Stay Home, Save Lives" 121

14 Pop the Weasel 129

15 "The City Is Up for Grabs" 135

16 Bigger than the Italians 143

17 "My Name Is Anjanette Young" 149

18 A City in Crisis 159

19 "Adults in the Room" 171

20 "Not a Gimme" 183

21 "False Prophet". 197

Epilogue: Breaking Up with the Mayor. 203

Acknowledgments 207

Notes. 211

Index. 235

PROLOGUE

CHECKERS

FOUR-YEAR-OLD IDRIS LOCKETT WON 2019's best Halloween costume contest for his impersonation of Chicago mayor Lori Lightfoot. His mother, Catherine, had picked Idris up from her cousin's home and found him in a jacket that was way too large for his little frame. The visual reminded Catherine of the city's new mayor, who often wore suits that exceeded the limits of her arms and legs. Sporting a blazer, pearls, and sprayed gray hair, Idris Lockett was called the "mini mayor" by his family. The hilarious look went viral, and the mayor's office posted on social media, "Nailed it." Lightfoot took notice of the adorable news stories and invited Idris, who had survived three surgeries to fix an underdeveloped heart, to City Hall for pizza.

Nearly four years later, Idris Lockett took an excused day from school to attend Lightfoot's final City Council meeting with his mother. They brought her a bouquet of roses and sat through five hours of aldermanic speeches, hoping to get a moment with the mayor and say thank you. She didn't give it to them. "I don't know what she had going on," Catherine told me, disappointed. "I just wish she could've come out in good faith."

Lockett wasn't the day's only snub. Lightfoot's mayoral predecessors had given speeches to the departing alderpersons touting their records together, but she was silent. Lightfoot told staff she didn't want to give multiple farewell addresses, but City Council members took it as one final act of contempt for their institution. Alderperson Tom Tunney, who vacillated between being Lightfoot's friend and foe over the years, texted to invite her to a gathering afterward with alderpersons. "I will not be in attendance," she texted back. "It's better that you all enjoy yourselves without my presence." Lightfoot also skipped the customary postcouncil news conference in what essentially amounted to a press boycott after losing reelection.

The day's events highlighted how much had changed in four years for Lightfoot and the city of Chicago. She entered the mayor's office with enormous promise, winning all fifty city wards against a political titan, only to be rejected by more than 80 percent of the city's voters, making her Chicago's first incumbent to lose reelection since 1983. Lightfoot's early months as mayor gave residents hope for change: safety, equity, ethics. But by the end, residents saw her tenure as a series of missed opportunities. Even though she landed a series of significant achievements, from pushing economic development as part of the Invest South/West initiative, securing a casino to boost Chicago finances, earning credit-rating upgrades and moving the Red Line South Extension steadily forward, Lightfoot's victories were overshadowed by her failures to bring people together. For her part, Lightfoot blamed the media. "We just literally need to go door to door because the cynical, 'we only care about website clicks' press will never give any of us, at any level a fair shake," she once texted US Rep. Robin Kelly.

The rise and fall of Mayor Lori Lightfoot raises important questions. How did she go from political wunderkind promising to make Chicago the safest big city in America, change its culture of corruption and villainy, and reform the long-troubled police department to sulking on her way out of City Hall? What can leaders across the country learn from Lightfoot and Chicago's experience about modern governance and the big issues facing cities? Where does the third largest city in America go from here?

Andre Vasquez, a former rapper turned Chicago alderperson, tightly summarized the problems Lightfoot faced through her only term in office: "It is objectively true that you had the hardest hand dealt to you of any mayor in the history of the city of Chicago." Roswell B. Mason, mayor during 1871's Great Chicago Fire, might quibble if he weren't dead. But the years 2019–2023 were indeed plagued by unforeseen catastrophes, from the global COVID-19 pandemic to civil unrest prompted by the police murder of George Floyd, which exacerbated Chicago's deep segregation and stirred tension over the dark legacy of misconduct by local cops.

No one could blame Lightfoot for causing these compounding crises, but that isn't the whole story. First-term governor J. B. Pritzker drew the same bad hand with Lightfoot and managed to fare far better, now serving his second term. An old political axiom often quoted at City Hall notes there are no permanent friends or permanent enemies, just permanent interests. In four years, Lightfoot managed to inflame them all with her handling of the issues and fiery response to negative feedback, which included a defiant declaration that "99 percent" of the criticism she received is racist and sexist.

Manny Perez, a political operative who helped run Jesús "Chuy" García's campaign for Chicago mayor in 2015 and helmed Lightfoot's successful runoff bid in 2019, has a saying: "Every campaign is on a path of self-destruction." Sometimes that's people fighting inside, destroying it from within. Other times, it's external forces crushing candidacies. The question is, what comes first, Election Day or self-destruction? Lightfoot made it to 2019 Election Day without self-destructing. Could she do it again?

To give herself a chance at making the April 2023 runoff, Lightfoot needed Black voters to back her campaign, and just enough white progressives along the lakefront who supported her original run to stay loyal. If that happened, Lightfoot thought she could pull off a win. Lightfoot understood that elections force choices between sometimes unpalatable options. Every campaign is an exercise in disproving the old adage "I wouldn't date you if you were the last man on earth."

When she was elected in 2019, Lightfoot seemed blessed with extraordinary political luck and skill. Her win of all fifty wards included her opponent's home base in Hyde Park. Before pivoting to politics, Lightfoot had broken barriers as one of the few Black female equity partners at the law firm Mayer Brown and had been a federal prosecutor. She was primarily known for her toughness and used her fighting skills to pound on her rivals. That worked for a campaign that turned into a brawl over government ethics and the other candidates' ties to indicted alderperson Edward Burke. To succeed in office, she would need a more strategic tack, which she proved herself incapable of taking. I think back sometimes to a comment Lightfoot made to me just before an antiviolence march. Noticing a couple ornate chess sets hand carved by members of a church in the Back of the Yards neighborhood, I asked Lightfoot if she played. She chuckled and responded that she's more of a checkers player. Her brother tried to teach her, Lightfoot said, but she wasn't able to get into the game. It showed over the next four years of chaos.

Heading into the February 2023 Chicago mayoral election, Lightfoot faced eight opponents, nearly all of them Black. There was only one certainty as the voters made their choice: the only white candidate, former Chicago Public Schools CEO Paul Vallas, would be headed for a runoff between the top vote-getters. Lightfoot was more than OK with that. The incumbent mayor was deeply unpopular with Chicago residents, who were disturbed by her combative style, dissatisfied with high crime, and distressed over diminishing quality of life, including frequent disruptions to schools and public transit service.

But Lightfoot thought she could fight her way into the second round, then exploit Vallas's toxic association with conservative Republicans and lack of charisma to beat him. In some ways, Lightfoot wanted to imitate the strategy Pritzker used to secure his own reelection: support the most conservative rival in the Republican primary, then coast to victory by reminding overwhelmingly Democratic voters and independents that the opposing candidate has taken extreme policy positions. The difference between Lightfoot and Pritzker, however, could be measured by his high job approval rating compared to her far worse marks from residents, as well as the vast difference between their campaign war chests. The billionaire governor spent millions to tear down a more moderate primary rival and build up Darren Bailey, a Republican state senator who had advocated for the rest of Illinois separating from Chicago, while Lightfoot struggled to raise enough cash to get her own message out. Still, Lightfoot knew many of the Chicago residents most dissatisfied with her leadership would still rather vote for her than a Republican.

And while Vallas had, in fact, been a lifelong Democrat, he spent years flirting with extreme conservatives and took money from right-wing donors, making him a tough sell to a large swath of Chicago. As election day approached, Lightfoot's team knew she faced a fight but thought she was in decent position.

Congressman Jesús "Chuy" García had entered the race as a presumed frontrunner, well-known from his 2015 run against Mayor Rahm Emanuel and generally well-liked. Lightfoot considered him a real threat, so she blasted away at him in campaign commercials, depicting him as a crook. García barely responded and didn't launch his own commercials until weeks later. In the meantime, García spoke in platitudes and shied away from the progressive policy positions that helped make him a household name. He never recovered the momentum he had on day one of the race.

While Lightfoot tried to cut off García, she reserved special scorn for Brandon Johnson, a Cook County commissioner and former educator backed by the Chicago Teachers Union (CTU), which had been her most vociferous critic since the 2019 election. For months, Lightfoot's strategy was to mostly ignore Johnson, believing that he lacked the name recognition to be a real threat. At one campaign stop that January, Lightfoot even mocked the CTU for giving him their support: "They've endorsed Brandon Johnson. God bless. Brandon Johnson isn't going to be the mayor of this city."

At the time she made that remark, however, Johnson was steadily rising in the polls, making connections with voters, performing well in debates, and charming the city. During one forum, Vallas mistakenly called him "Dr. Johnson," and he quipped back that Vallas had "added $100,000 to my student loans." CTU president Stacy Davis Gates had been one of Johnson's top supporters for years. She believed in him. She thought he could win, so she put her energy and significant clout toward making it happen. But she understood Lightfoot remained dangerous and never underestimated her. As an incumbent, Lightfoot could never be counted out, especially not in this city. "Chicago doesn't know how to break up with its mayor," Davis Gates said.

Lightfoot's rise to power would've been unfathomable through most of Chicago's history. For much of the twentieth century and into the twenty-first, the city of Chicago had been ruled by a small circle of men and their political machine. Richard J. Daley reigned as Chicago's boss for twenty-one years, from 1955 to 1976, through the construction of O'Hare International Airport and the Sears Tower, until his death. His son, Richard M. Daley, surpassed his father's record by one year, governing the city from 1989 to 2011 and leading a campaign to reinvigorate and beautify downtown at a time when people feared Chicago would decline. When Richard M. walked away from City Hall, the Daley family watched as his former lead fundraiser, Rahm Emanuel, took the throne.

Daley's effort to keep Chicago an attractive place to live also left the city with enormous financial problems due to his refusal to meaningfully raise taxes or cut services, leaving Emanuel with huge budget holes that he plugged with the largest property tax increase in the city's history. Emanuel, who had previously spent three terms in the House of Representatives followed by a stint as Barack Obama's chief of staff, worked tirelessly to spur corporate relocations to downtown, part of a strategy aimed at growing Chicago's tax base and gentrifying the city. The strategy was successful, but it led to criticism that Emanuel was "Mayor 1 Percent" and that he was only deepening Chicago's inequities. Under Emanuel, a narrative took hold that Chicago was a tale of two cities. Nobody pushed that criticism harder than Johnson and his allies, whose political philosophy was encapsulated by the slogan "For the many, not the few."

Despite criticism over his handling of the Laquan McDonald police murder, Emanuel had significant institutional support and political ambition. So his announcement in September 2018 that he wouldn't seek reelection stunned Chicago. Without an heir apparent, it also created the real sense of a city up for grabs. "This has been the job of a lifetime, but it is not a job for a lifetime," Emanuel said, drawing one big question: who would lead Chicago? Lightfoot had already entered at a time when other people were afraid of Goliath. Political heavyweights who had been afraid to take on Emanuel now scrambled to join the race for City Hall's top job. A historic field of fourteen candidates jockeyed to be mayor—including the youngest Daley son, Bill, who had succeeded Emanuel as Obama's White House chief of staff and now threw his hat in the ring to continue the family business; Illinois comptroller Susana Mendoza, a rising star in the state Democratic Party; and Cook County Board President Toni Preckwinkle, who was the Democratic Party boss of Cook County.

Federal prosecutors further roiled Chicago that November when FBI agents raided the office of powerful alderperson Edward Burke, a fifty-year veteran of the City Council who was suspected of extorting local businesses and had ties to all the new entrants but not to Lightfoot, who was still an underdog. As they plastered Burke's office windows with brown paper to hide their actions from reporters gawking outside, the feds transformed the electoral landscape into a battle between new and old, insider and outsider. Burke was reelected but lost all power as he resigned his chairmanship of the powerful City Council Finance Committee, creating drastic change for local government. Against this backdrop, Chicago residents cast their ballots on February 26, 2019, and, through a plurality, chose a candidate no one had seen coming: the political novice Lori Lightfoot. In the ensuing runoff, Lightfoot defeated Preckwinkle with 74 percent of the vote. That's the sort of margin both Daleys used to run up against political has-beens and nobodies. It was a stunning victory.

As a first-time candidate with limited political experience, Lightfoot presented an unprecedented blank slate to Chicago voters. No one expected her to win, and it was impossible to predict how she would govern. Yet the stakes couldn't have been higher. As a city, Chicago faced enormous headwinds. In the 2020 Census, Chicago gained a small amount of population but lost hundreds of thousands of Black residents. Chicago's Black population dropped 10 percent in the 2020 Census and went from more than one million twenty years ago to fewer than 800,000, leaving swaths of the South and West Sides empty. The result was a number of struggling neighborhoods often overlooked by the rich and powerful.

Alarmists have for decades said Chicago is at risk of "becoming Detroit," but that comparison has never proved apt. The city's economy is more diverse and vibrant, its location next to Lake Michigan too strong a lure for tourists and people trying to make a new life. The home of former president Barack Obama remains a metropolis, with major sports teams in each sport, one of the world's busiest airports, and several prestigious research universities. But what Chicago could face is a situation more akin to Philadelphia than New York—a perfectly lovely regional town but not a world-class city. Whether Chicago can maintain its global status is, undoubtedly, dependent on its political leadership and vision. For four years, that political leadership belonged to Lightfoot.

Some of Chicago's problems can be explained by forces greater than the mayor—national polarization, longstanding cultural and racial tensions, our plague years. But some are the result of her poor leadership at City Hall, a story that hasn't been told in full until now.

★ ★ ★ ★

I covered Lightfoot for the *Chicago Tribune* from the beginning of her political career, when she was a long-shot candidate and some of my colleagues thought she wasn't worth the time of day. We developed a strong relationship of mutual respect and shared humor. When editors asked me to follow her around during the first mayoral runoff, she texted me: "I heard you are being assigned to cover our campaign for the duration. A plus in my book." One day I recommended she watch *Bird Box*, a horror film starring Sandra

Bullock. After she watched it, Lightfoot approached me at a news conference to whisper, "That movie scared the shit out of me."

Our relationship changed over the four years that I covered her turbulent term in office, which included crime spikes, a teachers' strike, and a series of bitter feuds with alderpersons and state legislators. As her administration struggled, her interactions with me—as with many other members of the press—became less genial and often combative. She once emailed staff, "There will be nothing given as placed stories or friendly background to Greg Pratt" and ordered them to "under no circumstances" give me anything proactively. "Are we clear?" she wrote. Later, at a public news conference, she attacked me for raising a question about withholding bodycam video from a police raid victim, calling me "reckless and irresponsible—unfortunately, now, a pattern of his stretching back many months." The next day, she publicly apologized to me after her team informed her that she was wrong on the facts.

Through thousands of conversations with hundreds of sources, I've developed a strong understanding of how City Hall works and how it doesn't. Chicago has been a flashpoint in every major issue facing the United States, from income inequality and segregation to crime and poverty. In recent years, all of these issues have been magnified by the global pandemic, the murder of George Floyd, and racial reckoning in the country. Under Lightfoot, I've watched Chicago wrestle with COVID-19 and two rounds of riots that deeply harmed the city's psyche and continue to grapple with inequity in the public schools and the city more broadly. Consider Chicago's first congressional district, which stretches from Streeterville and Navy Pier downtown to the impoverished neighborhood of West Englewood. It has a life-expectancy gap of thirty years—people live on average to ninety in Streeterville, but just to sixty on the South Side. The median income is $100,000 in Streeterville, but only about a quarter of that in West Englewood.

More than anything, the city under Lightfoot struggled with crime and stalled police reform. In 2018 Chicago recorded 561 homicides, and that dropped to a still astonishing 492 in 2019, according to police statistics. By the end of 2021, that figure had spiked to more than 800—an astounding increase Lightfoot attributed to the pandemic and a lax judicial system, though critics said her police department has also contributed to the rise with poor leadership and misuse of resources. Perhaps her most consequential decision as mayor was to hire a former Dallas police superintendent, David Brown, as top cop.

In Chicago he struggled to fit in and left the department floundering. In 2021 more than 1,000 officers quit, but only 315 were replaced. Arrests were down by thousands. Morale was low.

As a candidate, Lightfoot promised she wouldn't lead "with her middle finger"—a reference to her predecessor Emanuel, who mailed a dead fish to a former colleague when he was young and making his name in politics. Despite her promise, Lightfoot's time in office saw a series of controversies, often created or exacerbated by the mayor's combative style. She has taken an approach to governance that led Alderperson Susan Sadlowski Garza, a longtime ally, to summarize her time in office this way: "I have never met anybody who has managed to piss off every single person they come in contact with—police, fire, teachers, aldermen, businesses, manufacturing."

The title of this book is drawn from a text message Lightfoot sent amid the riots in 2020, when she was exasperated with an alderperson's concern for the civil rights of people caught downtown. But it applies broadly to the political landscape she benefited from in 2019 and left behind. By the time Lightfoot sought reelection in 2023, the city was again up for grabs. She lost in the first round, defeated by Vallas and Johnson, two candidates who expressed polar extremes of the political spectrum. Eventually, the candidate she had most dismissed, Johnson, would emerge victorious to helm the city. In some ways, the past four years of Lightfoot's tenure as mayor are a model for how not to lead a big city. Her failures weakened the office. She lost control of Chicago Public Schools, alienated former supporters, and drove segments of the city crazy. Yet there's undeniably a lot to admire about Lightfoot. The job requires toughness, her most abundant quality. Most of all, she cared deeply about equity in a segregated city.

Over the many months I spent writing this book, people asked me if Lightfoot was aware that I was writing it. She was. I'll always remember the way she glared at me the first time we saw each other after I informed her communications director, Kate LeFurgy, that I was writing the book. To my regret, Lightfoot declined to participate in interviews or address questions about specific incidents mentioned in these pages. While I'm disappointed by the mayor's position, it doesn't change my ability to tell the story of the past four years in Chicago, which I spent sitting in the front row at City Hall, watching the power players, good government goo-goos, optimists, wannabes, has-beens, never-wases, and scoundrels jockey for influence. I hope you will learn from the good, the bad, and the ugly.

1 | THE BREACH
NOVEMBER 19, 2015

SOUTH SIDE ACTIVIST WILL Calloway packed into Cook County Judge Franklin Valderrama's twenty-third-floor courtroom at the Daley Center across from City Hall alongside community leaders, reporters, and lawyers to hear the judge's ruling in a case with deep implications for Chicago and the nation. Calloway had been involved with the city's police-accountability movement since 2012, when he met Martinez Sutton, the grieving brother of police shooting victim Rekia Boyd. A devout Christian, Calloway spent the days leading up to the hearing praying for a just ruling.

The issue before Valderrama was whether Mayor Rahm Emanuel's administration broke the law by withholding police dashcam video of a white officer shooting a Black teenager sixteen times. Emanuel lawyers argued the release would interfere with an FBI investigation into the killing. At the time, "ongoing investigation" was a common rationale to withhold footage of police officers shooting people, and the case would determine whether law enforcement would continue to shroud potential misconduct in secrecy. Valderrama's ruling also had the potential to reshape Chicago's relationship with its government and police department by exposing a profound injustice.

The October 20, 2014, shooting incident had started with a 911 caller reporting that a young man was breaking into trucks near 41st Street and Kildare Avenue on the working-class Southwest Side. Responding police officers followed Laquan McDonald near a Burger King parking lot, where he walked with a knife in hand before he was shot by Officer Jason Van Dyke. Fraternal Order of Police spokesman Pat Camden told media at the scene that

1

McDonald ignored orders to drop the weapon and lunged at officers, leaving them no choice but to shoot him. McDonald, Camden said, had a "100-yard stare." Valderrama ordered the city to release the video, which fully exposed a cascade of lies about McDonald's murder. Following the judge's order, Chicago stood on edge as its residents absorbed one of the largest breaches of public trust in the city's history.

The police story of McDonald's killing had been unraveling for months. In a February 2015 article for *Slate*, journalist Jamie Kalven reported on the basis of the autopsy report that the boy had been shot sixteen times, front and back, and made known the existence of dashcam footage that captured the incident. CHICAGO POLICE HAVE TOLD THEIR VERSION OF HOW 17-YEAR-OLD BLACK TEEN LAQUAN MCDONALD DIED, the subhead read. THE AUTOPSY TELLS A DIFFERENT STORY. Kalven's story quoted the autopsy report and described McDonald clearly: "Six feet tall and 180 pounds, he had been wearing blue jeans and a black hooded sweatshirt. He had dreadlocks, the longest of which was five inches. He was, before his encounter with the police, in good health. A tattoo on his upper right arm read 'Quan.' Another on the back of his right hand read 'Good Son.' And on the back of his left hand were a pair of dice and 'YOLO'—the acronym for 'you only live once.'" The story noted inconsistencies between officers' version of events and the bullet holes in his body. It later won a national award for exposing the truth. But it didn't draw much immediate public attention or outrage, even as Emanuel was campaigning for a second term.

In April the newly reelected mayor's administration agreed to pay McDonald's family $5 million to settle the case, before a lawsuit was even filed. The city's top lawyer, Stephen Patton, testified at a City Council committee hearing, "The plaintiffs contend very vehemently that Mr. McDonald had been walking away from the police and was continuing to walk away from the police. And they contend that the videotape supports their version of the events." None of the alderpersons present challenged the settlement in any meaningful way, though Burke, a longtime police supporter whose ward housed the Burger King, questioned why responding officers didn't have tasers. Patton considered the settlement a smart use of city resources and an effective way to handle lawsuits stemming from police misconduct—closing a hot case early, saving the taxpayer money in attorney's fees and judgments. But to others, it reeked, particularly as the Emanuel administration fought to keep the video secret.

THE BREACH | 3

South Side alderperson Howard Brookins, who doubled as a criminal defense attorney, was later critical of the city for withholding the footage.

"I'm not worried about rioting or demonstrations. I need this to stop," Brookins said, according to the *Chicago Sun-Times*. "If you don't show the video and this continues to happen, then we're still headed down that path."

The Emanuel administration's argument for not releasing the video was plausible—it had long been the practice to withhold such evidence while investigations were pending, after all—but it proved to be illegal. The Illinois Freedom of Information Act is clear that only government bodies actively doing an investigation can withhold records. That means you can't file a request to get the records directly from the FBI if the Department of Justice is reviewing the case, but you can request them from the government body that keeps the records—in this case, Chicago. Calloway, an activist from South Shore, and independent journalist Brandon Smith sued the Police Department for the video, which culminated in the judge's order. The footage showed McDonald walking away as officers followed him from a safe distance. The situation is tense but under control when Van Dyke arrives on the scene and opens fire, unloading sixteen times in what is essentially an execution. His partner kicks the knife away from McDonald's limp body. None of the officers attempts to render aid.

While Kalven's story exposed the wrongdoing, acts of violence best encapsulate the expression "a picture is worth a thousand words." It's one thing to be told a shooting is wrong. It's another to watch footage contradicting an official story so clearly. Some advocates assumed the Emanuel administration would appeal Valderrama's ruling, but City Hall quickly announced it would obey the order. Kalven later recalled asking Patton why they didn't appeal, and he replied that they recognized they had lost control of the situation. When the video was released, it sent seismic shockwaves through the city, leading to a series of police reforms, broken careers, and new promises.

The McDonald video release occurred after Michael Brown's shooting in Ferguson, Missouri, which sparked a national conversation about policing and a roiling series of riots in the Saint Louis suburb. The video forced a reckoning for a city with a dark legacy of police misconduct epitomized by Jon Burge, a Chicago Police commander who learned to torture while serving in Vietnam and used electroshock to elicit confessions from Black and brown suspects, some false, robbing the justice system of credibility and hundreds of men their freedom.

The scandal's aftermath effectively ended Emanuel's career as an electable politician and changed the city's political trajectory. It also threatened to destroy all credibility and goodwill Chicago had with its residents. To counteract the scandal, Emanuel turned to Lori Lightfoot, a big law partner at Mayer Brown and former federal prosecutor who had spent time in the city's internal police shooting investigation agency to lead a newly formed Police Accountability Task Force. Calling herself a "girl scout" in the press, Lightfoot was eager to help shape the city's response. Police reformers with long memories, however, knew Lightfoot had been a part of the problem.

Originally from small town Massillon, Ohio, Lori Lightfoot grew up working class. Her father, Elijah, worked three jobs during her childhood. He later went deaf after a bout with meningitis, adding to the family's trials. Her mother, Ann, was a health care worker and served on the local school board. Their lives were molded by other tragedies: Lori Lightfoot's grandmother's husband was murdered by the Ku Klux Klan. As a kid, Lightfoot was a nerd who would stand up for herself and classmates. In high school, Lightfoot was her student body's president, with a "Get on the right foot" slogan, and led a boycott of bland cafeteria food. She then went to the University of Michigan, which was a financial challenge; she worked a summer factory job making cans for Tony Chachere's Original Creole Seasoning so she could go back to school in the fall. After earning a bachelor's in political science, Lightfoot gained admission to the prestigious University of Chicago Law School. Years later, during a WTTW television forum, Lightfoot said she was "very much afraid of failure" when she was younger and should have applied for undergraduate studies at Ivy League schools or on the West Coast but didn't "for fear of not getting in" or fitting in. But she made a big splash at the University of Chicago when she wrote an article about a Baker McKenzie law firm partner asking racist questions to prospective hires. Harry O'Kane, a litigation partner with more than twenty years at the firm, told a student "that the university loves to admit foreigners to the exclusion of qualified Americans," asked how the student would react to being called "a Black bitch" or the *n*-word by adversaries, and asked, "Why don't Blacks have their own country clubs?" The embarrassment was written up in the *Tribune* under the headline IMMENSE BLUNDER BY BIGGEST FIRM.

Geoffrey R. Stone, the law school's dean at the time, told me he had reported O'Kane's behavior to the firm, but Lightfoot responded, "'That's not enough. The firm needs to take more action to make sure its lawyers don't behave in that way again.' She urged me to tell the firm that it cannot interview our students until it does that. Lori was very compelling, and I then called the head of the firm again and said that the firm could not interview at UChicago unless and until it disciplines the lawyer and educates its lawyers not to behave that way again. The head of the firm agreed and did what Lori had suggested. She was bold, courageous, and right." The incident was Lightfoot at her best: diagnosing and exposing a problem with courage and moral clarity.

After law school, Lightfoot took a job with the US Attorney's Office, where she found mixed success. As a prosecutor, she was excellent—tough and capable of taking on heater (or high-profile) cases. She prosecuted John Thomas Veysey III, an arsonist. She also put away South Side alderperson Virgil Jones, who took a $4,000 campaign donation that was wrapped in a newspaper. At trial, Jones said he was "shocked" when he received the cash but couldn't explain why he then went into the bathroom and removed the money. Jones had also been caught on tape "spelling out his philosophy" when he told a cooperating witness that "'m-o-n-e-y' always came first." A *Tribune* story noted Lightfoot's posttrial declaration: "The alderman is an unrepentant crook."

She ran into a career-threatening incident in 2000, when a US Seventh Circuit Court of Appeals opinion ruled Lightfoot "had made a misleading statement to the court in a case involving the extradition of a fugitive," as *Politico* reported. The opinion, by Judge Richard Posner, reprimanded Lightfoot for what he called "professional misconduct" and was considered a major embarrassment, though she always defended herself from allegations of wrongdoing. Lightfoot later said she was "a junior lawyer following the advice of people who were much more experienced than me." Getting bench-slapped is a big deal within the legal profession and followed her for decades, though it's the sort of blemish nobody cares about except highfalutin lawyers.

Contemporaries recall Lightfoot as a hard-charging prosecutor with a mean streak, in the courtroom and at the office. Everyone respected her intellect, but she was considered controversial for how she treated people. For instance, the US Attorney's Office (USAO) traditionally held an annual holiday party with skits. In 2001 Lightfoot went on the show and riffed about a fellow prosecutor who had, as one colleague remembered, "a very warm relationship with a paralegal." They were allegedly having an affair, and Lightfoot publicized it for the whole office, shocking a hardboiled group of prosecutors used to the rough and tumble of crime. Not long after, new top prosecutor Patrick Fitzgerald sent word down that there would be no more skits. (Fitzgerald did not return messages seeking comment.)

She wasn't afraid to scrap with defendants, either, even in cases and hearings where she wasn't the primary attorney. Another story colleagues remember from Lightfoot's time in the USAO involved a sentencing hearing for Rodney White, a bank robber who took a woman hostage and became belligerent during his sentencing in front of Judge Charles P. Kocoras. "They got jails to fill. That's what's going to happen," White said, after a long rant. "And you a Jew, man. . . . What rights you got to try to oppress some other people, man, when you a Jew?"

Kocoras asked, "Are you finished, Mr. White?"

White repeated his question, then lashed out at Lightfoot, calling her "you little, short Gary Coleman look-alike."

"That's about enough, Mr. White," she said.

He responded, "Don't tell me nothing, bitch. Fuck you."

Depending on perspective, the story highlights Lightfoot's loyalty to a friend and her decency in the face of nastiness—or her tendency to suddenly wind up in a fight.

After nearly six years at the USAO, Lightfoot expressed dissatisfaction with her career advancement and became open to new opportunities. One day, Lightfoot received a voicemail on her office line from Norma Reyes, who served as a high-ranking aide to Mayor Richard M. Daley. "She indicated to me that she was interested in having me apply for the job, and I considered that. I agreed to apply. And then I interviewed with a couple of people and did some due diligence, was offered the job," Lightfoot later recalled. The offer was to head the Office of Professional Standards (OPS), a unit within the Chicago Police Department that reported up to the city's top cop. Her job was to review allegations of police misconduct, notably instances of excessive force. If it sustained allegations, the agency would refer disciplinary charges to the Chicago Police Board, which would vote on the outcome in a sometimes yearslong process.

Although it was meant to appear robust on paper, the police-accountability system Lightfoot inherited in the summer of 2002 was a model of failure.

Over the years, the agency's own leadership privately acknowledged its deep problems. The city's first Black mayor, Harold Washington, appointed University of Illinois at Chicago professor David Fogel to lead the agency in 1984, and he held the position until 1990, when he retired. As head of OPS, Fogel wrote a memo stating that "a good number" of OPS investigators were "irremediably incompetent" and "part of the inherited politically corrupt heritage of pre-Washington days." In the memo, Fogel said "the troops"—meaning cops—loved OPS because the agency "actually operates to immunize police from internal discipline, increases their overtime, leads to an enormous paper storm, and has institutionalized lying."

Because it was based within the department, OPS remained cozy with cops, a tough challenge to balance for investigators who had to be feared and thorough. It was one they often failed at. Lightfoot replaced Callie Baird, who had been a public defender and married Nick Ford, a one-time prosecutor who became a Cook County criminal courts judge. John Conroy, whose career was defined by reporting on police torture and misconduct, wrote a stunning paragraph in a 2006 story that focused on Ford and the justice system:

> Lawyers who defend police-torture victims in Chicago long ago reached a harsh conclusion about Cook County's criminal judges: most have a vested interest in refusing to acknowledge police brutality. Now these lawyers can point to a case so extreme it's almost funny: a judge who apparently ruled on his own performance as a prosecutor, deciding there was no taint to a confession that the judge himself had written. Judge Nicholas Ford passed judgment on assistant state's attorney Nick Ford. Ford had no problem with Ford's work.

Lightfoot was well aware of the problems in OPS and tried to address them head-on for the media. In one interview, Lightfoot promised not to be "window dressing," according to a *Chicago Defender* profile that praised her as "petite, apparently feisty and scheduled to take the reins."

"I realize that accepting this job is accepting many challenges," Lightfoot said. "I pledge that we will be working to assure that to serve and protect applies to all citizens. This great city deserves nothing less. That has been and will be my guiding principle."

"As a citizen, I know there are some inherent and long-standing tensions among the community served by OPS," Lightfoot said when she was appointed, according to the *Sun-Times*. "We can do better. Everybody recognizes that. And we will."

Years later, Lightfoot spoke of her time at OPS as an era of reform when she enforced strict rules on cops, particularly Rule 14, informally known as "you lie, you die." In truth, Lightfoot ran the agency in a way geared at protecting the system's legitimacy and promoting the bad-apple theory of policing that most problems are isolated.

In April 2003, for instance, a group of several dozen officers dragged four men out of a van. Some cops kicked the men as other officers held them down, the AP reported. Lightfoot said OPS was working "to complete the investigation so that there's no concern out there that the things depicted on the video are commonplace in the department." An officer was later indicted in the case. For some, that is reassuring, but it points to wider issues going unaddressed. Why did the officers feel they could stomp on suspects? Would anyone have been charged without video and the resulting media outrage?

Lightfoot pushed back on criticism as head of OPS. She argued with activists over the death of fifty-five-year-old May Molina, who died while in police custody after allegedly ingesting heroin packets and not being given medical treatment. Confronting a group of activists who were upset over Molina's death, Lightfoot argued with Aaron Patterson, a former death-row inmate who was pardoned by former Republican governor George Ryan amid claims that he had been wrongfully convicted of murder. "We will not turn this into a circus," Lightfoot said at the time, according to the *Tribune*. "I have offered to meet with you. You don't want the terms of the deal." Molina's family won a $1 million verdict from a jury in federal court nine years after her death, as her team argued "that Molina's death was not an isolated incident but the result of widespread problems in the system," as the *Tribune* reported.

In a 2013 story by the *Windy City Times*, Lightfoot summarized her view of OPS, saying the job entailed "walking a difficult line between maintaining the integrity of the department and handling complaints against it." She proved to be a protector of the system and a prosecutor of individuals. In some ways, her time at OPS legacy was well-defined by what happened on November 15, 2002, a day she started with an overnight call to the scene of a police shooting before heading over to a deposition with the city's most prominent civil rights attorney, Jon Loevy.

In the middle of that night, Lightfoot rushed to the scene of the police shooting at Willie's Hideaway Lounge, a dive bar in the city's Bronzeville neighborhood on the near South Side, where an officer and two suspects had been wounded. Chicago cops reported in official documents they were off duty and shooting pool when two gunmen walked in, announced a robbery, and ordered everyone to the floor. As one of the robbers searched patrons for cash, a detective reported he was lying near the bar and tried to discretely reach his pistol. The gunman noticed the detective moving and asked if he was police. The detective said no, but the robber put it together when he saw the star on his belt and empty holster. "You are the motherfucking police!" he allegedly shouted, according to police records, before opening fire on the detective, who shot back. Two bullets pierced the tavern wall near the women's restroom. Both robbers were shot as they fled. Officers with a local public housing unit later arrested one of the offenders, who left a trail of blood on a nearby building's front steps.

The day of the shooting at Willie's Hideaway Lounge was already scheduled to be busy. Lightfoot spent the night at the shooting scene, then made her way to an early afternoon deposition with Loevy in a wild case brought by George Garcia that illustrated broader problems with the city's police-accountability system. Garcia alleged that he had been good friends with a police officer, Zamir Oshana, but their relationship soured when Garcia and his girlfriend broke up and Oshana started seeing her a week later. Garcia kept in touch with the ex-girlfriend, however, so Oshana got mad and threatened to beat Garcia up. As if the drama wasn't convoluted enough, Garcia threatened to show the police department a photo of Oshana flashing the Latin Kings gang sign with his fingers, adding an element of blackmail to the mix.

On February 2, 2001, Garcia had been at his uncle's restaurant when he saw Oshana's truck circling outside. He went to a nearby police station and told the cops about the photo and Oshana's threats to beat him up and returned to the restaurant, where he saw Oshana and a man he didn't recognize. "Come here, you bitch, I want to talk to you," Oshana said, according to court records. The other man began to push Garcia, and when Garcia tried to get away, the man identified himself and Oshana as cops and beat Garcia. The two men tried unsuccessfully to pull Garcia into Oshana's truck. When Oshana went to pick up a metal garbage can, presumably to beat Garcia with it further, he ran to the police station and reported the assault. All told, Garcia had a broken nose, fractured eye orbital, and serious hip injuries. Police told him the Office of Professional Standards would take over the investigation.

Garcia hired Loevy to sue the police department. The lawsuit brought a novel and aggressive claim: Loevy argued, as the *Sun-Times* reported, that the city was so lax in disciplining off-duty cops for beating people "that it created an environment that effectively encouraged it." Loevy summoned Lightfoot for a deposition to establish OPS policies and procedures. Years later, Loevy still remembers how combative she had been. And Lightfoot still brags about it.

Depositions are often a game of cat and mouse, an exercise in not answering the question and finding your way around an issue. Asked if she made changes to the organization, for instance, Lightfoot said, "I helped get air conditioning on the weekends. I helped get email up and running in the office." She then listed modest changes to operating procedures but repeatedly ducked and dodged when asked about substantive matters, including the number of investigators at the department. "Is that the right amount of staffing for the mission of your organization?" Loevy asked.

"I think that's an impossible question to answer," she answered.

Loevy asked, "Would OPS run better if there were more investigators?"

Lightfoot responded, "I'm not exactly sure I know what you mean by run better." Finally, she said, "Better to me suggests that there is something wrong with it now, and I don't agree with that assumption."

Similarly, Lightfoot defended the organization when asked if, in her view, OPS runs efficiently and effectively.

"I believe that given what our mission is, given what our resources are, that we do a very good job addressing the very significant and important function that we serve, both within the department and for the community," she said.

At one point, Loevy asked about civil rights violations.

"Do you know what the sustained rate was for civil rights violations before you got there?" Loevy asked. After Lightfoot's attorney objected to civil rights violations, Loevy clarified, "If we were to break down OPS investigations by category of allegations, one of the categories is civil rights violations, including things like excessive force. Are you familiar with that category?"

"I'm familiar with the category of excessive force, but I'm not familiar with it as characterized as a civil rights violation," Lightfoot said.

"Are you familiar with any category as civil rights violation?" he added.

"Not to my knowledge."

Lightfoot is an intelligent, gifted attorney; with that context in mind, her answers were preposterous. Excessive force being a civil rights violation is the sort of knowledge you gain as a law student.

Loevy and Lightfoot fought over other critical issues, including the sustain rate of complaints. Most of the time, allegations of wrongdoing went nowhere. Officers would tell you that's because most are false, but advocates said they were poorly investigated and the investigations were biased. Much of the deposition focused on this subject, where Lightfoot was evasive and noncommittal. Lightfoot repeatedly said she wasn't aware of the department's sustain rate regarding excessive-force investigations before she got there. Nor would she venture to give an opinion on the figures.

"Would it surprise you that OPS has sustained 5 percent of excessive-force allegations in the year 2000?" Loevy asked.

"As I said, I don't have any knowledge as I sit here today about what the rate was so I can't say if it would surprise me or not surprise me," Lightfoot answered.

Similarly, Loevy asked, "Would you find there to be a problem if Chicago sustained 5 percent of the excessive force allegations in the year 2000?"

"As I said before, I am not prepared to make judgment about a number that I, as you said, don't know is true. It sounds like you may possibly be making it up, which gives me some pause," Lightfoot said. "And even if it is true, without knowing what the specific factors were that went into that, I'm not in a position to sit here and Monday morning quarterback that and second guess that."

Later, Loevy tried to press Lightfoot on whether she'd be troubled by 95 out of 100 cases are unsustained and got a similar answer.

"You're asking me would it trouble me, and what I'm saying to you without knowing more, I wouldn't as a prudent lawyer be in a position to answer that question. It's not my job and it's not my practice as a lawyer, whether or not I'm at OPS or in anyplace else, to simply make knee-jerk assumptions, observations, judgments without knowing specifics. That's not what I do, that is not what I have ever done, and that is not what I will ever do."

At one point, Lightfoot's lawyer bickered with Loevy over whether he was raising his voice. Lightfoot then jumped in and said, "For the record, I don't care if he raises his voice. I don't care if he gets red in his face. Let's just get through this." Loevy objected to the accusation and called a recess.

"I'm not making an accusation," she said. "I'm making an observation based upon the rising level and the tone and the sarcasm and the volume of your voice at different times. The fact that you have got your red face, the fact that you're using your hands in a vociferous manner. I don't care if you do any and all of that, let's just get through this."

The deposition went further off the rails when Loevy asked if Lightfoot intended to remain at OPS, and she responded, "I don't see how that is any of your business. . . . I find it insulting because I have been on the job for three months, and that suggests I'm some frivolous person that is going to flit off," Lightfoot said. Loevy repeatedly countered that he didn't understand why it was insulting, and the exchange ended with her saying, "That is none of your business. And I'm going to tell you again it's none of your business. You're not the chief of police, you're not the community out there, and it's none of your business in a 30(b) deposition to ask me that kind of question."

The encounter with Loevy has a few revealing postscripts. Garcia won the case alleging lax discipline by the city a year later, as a jury awarded Loevy's client $1 million.

Twenty years after the deposition, Lightfoot was mayor and responsible for the city Law Department as it confronted wrongful-conviction cases and excessive-force complaints. State's Attorney Kim Foxx hosted Lightfoot at her office to speak about upcoming exonerations tied to corrupt detective Reynaldo Guevara, who has been accused of being a serial framer. While they were going over Foxx's plan to drop cases against more than a dozen Guevara victims, Lightfoot bragged that she had gotten the better of Loevy during a deposition they once had and ripped him as a poor lawyer, an aside that shocked people in the room for what it said about her mindset and priorities. Loevy has won hundreds of millions of dollars for civil rights clients and earned exonerations for dozens of men who were wrongly convicted, their lives forever scarred.

As for OPS, a 2007 *Tribune* investigation found the city's police system was broken and Daley disbanded the agency, moving police accountability to a new agency outside the department and renaming it the Independent Police Review Authority. Lightfoot had gone by then, having left OPS in 2004 for Mayer Brown, where she made big money representing the well-heeled. There, she continued to be known as a tough colleague—when she was upset with someone's work, she'd share that with people far and wide—but also earned a reputation for excellence. Lightfoot made a couple brief stops in the Daley administration to help solve problems and respond to scandals—Daley asked her to take on procurement reform after controversy over contracts, for instance. Part of the politicians' playbook is to hire someone clean of an issue to sterilize it, giving themselves cover. These stints were relatively short, but she started to draw more attention. Cook County commissioner Larry Suffredin, for instance, approached her about running for Cook County state's attorney in 2012, a run she considered but declined.

That year, Fitzgerald left the US Attorney's Office, and Lightfoot saw the opportunity to be appointed as his replacement. Arguing that the office had never been led by a person of color or a woman, Lightfoot launched a public campaign to get herself appointed Chicago's top federal prosecutor. Mark Flessner, a longtime Lightfoot friend from the USAO and future top lawyer at the city of Chicago, recalled Lightfoot's deep disappointment when she lost the position to Zach Fardon, who was straight out of central casting for white male lawyer. "She was crying," Flessner said. "It was so upsetting."

Also in 2012 the city appointed Lightfoot to represent it in a lawsuit brought by Christina Eilman, a California woman who had been arrested at Midway Airport while having a bipolar breakdown and later was released "in a high crime neighborhood where she was abducted and sexually assaulted before plummeting from the seventh-floor window of a public housing high-rise," as the *Tribune* reported. It was an absolute nightmare of a case, a horror for the Eilman family, and a financial time bomb. Although the city denied that it lacked confidence in the trial team, it did. Emanuel's top lawyer, Stephen Patton, knew the city didn't have the right horses to keep from being pilloried. They had done some exercises to practice for the case and were making mistakes, like attacking Eilman and suggesting the blame for the attack fell on her—a line of reasoning that would've done nothing but infuriate jurors. Patton thought Lightfoot would be able to land the case with a more reasonable settlement than the $100 million the family was pursuing. In the end, the lawsuit was settled for $22.5 million, an astonishing sum that could've been higher without Lightfoot's quality legal work at the top. Soon, Emanuel would turn to her again.

2 | "SIXTEEN SHOTS AND A COVER UP"

IN THE MID-2010S, LORI Lightfoot became a prolific commenter on police-misconduct cases, where she would take media questions and explain thorny issues. As reporters, we often look to "experts" for context: former prosecutors to talk about prosecutions, ex-cops to talk about cops, academics who have studied an issue and can speak from the outside. It's important for journalists to try to gain as much context and knowledge as possible. When a grand jury in Missouri declined to indict Darren Wilson, the Ferguson cop who shot Michael Brown, Lightfoot questioned the lack of transparency by St. Louis County prosecutor Robert McCulloch because he didn't explain why Wilson believed he needed to use lethal force. "Why were those shots necessary?" she asked, according to Bloomberg.

Lightfoot spoke against proposals to open special prosecutor investigations every time a cop is involved in a shooting, a popular idea with some activists worried that prosecutors are reluctant to investigate their colleagues in the police department, whom they rely on to bring cases. Aside from the challenges of a learning curve, she told the *Sacramento Bee*, "It's very demoralizing to police and the state's attorneys." Her thoughts were in line with Mayor Rahm Emanuel, who had long expressed concern about police morale and what he called the "Ferguson Effect." In a private meeting, reported on by the *Washington Post*, Emanuel told US Attorney General Loretta Lynch, "We have allowed our police department to get fetal and it is having a direct consequence."

Still, Emanuel and his team understood the city had problems with its police department and oversight. What to do about it was the hard part. His deputy mayor for public safety, Janey Rountree, a gun policy expert, had been impressed by Lightfoot after a panel discussion focused on gun violence in Chicago and possible solutions. Rountree had spoken with Lightfoot about the connection between state and regional gun laws, gun trafficking, and gun violence, in addition to the potential role of federal prosecutions of gun traffickers and variations in prosecution rates among the US Attorney's Offices.

The administration was having particular problems with the Police Board. According to a *Sun-Times* investigation, Police Superintendent Garry McCarthy was losing most of the cases in which he wanted to fire an officer. Out of twenty-five requests, the board only fired seven. Of the eighteen who kept their jobs, thirteen were found not guilty of wrongdoing and restored to duty, and five others were either suspended or reprimanded for misconduct, according to the newspaper. Police discipline across the country was lax, but Chicago's disciplinary panel was especially soft. Emanuel officials liked that Lightfoot had been at OPS. They also had a perception that she was propolice, as the ideal candidate could make changes without hating cops. Emanuel chose Lightfoot to head the Police Board.

"We've seen with what's happening around the country that the public demands and expects that, when there are serious allegations of misconduct by police officers, that those charged with doing investigations and rendering final judgment will act in a fair and expeditious manner," Lightfoot said, according to the *Sun-Times*. "I will be working hard to make sure the Police Board lives up to those standards. I obviously have a lot of information I need to understand about where they are and the challenges they face. That will be job one for me."

Before alderpersons approved her appointment, Lightfoot expressed her concern for both sides. "Many of our communities are hurting and are ravaged by crime. They need the police. And we need the police to be successful in fulfilling their important duties. But that work needs to be done in a way that is respectful to the communities and the individuals they serve."

Not long after, the McDonald scandal broke. The city had withheld the video but was ordered to turn it over, unleashing charges of "16 shots and a cover up." She was one of the first people to defend the city. A *Tribune* article from November 26, 2015, noted the city's Independent Police Review Authority (IPRA)—created after OPS was dissolved—"opened an investigation into the shooting within hours, and Van Dyke was stripped of his police powers nine days after the shooting. The police review agency forwarded the evidence to prosecutors, then suspended its investigation so that it would not interfere with the criminal probe."

"For the piece of the process that the city controlled, the process worked," Lightfoot said, according to the *Tribune*. "IPRA was on the scene that night, it immediately began an investigation and once it conducted its preliminary investigation it determined this was a matter that needed to be reviewed by law enforcement."

This statement by Lightfoot best encapsulates a theory journalist Jamie Kalven once shared with me about "cover up by investigation." The idea is that agencies say they're looking into a matter, then sit on it indefinitely, creating a veneer of respectability but really covering up. Officials at City Hall and State's Attorney Anita Alvarez's offices have long resented the Department of Justice for how it handled the case, as the FBI opened an investigation but never brought charges. They argue their hands were tied by the feds' inaction. But the public never believed Alvarez would've brought a case without the judge's order demanding the video's release. In fact, Alvarez charged Van Dyke on the same day the video was ordered released, a move also widely believed to have been aimed at preventing riots.

What followed was a firestorm and a series of textbook attempts at damage control. First was to fire someone high-profile. Emanuel was initially reluctant to dismiss Garry McCarthy, who had led the city Police Department to a few years with reduced crime and who was widely respected by the mayor's team. But the controversy showed no signs of stopping, so he fired McCarthy as a sacrificial lamb on December 1. Next was to announce a blue-ribbon commission that could address the issue. That same day, Emanuel announced the Police Accountability Task Force with Lightfoot as the chair and involvement by city inspector general Joe Ferguson, who was particularly well-regarded by the media. Part of the idea was to be proactive and get ahead of the Justice Department, with the hope that they could show the feds Chicago was taking it seriously and avoid a pattern-or-practice investigation that would lead to a costly and contentious consent decree. (Pattern-or-practice investigations come from "a federal law that bans 'a pattern or practice of conduct by law enforcement officers' that deprives people of their constitutional rights," as the *Tribune* reported.) It was wishful thinking by the administration, as the scandal was too large to hope for Obama officials to ignore.

"The shooting of Laquan McDonald requires more than just words," Emanuel said in a statement. "It requires that we act; that we take more concrete steps to prevent such abuses in the future, secure the safety and the rights of all Chicagoans, and build stronger bonds of trust between our police and the communities they're sworn to serve."

Finally, there was an alphabet soup reshuffling of the city's police oversight body. OPS had been dissolved in 2007 amid scandal and transformed into the Independent Police Review Authority. Immediately there was clamoring for a new agency, which eventually became the Civilian Office of Police Accountability.

As Emanuel made moves to address the crisis, he found himself at odds with senior leaders of the Democratic Party. At first, Emanuel said it would be "misguided" for the Department of Justice to get involved. But he changed his tune after Illinois Attorney General Lisa Madigan and Democratic presidential front-runner Hillary Clinton called for a DOJ review.

A *Tribune* story highlighted the pros and cons:

> On one hand, ending up with federal investigators and a judge driving change in the department would partially insulate Emanuel from rankling the city's 10,000 police officers, some of whom might be resistant to changes and all of whom live in the city, belong to an influential union and vote. On the other hand, sitting at the helm of a City Hall where a federal eye is needed to ensure proper conduct from cops could leave Emanuel looking like an ineffectual leader unable to deliver changes in a police department with a long history of excessive force and corruption.

That wasn't enough to quell the controversy, however. More than a week after the about-face, Emanuel called a special session of City Council to give what is known as the "code of silence" speech. In it, Emanuel acknowledged something long argued by criminal justice reformers and activists that had been denied by the city's police department: police officers protected one another, explicitly and implicitly, by looking the other way. It was essentially an acknowledgment that the thesis of Loevy's 2002 Garcia lawsuit was valid.

"We all have grieved over young lives lost again and again to senseless violence in our city. Now more than ever we need good and effective policing.

We cannot have effective policing if we turn a blind eye to extreme miscon- duct—as we saw its worst in the tragic case of Laquan McDonald," Emanuel declared to alderpersons. "We cannot ask citizens in crime-ravaged neighbor- hoods to break the code of silence if we continue to allow a code of silence to exist within our own police department. We cannot ask young men to respect officers if officers do not respect them in kind. Respect must be earned. Respect is a two-way street."

The Chicago Police Board made recommendations for new superintendent finalists, putting Lightfoot in position to influence the city's direction. Days later, the Police Board launched its search for a McCarthy replacement in earnest by requesting several essays on policing. As the *Sun-Times* reported, candidates were asked to define "accountability in the context of policing," identify the "best practices for early-warning systems" for officers whose actions trigger multiple citizen complaints, and explain how they "assess and address bias-based policing." They were also asked to articulate their philosophies on use of force, investigations over officer incidents, and how they would confront "significant distrust" between citizens and police. Lightfoot floated the idea of a hotline for officers to report each other and break the code of silence, a move that suggested to City Hall she was enjoying the spotlight.

In the middle of February 2016, the Police Accountability Task Force rec- ommended a sixty-day release window for police-shooting videos. The idea was to ensure "ongoing investigation" didn't get used again to indefinitely prevent release of a video. It was generally received well and marked a critical moment. Historically, prosecutors and police agencies would argue against disclosing anything due to ongoing investigations. Still, the time frame is longer than what's allowed under statute—five days to respond to a Freedom of Information Act (FOIA) request—but it's generally regarded as a reasonable compromise.

Lightfoot's first significant, outward conflicts with Emanuel started that month, when the media got wind that Cedric Alexander, the public safety director of DeKalb County in Georgia, was a frontrunner in her search for a new police superintendent. In mid-March, the Police Board announced its finalists, including Alexander. Lightfoot was quoted in the *Sun-Times* saying, "He is a different kind of person than what we've seen in the police department in quite a long time. He can talk the language of policing. But he can also talk the language of community." A March 22 *Tribune* story noted Lightfoot was lobbying for Alexander, though she denied it.

Emanuel was dissatisfied with the options and aggravated by what he considered a Lightfoot pressure campaign. Some of that spilled out in public after Alexander claimed that Emanuel called to offer him the job, then took it back, a series of events denied by City Hall. Emanuel was worried about morale as crime spiked, and he felt pressure to hire from within. Refusing to be boxed in, Emanuel rejected all three choices and selected Eddie Johnson, a longtime Chicago cop who had been chief of patrol for just three months when he was tapped to lead the department. It was an extraordinary move by Emanuel, who had to get the City Council to pass a law allowing him to circumvent the process and simply select whomever he wanted.

Emanuel had thrown away months of work, angering Lightfoot. There were also concerns that Emanuel's decision undermined the Police Board's credibility and her own as she was still working on the Police Accountability Task Force. Johnson proved to be a skilled political operator, often charming audiences and activists with a good sense of humor and levelheaded approach. At his introductory news conference, Johnson said he wanted to focus his remarks "on one word. It is at the heart of good policing, safe communities and it's the simple challenge facing Chicago today. That word is trust. Trust between the police and the people we serve. Trust between the rank-and-file and the command staff. Trust between police and elected officials and community leaders. And trust among police officers, who both must watch each other's back and hold each other to high standards."

Spurred by anger over the process, Lightfoot had a different reaction to the hire, which she confided in a friend who was working with her on the police accountability task force report: "Not only is he a fuck up, but he needs a new kidney." (A year later, Johnson received a new kidney from his son after fighting health problems.)

In mid-April, the task force released its report. Many activists had low expectations, but she dramatically exceeded them with a presentation that concluded Chicago Police have "no regard for the sanctity of life when it comes to people of color."

The report was deliberately pointed. Part of the idea was to identify the problem clearly and pressure the city to handle it right. The idealistic goal was to rise beyond the traditional panel that collects dust for years. "We made it very hard for people to ignore what we were saying," Lightfoot said, according to the *Sun-Times*. "This is a historic time." But it infuriated Emanuel and others who were upset with the strength of its conclusions and the position it left the city in. From a corporate lawyer standpoint, it really boxed in the city government.

"I don't really think you need a task force to know we have racism in America, we have racism in Illinois or that there is racism that exists in the city of Chicago and obviously can be in our departments," Emanuel said, according to the *Tribune*. "The question isn't, 'Do we have racism?' We do. The question is, 'What are you going to do about it?'"

One of the report's conclusions was to dismantle IPRA, which didn't even last a decade. Emanuel also accepted its recommendations about video releases, faster investigation into alleged misconduct, holding more meetings with community groups, and expanding training on mental health cases, the *Tribune* reported. In mid-May, Emanuel abolished IPRA and replaced it with the Civilian Office of Police Accountability. The department also hired Anne Kirkpatrick, who had been a finalist when Johnson was chosen, to help implement the recommendations.

The Lightfoot team kept Emanuel in the dark about what was happening and deliberately didn't brief him. "He'd be out there spinning his ass off," Lightfoot told one person. While Emanuel was angry about a lack of a heads-up, he accepted and acted on most of the task force's key recommendations.

Over the next few months, the prospect of police reform darkened when Donald Trump won the 2016 presidential election. It threw the entire possibility of a consent decree into turmoil. Many advocates for police accountability had come to believe a court order documenting and enforcing steps for reform would be the most effective way forward. Emanuel had signed an "agreement in principle" with the Obama DOJ to negotiate a consent decree and also promised he'd get reforms done "with or without" a consent decree, which seemed to some like an attempt at lowering expectations. Emanuel officials spent months frustrated with the Trump administration because they wanted clearer guidance and partnership. In April, new attorney general Jeff Sessions made clear he was uncomfortable with consent decrees during an interview with *The Howie Carr Show*, a New England–based conservative radio program:

> I do share your concern that these investigations and consent decrees have the, can turn bad. They can reduce morale of the police officers. They can push back against being out on the street in a proactive

way. You know New York has proven community-based policing, this CompStat plan, the broken windows, where you're actually arresting even people for smaller crimes—those small crimes turn into violence and death and shootings if police aren't out there. So every place [with] these decrees, and as you've mentioned some of these investigations have gone forward, we've seen too often big crime increases. I mean big crime increases. Murder doubling and things of that nature. It's just, we've got to be careful, protect people's civil rights. We can't have police officers abusing their power. We will not have that. But there are lawful approved, constitutional policies that places—New York is—the murder rate is well below a lot of these other cities that aren't following these tactics.

In May, the Chicago Police Department released rules for use of force that it hoped would lead to more de-escalation.

That June, Emanuel came up with a "memorandum of agreement" with the DOJ that would have an independent monitor but no court enforcement. The Emanuel administration shared it with Lightfoot, who gave feedback that was critical but didn't raise too many alarms with City Hall, which then floated the plan. Lightfoot then went public with her criticism, which Emanuel staffers felt was much harsher in the press than it had been behind closed doors, as she called it a "fundamentally flawed" document that "will not advance the cause of reform." She told the *Tribune* it amounted to "indulging in fantasy."

"The mayor and his people need to recognize they don't have unilateral control moving forward on reform in Chicago. They just don't," Lightfoot said. "All this firestorm of controversy that has come since they decided to leak late on a Friday afternoon that they had an agreement they already sent to the Department of Justice—the anger that's out there over that is not going to decrease. It's only going to increase if they don't understand many people are involved and necessary partners in this narrative." A person who spoke with her at the time said Lightfoot felt frustrated that she was being pressured to sign off on something she couldn't live with.

All the maneuvering underscored a stark reality: City Hall and the Police Department are incapable of monitoring themselves. There are too many political constituencies to serve, too many daily emergencies for them to effectively prioritize change without an outside agent forcing them to do the work. Consider the way OPS and its successor organization were disbanded as examples illustrating how city officials will sign paper and make promises, then let them fall by wayside. Watching events unfold was Lisa Madigan, the state's attorney general, who added pressure on the city and filed a lawsuit to force a consent decree requiring supervision of changes in police training, discipline, and use of force, a critically important step toward forcing progress.

Like her denunciation of the Baker McKenzie racist interview, Lightfoot's handling of the reform efforts after being appointed to the task force was arguably her at her best. But it also highlighted a certain opportunism from Lightfoot, who was angry with Emanuel and lashed out. Channeled effectively, that sense of grievance and clarity of purpose could do a lot of good for the city.

3 | SLAYING GOLIATH

THE FIRST TIME LORI Lightfoot emerged as a serious potential mayoral candidate was August 2016, when she took the stage at the Hideout with Chicago Public Schools teacher Erika Wozniak and journalist Jen Sabella for their show *The Girl Talk*. Once a month, Wozniak and Sabella brought influential women into the bar for a conversation. Lightfoot was one of their first big guests. Longtime Chicago journalists Ben Joravsky and Mick Dumke had been hosting *First Tuesdays at the Hideout* for years, drawing in political nerds. Wozniak wanted to have a show for women, and the idea grew into a popular long-running event. That night, though, Sabella joked about all the TV news cameras showing up and noted that their YouTube channel had twelve views at the time. Lightfoot's comments throughout that evening drew raised eyebrows at City Hall, where she most notably talked about potentially running for mayor.

"People across the city have asked me about that question. I'm very comfortable where I am right now. I have a job I like," Lightfoot said. "But look," she added, "we all know that the status quo has got to change. We all know that the current way of doing things, and the historic way of doing things, has failed us. So I'm going to keep doing my part from where I sit right now to try to roll the rock up the hill and make some difference." Throughout the night, Lightfoot really unloaded on city government. She expanded beyond policing to criticize "other aspects of government." "I think people forget who they work for. They forget that they work for us. They work for you. They work for the taxpayers," Lightfoot said, before complaining about a major Logan

Square home renovation she went through with wife Amy Eshleman that was "a nightmare" because of the city. "I think people in that whole chain from buildings to planning to what have you forget that every delay is a job. Every delay is, some people that are not going to be able to work, to put food on their table, to build capacity in neighborhoods, because somebody doesn't want to move a piece of paper from this desk to this desk."

Lightfoot talked about transparency and policing: "We give our consent to the police department to operate in the ways that they operate. To use lethal force. To come into our neighborhoods and protect us. And when they don't understand that and when—they take that for granted or don't even appreciate or understand that that's a real problem. And it shouldn't be that I have to file fifteen FOIA requests, call people up twenty times or worse, which we're seeing a lot of now, filing lawsuits against the city, which by the way, waste more tax dollars, simply because the old way of doing it was delay, ignore, obfuscate. We have got to get to a place in every single city department, and we might as well start with the police department, where there's a hell of a lot more transparency than what there is now."

Tribune gossip columnist Kim Janssen, a salty Brit who is as talented as he is hilarious, was present and wrote a story about the night where he noted she hadn't closed the door on a mayoral run. When the story published, Lightfoot angrily accused Janssen of having "totally mischaracterized my comments." "I said quite clearly that I was not running for mayor," she wrote in an email, which he published. Lightfoot also cussed him out in a follow-up interview, which he enjoyed retelling in the newsroom.

Despite Lightfoot's denial, however, the idea of running for mayor was starting to percolate in her head. Mark Flessner, her good friend and advisor who later became her campaign treasurer and top lawyer, recalled her talking about it for at least a year before she announced. He recommended she not run: "I warned her how her life and her family life is gonna change dramatically, and she would have to be prepared for that," Flessner said. "I said, 'Those people are gonna come out of the woodwork,' and that turned out to be true."

As Lightfoot continued exploring the idea, she told people she wanted to make a difference and bring lasting changes to the Police Department, which badly needed reform. Emanuel only cared about the business community and construction cranes in the sky but didn't focus enough on other issues, especially neighborhoods, she told confidantes. One person asked Lightfoot if she thought she could actually defeat Emanuel. "I know I can make it really hard for him to win," Lightfoot said.

Running for a third term was a challenging prospect for Emanuel. He had been reelected in 2015 after spending more than $24 million to beat back a progressive challenge from then Cook County commissioner Jesús "Chuy" García, a left-wing icon who had worked with Mayor Harold Washington in the 1980s. President Barack Obama had jumped in to support Emanuel, helping him get over the hump in that race after a first term where his popularity among Black voters suffered due to his decision to close fifty low-enrollment schools, the largest mass closure in the nation. The McDonald case didn't hit until after his reelection was secured, but it badly wounded him, even as he had done transformative things to improve the city. As the *Tribune* later noted, "He [expanded] full-day kindergarten and pre-K, lengthened the school day, improved graduation rates, increased the minimum wage, attracted scores of corporate headquarters, [oversaw] a boom in downtown construction, laid the groundwork for a major expansion of O'Hare International Airport, bolstered the downtown riverwalk and managed to stabilize—although not fully fix—the city's shaky finances."

Emanuel pushed ambitious plans, like a Whole Foods in Englewood, one of the poorest neighborhoods in the country. He also brought Elon Musk into town for a proposed tunnel connecting O'Hare International Airport to downtown in minutes, an extravagance and luxury that was wildly unrealistic but drew positive attention to the mayor's "vision." (This is one of the ways politicians get attention: announce something big, even if it's a pipe dream.)

Even with his challenges, Emanuel bragged that he was six for six in electoral races. His team worried about former Chicago Public Schools CEO Paul Vallas and former police superintendent Garry McCarthy. Vallas had pursued work for the administration and been rebuffed; McCarthy had been fired. Both men had clear potential lanes among white, conservative voters in the city, who aren't strong enough on their own but can boost a candidate with sizeable support into a runoff.

Lightfoot met with Emanuel in the summer of 2017, when her term as Police Board president was up and a potential mayoral campaign loomed over their heads, about possible reappointment. Emanuel was frustrated with her public comments and concerned about her running for mayor, less because she was someone he feared but more because he thought it was a problem for the board if she ran because it would raise questions about political motivations for its rulings. He publicly declined to commit to reappointing her, telling media, "I'm going to look through it, and I look forward to talking to . . . Lori, like other board members, about where we've got to go." Days later, they met for an uncomfortable talk, and he acknowledged the tensions they'd had but said he wanted to "reset from a place of openness and honesty." Lightfoot said that made sense to her. He asked her straight up if she would run for mayor, and she denied it.

Emanuel came out of the meeting boasting to staffers that she said no. Weeks later, she bought campaign websites Lightfootforchicago.com, Lorilightfoot.com, and Lightfootformayor.com. It's one of the top points Emanuel people make when they say she isn't trustworthy. For her part, Lightfoot says she wasn't running for mayor but wanted to keep her options open. It's a level of hairsplitting that makes someone hard to trust.

As Lightfoot publicly waffled, others entered the race. It wasn't a particularly robust field as Emanuel scared off candidates with his millions and long career as a political operative. In April, Dorothy Brown made her announcement to the strains of "She's a Bad Mama Jama." It was an entirely appropriate song. As Cook County circuit court clerk, Brown controlled key operations for the court system, one of the most byzantine and failed structures of government in the Chicago area. Decades after computers became widespread, its digital system barely worked, and it was still using carbon paper. Worse, Brown was under federal investigation for years over bribes and kickbacks. She avoided being charged, but a key aide was indicted in 2017 for lying to a federal grand jury when asked in two separate appearances about pay-to-play allegations in the clerk's office.

Despite all the baggage, Brown kept winning reelection due in part to her support from "the church ladies"—older Black women voters who worship every Sunday and gave her their backing. Circuit court clerk generally doesn't attract big-hitter politicians either, allowing her to skate.

Vallas, who had previously run campaigns for governor and lieutenant governor in 2002 and 2014, respectively, had offered to help the Emanuel administration in the mid-2010s, as the school district suffered through an inept superintendent and then a crook who was indicted on federal fraud charges. But he was rebuffed and complained publicly that he had been told he didn't pass "the loyalty test." Vallas led Chicago schools in the 1990s, when

Mayor Richard M. Daley turned to him to modernize the district. He built numerous new campuses, ordered accountability measures for progress on schools, ended so-called social promotion that allowed students to pass when they were really far behind, and put a higher emphasis on test scores, which made him a celebrated figure in the 1990s. From there, Vallas rebuilt New Orleans schools after Hurricane Katrina and went to Philadelphia, with mixed results at each stop, as critics accused him of financial mismanagement and short-term slash-and-burn tactics.

A loquacious wonk, Vallas opened his campaign with a blistering attack on Emanuel's governing style. "It's all about the next election, it's all about loyalty, it's all about fundraising, it's all about intimidating quality people out of the races by flashing your fundraising potential, it's all about pay-to-play," Vallas said, according to the *Tribune*. "I'm running because there needs to be real change." He also attacked Emanuel personally, saying, "People don't like the mayor. Sorry, they don't like you. You're a bully. You intimidate people."

One of the great characters in Chicago, Willie Wilson, also entered the race, his second run for mayor. Wilson is a Black gospel singer and business-man who had a long relationship with Ray Kroc of McDonald's, owned several franchises, and sold medical supplies. His 2015 candidacy fizzled, though he had a small but enthusiastic base of Black churchgoers. During one event, Wilson referred to a bunch of reporters as "whiteys," denied saying it, then apologized, saying he meant no offense.

As a citizen, Wilson gained prominence for his cash giveaways. One day, Wilson handed out more than $200,000 in cash and checks that led to criti-cism that he was buying votes. He denied it, noting that he had been giving money away since the 1990s—earning a glowing profile in the *Wall Street Journal*—and was just doing his thing. The only thing that changed was that he was a candidate. "My money that I worked hard for, as long as I'm not breaking any laws of the United States of America, I have a right to do what I want to do with my own money, all right?" he said. "So my own money, I'm not going to pass up a person on the street who's laying down, don't have legs and needs money for food to eat. You have to lock me up and die first before I will stop that."

One of Wilson's close allies, former state senator Rickey Hendon, who had attempted to bully Barack Obama when they were in the statehouse together, ridiculed the idea that he was buying votes. "Buying votes on the West Side,

South Side, votes about $5, $10," Hendon said. "So if Willie Wilson is giving somebody $3,000, as an adviser, I'd be like, you're overpaying by 1,500 percent. Because if we wanted to buy votes, it's 5, 10 bucks on the West Side and South Side, so let's just be real about that."

Wilson fought back another way: "I'm just tired of white people telling me what to do. With my own money. I didn't use taxpayer dollars."

Calling himself a "conservative Democrat," Garry McCarthy entered the race in early 2018. Originally from New York, McCarthy faced an uphill battle as he was harsh in his assessment of the city's position. "Between the taxes, our economy, the schools and the crime rate here, we're a laughingstock in America," McCarthy told the *Tribune*. "The prevailing thought about Chicago is we're on our way down in all those areas, and they all infect each other, and nobody seems to get that. It's almost like a 'Wake up, Chicago' moment." It was widely panned at City Hall as a revenge tour against Emanuel, a move he denied. "While I am very emotional, that's not my motivation here," McCarthy said. "Why would I possibly take on turning around one of the largest American cities in the right direction? Because I'm annoyed? No. I'm doing it out of a sense of obligation as a public servant and that's what motivates me."

Lightfoot watched it all unfold, unimpressed by the rival campaigns. As she mulled a bid, Lightfoot told people she wanted to raise $1 million by the time she announced. She called around, visiting with key figures throughout the city, from former mayor Daley to Cook County State's Attorney Kim Foxx. Her pitch hammered Emanuel for not caring about the Black community or fixing police oversight. She also cited her work with the Daley administration and the Police Accountability Task Force. But people who talked with her got the distinct impression she was trying to hide her efforts from Emanuel.

In April 2018 Lightfoot attended a speech by Eddie Johnson to the City Club of Chicago, where she demurred. Despite the kerfuffle over Johnson's appointment, the two developed a positive working relationship. "If I were to make that decision, then I'll obviously announce it in an appropriate fashion, but I'm not there yet," Lightfoot said, according to the *Tribune*. She acknowledged the problems for a potential run: "Look, taking on an incumbent mayor who has capacity to raise unlimited amounts of money, and in the third largest city in the country, given the number of crises we have, is a very serious matter," Lightfoot said. "And I'm hearing from lots of folks across the city, and frankly, across the country, who are very encouraging. But this is a decision that has to be made by me and my family, because we're going to be putting ourselves out there and asking citizens of Chicago to take us seriously."

Asked whether she was close to deciding, Lightfoot responded, "Ah, come on now." But she also took a potshot at the city's violent crime levels, which were on pace for double-digit decreases after a spike in 2016 that followed McCarthy's firing. "Thank God they're making progress," Lightfoot said. "Of course, people ask, how did it get this bad in the first place?"

Lori Lightfoot resigned from the Police Board in early May, then announced her run. Years later, she gleefully recalled her relationship with Emanuel in a *New York Times* interview. "He supposedly once said to somebody about me, 'I gave her a platform and a microphone, and she took it and shoved it up my ass.'"

Lightfoot announced her campaign at the Hyatt Regency Chicago, where she focused on police accountability and racial equity. "I'm here to talk about a new progressive course for our city where equity and inclusion are our north stars," she said, denouncing Emanuel for an "'us versus them' style of governance." She did not come close to meeting her goal of $1 million by launch date, but she did report an impressive $243,000 from seventy-eight contributors, a sum that made her the top fundraiser against Emanuel.

In the early days, people remember Lightfoot enjoying the attention of people wanting to meet her and talk policy. She had been a big-time lawyer, not a politician, and enjoyed the novelty. Running for office is a slog. But it can also be a thrill. Candidates get to go on television, talk to the media, and reach a level of quasi celebrity that some find intoxicating. Lightfoot's early campaign ran into headwinds. While she attempted to portray herself as a progressive alternative to Emanuel, she didn't embrace particularly left-wing policies. She did an interview with liberal website ThinkProgress in which she attempted to put herself in the same wave as Alexandria Ocasio-Cortez, the socialist who unseated a powerful white moderate congressman in a shocking election. "There is a wave of women, and particularly women of color, who are standing up and saying we believe we have a right to have access to tools of power," she said, according to the site. "We're going to stand up, we're going to uplift voices, [and] we're going to fight every day." But the site took issue with her for raising her working-class background—it noted she had been a corporate lawyer, while Ocasio-Cortez had been a bartender. She wouldn't say she would support abolishing US Immigration and Customs Enforcement (ICE), something even New York City Mayor Bill de Blasio had advocated. And she criticized Medicare as "not an incredibly well-run system."

It was an early example of a recurring future theme: Lightfoot using identity politics to say she's progressive while taking on moderate stances. One of the people she had around the campaign, Lisa Schneider Fabes, wanted Lightfoot to meet with charter school groups, which others fought. It raised questions about her core philosophy. Some felt she was real about helping working-class people. But her political north star was a mystery. More aptly, she's a corporate lawyer who appreciates the status quo for what it is while trying to change things around the margins. She appreciates order.

Foxx visited Lightfoot's campaign office at one point in those early days and received a phone call later from Emanuel advisor David Spielfogel warning her about the candidate. The message was essentially *I hope you know that Lori is crazy*. Or it was *I hope you know that Lori is untrustworthy*. Some memories differ. But the gist was the same: *Stay away*.

That August, Lightfoot proposed an ethics-reform package, including term limits for the mayor, prohibiting officials from having side jobs that conflict with their city employment, giving City Council its own lawyer, and removing the workers' compensation program from Alderperson Edward Burke's Finance Committee. She also said she would increase compliance with the Freedom of Information Act, which Emanuel frequently and flagrantly violated. Furthermore, she sparred with the mayor after he made controversial comments about a lack of accountability in the Black community in response to upticks in crime. Emanuel said children need the structure of family and faith and asked "that we also don't shy away from a full discussion about the importance of family and faith helping to develop and nurture character, self-respect, a value system and a moral compass that allows kids to know good from bad and right from wrong." That part of the discussion "cannot be off-limits because it's not politically comfortable," Emanuel said. It was widely panned as lecturing and moralizing, and Lightfoot criticized him in the *Tribune* for "victim shaming." "He doesn't see us. He doesn't have empathy and understanding for what's really going on, and the complexity and the nuance in these neighborhoods. He doesn't get it, and that's why he's not going to be mayor again." She also compared him to a "migratory bird." "He makes so few stop overs in real neighborhoods in the city, that's it's like a rare sighting."

On the whole, however, Lightfoot's early candidacy floundered, as most do. The beginning of a campaign, especially more than half a year before an election, is a period where most members of the public aren't paying attention, and the candidates themselves are testing out their lines and figuring out what lane they're going to occupy. Her team felt optimistic Lightfoot would be able to press Emanuel on policing and reform, in particular, but the prospect of a direct confrontation was a ways off.

Other candidates kept coming out of the woodwork, such as Amara Enyia, a public policy consultant and director of Chicago's Austin Chamber of Commerce. The daughter of Nigerian immigrants, Enyia compared her long-shot campaign to the bawdy band of misfits from *The Lord of the Rings* who were trying to get the ring to Mordor. An interesting challenge came from Jerry Joyce, whose father, state Senator Jeremiah Joyce, had been one of the most powerful politicians in Illinois for decades.

A 1996 *Tribune* story about Jeremiah Joyce was headlined LIKE GOD, YOU KNOW HE'S THERE. It was a family of leaders. Jerry Joyce was a well-respected lawyer in Southwest Side Beverly and family man whose wife, Jannine, was a successful doctor. His brother Kevin was a state representative, while brother Mike went by the nickname "Pickle" due to the shape of his nose and was married to Muhammad Ali's daughter. But the family suffered a setback when Emanuel, in one of his first big fights as mayor, took a lucrative airport concessions contract from the Joyce family and gave it to another vendor. Jerry Joyce denied the episode led to his run, but he decided Emanuel was vulnerable and could be beaten in a runoff. The calculation was that he was too unpopular to get reelected in a one-on-one race and, in a multicandidate field, it would be easier to make a runoff. The challenge for Joyce would be standing out in a crowded field, as he wasn't well known or particularly media savvy. During an interview with *Chicago Tonight*, Joyce was asked about his multiracial family—he and Jannine adopted children from Guatemala—and how it informs his worldview. "My children are my children. I think I have a great perspective either way, whether my children, I have a great appreciation for the adoption process. My wife and I are so blessed to have adopted our children. I have, if that's what you're getting to."

A political consultant joked to me that, if you combined Vallas and Joyce, you'd have a perfect candidate: one talks too much, and one doesn't say a word. Emanuel's political concerns had more to do with the landscape than the candidates in the field.

The weekend before Labor Day, a rumor spread through Chicago politics that Emanuel would be dropping out of the race. He had not formally announced his candidacy, and jury selection was scheduled to start in Jason Van Dyke's murder trial for killing Laquan McDonald. While Emanuel expressed confidence about his standing with residents, his poll numbers were lagging. Tuesday morning, his press office sent out a mid-morning note updating his schedule: "Mayor Emanuel will make an announcement." We all rushed upstairs to hear the news. I had a hunch, and the moment I saw his wife walk out with him, I knew. "This has been the job of a lifetime, but it is not a job for a lifetime," Emanuel said.

Without an incumbent, the campaign abruptly changed, sending rival candidates scrambling and creating a new dividing line: those who were willing to challenge Emanuel and those who weren't. Lightfoot put a brave face on the situation, telling the *Tribune*, "This is undeniably big news, but it doesn't change what we're fighting for. It doesn't change the needs of people all across this city. We live in a city where violence is far too prevalent. We live in a city where many people continue to live in poverty and struggle with chronic unemployment. We still live in a city where children must travel long distances each morning in hopes of a decent education. . . . The us-versus-them mentality continues to divide our communities, and we still need a leader to unite our city, and I plan to be that leader."

A day later, Emanuel took to the airwaves with a highly disrespectful message during an interview with WGN-Radio host Steve Cochran, who asked if the next mayor was already in the race. "No," Emanuel responded. "I don't think so. And here's the thing: the public knows that this is a very big job, and the mayor cannot be a one-trick pony. You can't just speak on one issue. You got to do economic development, you got to do education policy, you got to be able to get money out of Springfield and Washington. You've got to have an ability to actually invest in our neighborhoods, transportation, libraries, schools, and park system." It was classic Emanuel: pumping up the job to pump himself. The list of candidates, Emanuel added, "is not done. It's going to shake out for about a month, and then the voters will make a smart decision of who can fill that office. And what I mean by that is, you're not going to shrink the mayoralty, and there's got to be a mayor that actually fills this job."

4 | PIRATE BOOTY

MINUTES BEFORE RAHM EMANUEL publicly announced his decision not to seek reelection, he made sure to give Cook County Board President Toni Preckwinkle a courtesy notice privately letting her know. A former schoolteacher turned alderperson, Preckwinkle wielded enormous power and influence over local politics. She had served on Chicago's City Council for nearly twenty years before she was elected Cook County board president in 2010. From there, Preckwinkle rose to become Cook County Democratic Party chairwoman and, in 2016, helped elect her chief of staff, Kim Foxx, as the county's top prosecutor. Now, her sights were set on the mayor's office.

The seventy-one-year-old Preckwinkle rushed across the street to her political office, where she called every union leader she could to lock in their support. Preckwinkle long dreamed of becoming mayor but had decided not to challenge Emanuel in 2015, a decision that disappointed her progressive supporters. She would not miss out on another chance to run.

Very quickly, progressive labor groups got on board. Tom Balanoff, the legendary head of the Service Employees International Union (SEIU), immediately let his colleagues in the labor movement know: if Preckwinkle runs, he's all in. Some of them were taken aback by the force of his support.

Lightfoot watched Emanuel's news conference and immediately went into her office, shut the door, and also began dialing for support. Despite her public words to the press, Lightfoot advisors immediately understood the dilemma she faced with more candidates getting into the race, particularly Preckwinkle, who could make every progressive argument with far more weight. Lightfoot called Cook County Democratic Party executive director Jacob Kaplan and left a voicemail asking to connect with Preckwinkle. He passed it onto Preckwinkle, who did not call back.

As soon as Emanuel bowed out of the race, Illinois Comptroller Susana Mendoza emerged as a potential candidate. A former Southwest Side state representative who had run for city clerk and won, Mendoza had built a reputation as a ferocious campaigner. Under Republican Illinois governor Bruce Rauner, Mendoza got elected state comptroller and battled fiercely on behalf of the state's Democrats. She did impressive work rebuilding Illinois finances and paying off long overdue bills from Rauner's disastrous budget stalemate with the legislature.

Mendoza brought a vibrant personality. The day after Emanuel dropped out, Mendoza took the stage at City Club of Chicago for a previously scheduled speech. "We need to find a worthy successor to Mayor Emanuel," Mendoza said. "Anybody have any ideas?" It was a cheeky way in for Mendoza, who had been a protege of Illinois Speaker Michael Madigan and powerful alderperson Edward Burke. She had made a name for herself after a 2017 incident where a man crashed his black pickup into several cars. Mendoza had been bicycling with family and confronted the man, who claimed to be a police officer, following him after he fled the scene. "Say cheese!" she told him, while taking video on her phone.

The man, it turned out, was John "Quarters" Boyle, a legendary character who had been convicted in 1992 of stealing millions in coins from the Illinois State Toll Highway Authority, but nevertheless got hired by the city to oversee a program that led to him pleading guilty for extorting bribes.

Mendoza was immediately intrigued by the possibility of running for mayor. She did not have as close a relationship with Emanuel as some assumed, but they had been close allies. After he was sworn in as mayor in 2011, Mendoza visited him with a bottle of Midol as a gift—a not-so-subtle reference to his days as President Obama's chief of staff and reports that he once told a male staffer, "Take your fucking tampon out and tell me what you have to say," as Lisa Donovan once wrote. For Mendoza, a potential run had problems. She was up for reelection as comptroller in November 2018 and concerned about the optics of immediately seeking another job. Publicly, she repeatedly said it was "let's see," but she was privately amped and working toward it. Just before the November election, however, her campaigns were rocked when a television ad announcing her run for mayor leaked to the media. AL Media, a prominent political campaign firm, was apoplectic. Clients raised concerns about security.

AL Media sued Tony Williams, a contractor working with the firm, alleging he was on his way out when he sat for an exit interview on October 30, 2018. During the interview, Williams asked about Mendoza's potential campaign. On his last day at work, November 2, Williams allegedly texted an AL Media worker to tell him he'd be late to work. The firm later learned that a television reporter had received a copy of the video, causing AL Media to launch an investigation. Video access records reviewed by the firm showed Williams had downloaded it, and the ad's ensuing publication cast bad juju over the real announcement.

Perhaps the biggest surprise to enter the race was Bill Daley, the son and brother of two previous Chicago mayors. Daley had succeeded Emanuel as President Obama's chief of staff when Emanuel became the city's mayor. His potential candidacy was immediately floated, and it made for a strange fit. He had considered running for governor in 2002 and 2010, but didn't. He announced a campaign for governor in 2013 but dropped out afterward and vowed he wouldn't seek public office again. By 2018, Daley was a seventy-year-old with a controversial name, but he decided to finally put himself on a ballot and became the first major candidate to announce a run for mayor post-Emanuel.

He did not do a big campaign launch, however. Instead, Daley did a few interviews where he spoke about his family name and tried to hold himself above the fray. He had publicly complained earlier in the year that Emanuel kept blaming his brother for the city's financial problems, though Emanuel was always careful not to say "Daley." "I'm not going to change my name. That's not going to happen. Look, some people like us, some people don't. Some people like my brother, he got elected six times," Daley told the *Tribune*. "So, for his tenure, people were positive, obviously, based upon the results. I've got to go out and earn that. I don't take anything for granted."

Daley was clearly uncomfortable with voters, however, and members of the public. His attempt to run as a man of the people was an almost impossible sell. Since leaving the White House, Daley had worked in highfalutin corporate business. The *Wall Street Journal* in 2015 reported that J. P. Morgan hired a Chinese commerce minister's unqualified son for a job at Daley's recommendation, proving the old adage that you can take a Daley out of City Hall but you can't take City Hall out of the Daley. Despite his lack of interest in traditional campaigning, Daley's family ruled Chicago for nearly half a century, and his name loomed large. Business leaders, including billionaire Ken Griffin, rushed to give Daley money. One of Daley's first orders of business was to meet with Jerry Joyce to try to convince him not to run. They had potentially overlapping bases of conservative whites and city workers, and their families had known each other a long time. Daley met with Joyce a couple times. He tried carrots—including mentioning the 2020 state's attorney race, an allusion to him possibly supporting him for that job—and he tried the stick, mentioning that he would have a team ready to challenge his signatures to get on the ballot, an implicit threat to knock him off.

Joyce was not going to be bullied, however, and decided to stay in the race. Joyce figured his supporters wanted him, a consultant told him Daley couldn't win, and he wasn't even sure Daley would stick with the campaign, given his past history of flaking. While Joyce struggled as an orator, he brought together a vigorous campaign team that collected signatures around the city and showed a strong ground game.

Following Emanuel's departure, other long-shot candidates started making moves. Amara Enyia had known famous Chicago music artist Chance the Rapper through activism circles. He had been impressed by her advocacy for a public bank, strengthening local block clubs, and investing in the community, and her positions resonated. Chance's people reached out to Enyia. In one of their first conversations, Chance asked Amara Enyia which of the candidates they could not support. At the same time, Enyia and Chance said, "Lori Lightfoot."

In mid-October, Chance the Rapper tweeted a late-afternoon announcement for the next morning: "City Hall pull up." He arrived at 10:00 AM and tried to build suspense. "I want to work with somebody who is about change, somebody who is about our community, somebody who is about equity, somebody who is about fairness," Chance said at the packed news conference. "And the one person in my research of this wide-open race that's views align with me would obviously be candidate Amara Enyia."

If Enyia and Chance disliked Lightfoot, the feeling was mutual—and maybe even more intense. In the documentary series *City So Real*, a man said Lightfoot approached him to bash Enyia and said, "Amara doesn't have anything to say. She talks a lot but doesn't say anything." She privately called her a "fraud" and said the difference between them was "twenty-plus years more experience." Lightfoot had earned the ire of activists for how she handled police board cases, particularly the killing of Rekia Boyd, a Black woman who was shot by police officer Dante Servin, who opened fire on a group of people who were just hanging out. He had claimed he thought they had a weapon and quit before Lightfoot could rule on his case. But she had alienated activists by shutting them down when they got too animated at hearing.

Later, Chicago native Kanye West donated six figures to Enyia, helping boost her further even as rivals sought to make an issue of the rapper's relationship with Donald Trump. "He said he was thinking about coming back to Chicago," Enyia told the website Complex. "He wanted to give back to the city. He's from the South Side, so he's a native son, and when he was having conversations with folks as he was thinking about moving back that my name kept coming up."

"I asked him about the whole Trump thing because there was some controversy over, you know, what was going on with Donald Trump," Enyia said. "But he told me he doesn't support Trump's views. He said I don't support his views, but I believe that your platform, and your message, and who you are is what Chicago needs."

As the other candidates made moves and big names started entering the race, Lightfoot immediately took umbrage at the idea of opportunists joining with special interests to divvy up the spoils of power by scheming to take City Hall. The rush of big names looking to enter the race who weren't willing to challenge Emanuel rankled her well-honed sense of grievance.

"This notion that city government and the mayor's office is pirate booty ripe for the picking is offensive," Lightfoot told *Tribune* columnist John Kass.

While other candidates brought strengths and weaknesses, nobody entered the 2019 mayor's race with more power or clout than Preckwinkle. Lightfoot respected Preckwinkle and called around after the county board president entered the race to ask for feedback and what she should do. She didn't want to lose her relationship with Preckwinkle, whom she had previously supported with campaign cash. With Preckwinkle in the race, potentially hogging up what had been her lane, Lightfoot had a tough decision to make.

That became easier when *Sun-Times* gossip columnist Michael Sneed published a story suggesting that Lightfoot would drop out of the race to become Preckwinkle's corporation counsel. It's impossible to overstate how angry that story made Lightfoot. She called everyone, including State's Attorney Kim Foxx, to complain. "This is bullshit. This is Toni. They're trying to undermine me," she said. Although Preckwinkle and her team denied the leak, the damage was done.

"The insulting part of that is that it suggests I'm going to hand over my integrity to somebody like Toni Preckwinkle," Lightfoot said, according to the *Tribune*. "I'm not going to retreat from any party boss who's going to try to bully me out of the race. That's never happening. [Preckwinkle] is a party boss that was trying to bully me, absolutely, no question about it. And that has failed. And frankly we're going to continue to expose that and other things that are going on in the city."

While Preckwinkle appeared to be a formidable candidate, her campaign suffered a series of missteps that made it seem she was cursed from the beginning. Just before she announced her candidacy, Preckwinkle fired her chief of staff, John Keller, for what she called "inappropriate behavior on his personal time." Allegations emerged that after leaving a bar on Election Night 2016, he groped a woman in the backseat of a taxi. Later, the *Tribune* reported Preckwinkle had been warned of concerns with Keller's behavior months earlier, all of which cast a pall on her candidacy.

Not long after, the county inspector general released a report into a bizarre incident in which Preckwinkle's Chevy Tahoe security SUV was found abandoned near a southwest suburb overflowing with Preckwinkle political materials—a violation of county law that makes it illegal to use official vehicles for political campaigning. As I dug in on the scandal, Preckwinkle fired Delwin Gadlen, her security chief, who responded by giving me an interview where he lamented the betrayal by a woman he called a "mother figure." The situation was a personal and political embarrassment.

She had other problems. Preckwinkle had pushed a tax on sweetened beverages that came to be known as the "pop tax." While some progressives liked the policy, it hurt her badly with Black and Latino voters and was repealed by the county board. Mostly Black critics started calling her "Queen Sugar." During the annual Bud Billiken Parade, one of the top gatherings of Black residents, people on the side of route poured their sodas out in protest.

My reporting had been tough on Preckwinkle. In one story, I noted that she had given former alderperson Vilma Colom a promotion despite a hearing officer's previous recommendation that she be fired over allegations she made various offensive comments at work, including, "I can't stand these Mexicans." That story was based on internal records. For her part, Colom told me, "I am not a racist. I am not against Mexicans. I am not against anybody. Someone took bits and pieces of a conversation and spinned it for whatever reason they spinned it."

With SEIU firmly behind Preckwinkle, the Chicago Teachers Union was widely expected to come on board as well. Before it made a decision, Lightfoot attempted to get the union's endorsement, and it didn't go well. The union's firebrand president, Karen Lewis, had left her post in summer 2018 and was succeeded by Jesse Sharkey, her white socialist vice president. Part of Lightfoot's pitch to CTU, Sharkey recalled, was about making efficiencies and cuts. To Sharkey and Vice President Stacy Davis Gates, that sounded like the Emanuel administration.

"We're big government people," Davis Gates responded.

Their problem with Lightfoot's pitch echoed concerns raised in the Think-Progress interview. Lightfoot spoke a big game about equity and underdogs, but it never jibed with her conservative views on spending and taxes, or her history as a corporate lawyer. "Frankly, you take the rhetoric about equity and racial justice out of what Lori Lightfoot says, and she's a pretty neoliberal politician," Sharkey told me.

CTU decided to endorse Preckwinkle, who badly needed a game-changer to project an aura of inevitability, settle skittish donors, and reclaim the narrative. She got it December 8, when the union called a news conference to give her their support. With tens of thousands of loyal members made up of teachers and paraprofessionals who work in the city's public schools, CTU had the power and influence to reshape the playing field. CTU has long been a major influencer in the city's political campaigns. Its endorsements don't always lead to victory, but they instantly confer an air of credibility to any contender.

Standing in a Pilsen neighborhood union hall, Preckwinkle accepted the endorsement by outlining her support for a fully elected Chicago Public Schools school board, a freeze on charter schools, and a moratorium on school closings, deep scars from 2013 when Emanuel closed down fifty schools. Preckwinkle, who first wanted to be a cowgirl but became a teacher, recalled her own journey as a young girl in Minnesota. Working in schools helped prepare her for politics, Preckwinkle said, because teachers have to deal with many "constituencies," including parents and administrators. Preckwinkle beamed throughout the announcement, celebrating the "incredible enthusiasm and optimism" of young people and clearly relishing the moment. She was confident that the union could help carry her into City Hall.

The period before CTU endorsed Preckwinkle generated another behind-the-scenes story, one Lightfoot shared widely even though she wasn't part of the alleged conversation. The story goes: Jesús "Chuy" García, who was headed for Congress, met with the teachers' union as he considered possibly making another mayoral run and was asked if he would be willing to serve as a one-term mayor and then endorse Brandon Johnson, a CTU leader who had just been elected to the county board but had yet to serve a single day in public office, as his successor. CTU leaders deny the story, saying the conversation was mischaracterized, but Lightfoot would often recount the encounter as proof that the union was cravenly pursuing power. It said a lot about CTU to her.

One of the darkest arts in Chicago politics is ballot challenges. The most famous story came when State Senator Alice Palmer ran for congress and anointed attorney Barack Obama to be her successor. However, she changed her mind and decided to seek reelection, aggravating Obama, who said, "I am disappointed that she's decided to go back on her word to me." He challenged her signatures and got her kicked off the ballot.

Businessman Willie Wilson mounted a challenge against activist Ja'Mal Green, a young twentysomething who had announced he would run for mayor. Wilson advisor Rickey Hendon, the flamboyant former state senator, challenged Green's petitions, sparking a war of words on social media that led to some tense confrontations and one encounter where they looked like they were going to fight in the Board of Elections. Hendon later complained that Green yelled, "Yo mama!" at him, and Hendon vowed to challenge Green's signatures no matter what office he runs for, whether it's "dogcatcher or booty kisser." Green dropped his candidacy.

Joyce filed a challenge against Bill Daley, though he later dropped it.

The proper purpose of ballot challenges is to prevent people from getting on the ballot because they broke rules. Often, however, candidates file objections just to tie up their opponents. Preckwinkle mounted challenges against Mendoza, Lightfoot, and Dorothy Brown but was only able to kick Brown off the ballot. The other two objections solely existed to aggravate Mendoza and Lightfoot, with the latter furious with Preckwinkle for wasting her campaign money and time heading into the holiday season.

"As city employees, they're gonna be working overtime on these petitions challenges at night and on the weekend. They're gonna be working on Christmas Eve," Lightfoot said. "Merry Christmas, Toni Preckwinkle. We should just give her a bag of coal."

Those were some of the Lightfoot campaign's darkest, most grueling days. She had also broken her hand and was walking around with a cast throughout the fall. Although staffers were confident in their position, the process is mentally exhausting and requires significant resources to fight. "This is a rigged game that is designed to stop competition, to protect incumbents, and not allow ordinary people who care about the city to have access to the ballot," Lightfoot angrily said at one point, threatening that she'd be "filing a motion to sanction the lawyers who brought what we call specious, meaning complete nonsense claims" if they were in court.

Lightfoot celebrated when Preckwinkle dropped her objection, saying, "I will be the first and only out LGBTQ candidate to be on the ballot for mayor of the City of Chicago. We slayed the machine today, but they will regroup and come back. The Toni Preckwinkle that presented herself back in the day as a reformer is gone. She is the paragon of the status quo, and we will fight on to victory on February 26."

To raise morale, Lightfoot took her campaign team Christmas caroling. When one staffer objected, Lightfoot said, "Sometimes you just have to do what the boss wants."

5 | BUTCHER PAPER

SURVIVING THE PETITION CHALLENGE and making the ballot gave Lori Lightfoot something to celebrate. But while Lightfoot had assembled a strong team of hungry staffers, volunteers, and consultants, her campaign wasn't really going anywhere until an enormous corruption probe began spilling into public view. Days after Thanksgiving, Alderperson Danny Solis announced he wouldn't run for reelection. For decades, Solis had been one of the most influential members of City Council, a close confidant of Mayors Richard M. Daley and Rahm Emanuel, and chairman of the powerful Zoning Committee that oversees big-money construction projects. Solis had been appointed to represent the Pilsen neighborhood in the mid-1990s, after his predecessor, Ambrosio Medrano, went to prison as part of Operation Silver Shovel, one of the most extraordinary corruption scandals in a city known for them.

In that case, the federal government worked with an informant, John Christopher, who was part of a massive illegal dumping operation in Chicago's North Lawndale neighborhood, where contractors dumped a six-story pile of debris dubbed "Mount Henry" for the local alderperson, which Robin Amer chronicled in *The City* podcast with *USA Today*. Medrano pleaded guilty to extortion for taking $31,000 in bribes to help secure illegal dump sites in Black and Hispanic neighborhoods for Christopher's company, the *New York Times* reported. (If you think Medrano learned a lesson from his conviction, think again. After being freed from prison, Medrano became ensnared in two new corruption cases involving hospital supplies and kickbacks and got sent back behind bars.)

47

Solis appeared on public television station WTTW to discuss his retirement and was asked about Alderperson Edward Burke running for reelection. Burke was facing a challenge from Jesús "Chuy" García's political organization in the Southwest Side's Fourteenth Ward, which had once been white and Polish but is now majority Latino. Burke took over the Fourteenth Ward seat in 1969, after his father, Joseph P. Burke, died of cancer, and became the longest-serving alderperson in Chicago history.

Known for his pinstripe suits, Burke had been a key opponent of Mayor Harold Washington during the 1980s and maintained uneasy relationships with Daley and Emanuel, who allowed him to remain Finance Committee chairman rather than risk a gnarly confrontation with the vicious power broker. On the side, Burke was a property tax attorney and even represented Donald Trump on Chicago appeals. To critics, Burke was a walking model of legalized corruption, as he would frequently recuse himself from City Council votes after presiding over hearings related to his clients' business. Journalists David Kidwell, Patrick Judge, and Dan Mihalopoulos wrote a startling story noting he had "presided over a heated three-hour hearing on a taxpayer subsidy for Illinois' largest Catholic health system, Presence Health, heaping praise on witnesses and sparring with opponents before announcing his abstention during the roll call vote at the end." Despite the baggage, Burke was well-liked by other alderpersons, in part because he would generously allow his staff to do work for other members of City Council.

"I think Ald. Burke should reconsider," Solis said in the interview. "You got money, you got a great family, you got grandkids. Why do you want to run?"

✳ ✳ ✳ ✳

Days later, I was in the lobby at City Hall when I spotted Carol Marin. She is one of the best reporters in town but not a daily presence in the building or at news conferences. I remember thinking something must be going on. Our colleague Bill Ruthhart got a tip later that morning "that something strange is going on at Burke's City Hall office." Reporter John Byrne went up there and saw that brown butcher paper had been posted over the windows. News that the FBI was raiding Burke's office echoed through the building like a thunderclap. I rushed out to Burke's ward office on the Southwest Side and it, too, was being raided by the feds.

"I've been in office for forty-nine years. I've been under investigation in the past. Nothing has ever come of it, and I've always cooperated," Burke told the press outside his home, downplaying the situation. "And I'll cooperate with whatever this investigation is."

To say the raid changed everything is an understatement. I worked on a story with Ruthhart and Byrne afterward focusing on the "political silence" in the aftermath of the Burke raid. City Hall veteran Gery Chico, Bill Daley, and Toni Preckwinkle all refused interview requests by the *Tribune* about the charges and their relationships with Burke. Mendoza released a bland statement: "This news is extremely troubling, and it's exactly the kind of politics we need to get away from in Chicago," she said. There was good reason why: Mendoza had her wedding ceremony at the Burke home. We also found a photo gallery of her wedding reception at a Joliet banquet hall that showed Mendoza and her husband posing with Burke while smiling. Another shot showed the couple laughing as Burke smiled with his fist in the air, seemingly mid-anecdote. Chico had been close friends with Burke, who praised him to the *Sun-Times* when asked about the mayor's race. "I like Gery Chico," Burke said. "As you know, he and I go back a long way. He worked for me here in City Hall. And there's probably nobody more qualified than he is." As a fellow old white man whose brother had allowed Burke to remain as Finance Committee chairman, Daley was in no position to criticize Burke.

Oddly, Preckwinkle took the worst hits after it was revealed Burke hosted her at his home in Gage Park for a fundraiser that offered the status of chair for $10,000, cochair for $5,000, and sponsor for $2,500.

Lightfoot smartly trained her fire on her rivals with sharp criticism. "It seems all these other folks are running for cover and don't want to talk about him, but frankly, that underscores the fact that we've got different factions of the political machine manifested in Mendoza, Preckwinkle, Daley, and Chico and others who don't want to rock the boat because they are very much wedded to the status quo," she told the *Tribune* for our story. "It's telling that they aren't willing to step up and say, 'Look, this guy has been in office way too long, he's been allowed to amass way too much power.'" Lightfoot continued:

> It's just astounding to me. You cannot call yourself a progressive,
> you cannot tell people you are for them, that you are going to put
> them first, that you have a different vision and you want to have a

different compact with government if you are not speaking up about this issue. It is unacceptable. This is a guy who has a lot of power, power that he doesn't deserve, and we've got to talk about this. It has implications for the Finance Committee. We have a lot with city finances to work out, so how is that going to work with this cloud of an investigation hovering over this man? If not now, when? When are we going to break from the past?

Pretty soon, Lightfoot's regular stump speech focused on "the broken and corrupt political machine." I remember talking to high-ranking Mendoza and Preckwinkle advisors during the election. I said Lightfoot was well positioned to benefit from a corruption scandal overtaking other issues. They were dismissive. A Preckwinkle advisor told me, "Lori needs to smile more."

The next few weeks after Burke was raided were excruciating. Every Thursday, we would sit around the newsroom waiting to see if Burke would finally face federal charges. (I would wear nicer clothes so I wouldn't look too schlubby if I needed to head him off somewhere.) Then, the first week of January, federal prosecutors charged Burke by criminal complaint for allegedly using his position as alderperson to try to steer business to his private law firm from a company seeking to renovate a Burger King in his ward. Coincidentally, it was the same Burger King involved in Laquan McDonald's murder.

Most remarkably, the complaint alleged Burke asked one of the company's executives to attend an upcoming political fundraiser for "another politician," who was identified as Preckwinkle. The Burger King executives weren't able to attend but did send her a $10,000 check. It raised nasty questions about Preckwinkle and Burke. Why was he trying to help her so badly? (That question has never been answered.) Was she aware of his efforts? (She says no.)

Unfortunately for Preckwinkle, I reported soon thereafter that she had given Ed Burke Jr. a job. I'd been working on the story before the charges, but the county provided me the records showing she had hired him to be training and exercise manager for the county's Department of Homeland Security and Emergency Management right as the criminal charges hit.

Our story also showed he had gotten in trouble at Preckwinkle's office. In October 2017, Burke Jr. was asked to submit "some type of work-related e-mail" as proof that he had worked on specific dates from December 2016 to April 2017. He had emailed the county, "Are the written timesheets not enough?" He said he couldn't help any further. That December, Burke Jr. left for reasons that aren't clear.

I spent the next few weeks beating up Preckwinkle for her relationship with Burke. I wanted her to acknowledge whether she had spoken with the alderperson about a job for his son. She kept dodging the question when asked. Her press team objected to the questions, and I shot back, "If you could say that she didn't speak to Burke, you would." They would hem and haw but never dispute that, at least not in plain simple English, because they couldn't. That's a real lesson, by the way. If flacks can truthfully say something, they will say it. (Flacks will straight up lie to you, but most try to avoid that.)

During a *Tribune* editorial board meeting, Preckwinkle also was asked about my previous story. She sidestepped it repeatedly. First, Preckwinkle said Burke Jr. was "an employee of the county for more than twenty years. He had a training job in the sheriff's office and transferred to the department of Homeland Security in a similar function."

When she was asked if the Burkes or anyone associated with them asked her to hire Burke Jr. or put his résumé at the front of the line, she simply said, "There was an opening in the Department of Homeland Security, and he met the qualifications and he was hired for that position." When they asked if he was given special treatment, Preckwinkle said, "This is a Shakman-exempt position. We hired him in that Shakman-exempt position," referring to jobs where they're allowed to hire for political reasons.

The "answers" pissed me off to no end. She wasn't answering the question. And they highlighted one of the more incomprehensible facts about the campaign: Preckwinkle would literally read answers to questions from a sheet of paper everywhere she went, an attempt at avoiding verbal gaffes that sucked the life out of her candidacy and made her seem like a robot. The evasive answers didn't stop me. I kept digging into a tip that Burke Jr. had been under internal investigation for allegedly making inappropriate sexual comments at the sheriff's office when Preckwinkle hired him. The records were pretty astonishing. One investigation began after a female sheriff's employee alleged that Burke Jr. was "consistently disrespectful of women," talked about sex acts, and would leave the office by saying, "I'm leaving, going to watch the girls on Rush Street," as I reported for the *Tribune*. Records also said Burke Jr. called himself "the law," claimed to have "tapes" that would "humiliate" Thomas J.

Dart, sheriff of Cook County, and vowed to run for sheriff and fire a bunch of employees when he won.

Eventually, Preckwinkle called a press conference with what she said was "a growing coalition of elected officials" to discuss "her plan to dramatically expand the city's investment to help small businesses in Chicago's Black and Brown communities." The press release continued: "Toni enjoys broad support from electeds across our city, county, and state because she's a proven fighter who's unafraid to take on the good old boys club." The news release mentioned Alderperson Scott Waguespack, a progressive champion who had feuded for years with Emanuel over left-wing issues facing the City Council. On everything, he had been a critic, and his voice was widely respected. When we showed up to the news conference, I took special notice of his absence.

During the news conference, I asked again if she had spoken to Burke about his son. To my surprise, she finally admitted it. "I had a meeting with Ed Burke," Preckwinkle said. "He shared with me that his son was looking for a new opportunity." She got defensive: "I had one or two meetings a year with Ald. Burke out of a thousand meetings." And she denied repeatedly that he was her "ally." I remember walking out of the meeting exhilarated and confused. She had confirmed that she spoke with Burke, which was obvious to anyone with a brain but which I wouldn't have otherwise been able to prove.

The Burke scandal was clearly grating on Preckwinkle, but it was also boosting Lightfoot. At the first forum after Burke was charged with corruption, Lightfoot shined while Preckwinkle skipped the debate entirely, looking to avoid uncomfortable questions. In her absence, Mendoza held up Preckwinkle's name plate in mocking fashion and slapped Chico after he called her "Susan." "The A is not silent, and neither am I," she said. Later, the moderators asked each candidate a staple of political forums: if not yourself, who would you be voting for in the election? Several candidates, including Daley, said they would support Lightfoot.

Buoyed in part by the affirmation of her rivals, Lightfoot left in a good mood. On the way home, Lightfoot stopped with her wife, Amy Eshleman, to fill up the car. In a singsong voice, Lightfoot said, "Yeah, I'm running for mayor. Yeah, I pump my own gas."

★ ★ ★ ★

In late January, the federal government gave Lightfoot something else to smile about when an affidavit in support of the warrant to search Solis's home and offices was obtained by the *Sun-Times*. It revealed Solis had been under investigation for years and caught him on tape talking about prostitution. "I want to get a good massage, with a nice ending. Do you know any good places?" Solis asked political operative Roberto Caldero. He followed up, "What kind of women do they got there?"

"Asian," Caldero said.

"Oh good. Good, good, good," Solis said. "I like Asian."

Solis had also asked Caldero for help getting "blue medicine," a reference to Viagra, which Caldero said had become more expensive due to the Affordable Care Act. Solis was also caught on tape soliciting campaign cash from lobbyist Victor Reyes, who angrily complained that he hadn't sent him business. "How about anything? How about anything, Danny?" Reyes said. "How about anything. Not just the big one. How 'bout one fucking thing."

Reyes then noted that Alderpersons Roberto Maldonado, Joe Moreno, and Ricardo Munoz sent him business as Solis promised to get him help. Solis wasn't charged with a crime, but the revelations shook City Hall and angered colleagues. "The political machine is crumbling," Lightfoot tweeted.

After the initial revelation, Lightfoot held a news conference to press her advantage. "Voters don't want a candidate who is tied to this ever-deepening corruption scandal and I hear that from people all over the city. Even beyond this election cycle, Chicagoans are sick of government where individuals serve themselves at the expense of taxpayers," Lightfoot said. "We're sick of aldermen lining their own pockets instead of focusing on uplifting the quality of life in their own neighborhoods."

Although the focus on corruption helped her, it was still slow-going. Lightfoot expressed frustration at one forum that they weren't allowed to challenge one another, saying the "challenge with these forums is you don't get to follow up and call nonsense on things that you hear people say, and that's incredibly frustrating." At a separate forum, Lightfoot criticized Mendoza, Preckwinkle, Daley, and Chico for skipping events, with particular focus on Daley. "Bill Daley has barely been out here. Maybe his strategy is to raise a bunch of money and only go on TV, but I don't think that's the way you can be mayor," Lightfoot said, as reported by the *Tribune*. "Neighborhoods are starving. They want to be heard. They want to be respected, so coming out to these kinds of events still has enormous value."

Daley fired back in a rare comment: "Some of these people in this group would go to a door opening, because they have nothing else to do. I'm not going to be dictated by the schedules of people who are looking for anything to get a few people in a room and think that they're going to get points by kicking the hell out of me with a bunch of lies or rhetoric that heats up a crowd. Why would I want to do their work for them? Forget it. I don't need to do that." The problem for Daley was that, from the media's perspective, he wasn't doing anything other than running TV commercials, which are important but can't be everything in a competitive field.

Chico, for his part, dismissed the importance of the ongoing corruption case. "Never to rarely do I get asked by voters about all of this. I just don't," Chico told the *Tribune*. "The question people ask is, 'What are you going to do to make my life better?'"

Despite Chico's comments, Lightfoot was starting to pick up steam, and it was directly related to the corruption issue. She was starting to break through into the top tier but wasn't quite there. The local Fox station kept her off the main stage, which she complained about for years as putting her at the "kid's table." Still, her campaign team felt she needed to get on television, and to do that, Lightfoot needed more money. The team was stretched thin. Nadia Perl, her excellent press secretary, was essentially doing several jobs. Lightfoot made a series of phone calls to potential donors, telling them her candidacy was viable but would need more money to launch television ads and get over the top.

As she struggled to get donors, campaign chief of staff Rob Fojtik told Lightfoot she should write herself checks to pay for the ads, which she did not appreciate. "You think I make all this money!" Lightfoot ranted. "Fuck you!" (Lightfoot reported making an average adjusted gross income of $971,626 from 2014 through 2017 on her tax returns.) She talked about paying for her daughter's private education and supporting her extended family. He held the phone away from his head as Lightfoot yelled, and she hung up.

Later, Lightfoot called back, and he expected her to apologize or take a calmer tack. Instead, Lightfoot yelled at him some more. Fojtik, who went to work for Lightfoot early and was a key player in her campaign, called campaign consultant Joanna Klonsky, who talked Lightfoot into making the investment, perhaps the single most important act of her campaign.

One of the initial attempts at making the commercial involved a steam-roller. Lighfoot was sarcastic about the idea. "Oh, so you're gonna put the lesbian in, what, a tank top on a steamroller?" a staffer recalled. But then Beacon Media brought an outstanding ad with photos of Chico, Preckwinkle, Mendoza, and Daley appearing first on the dimly lit screen. "The truth is, they're all tied to the same broken Chicago machine. Except me," Lightfoot said, as the lights flick on and she appears on screen. "I've prosecuted corrupt aldermen and held police accountable. Now, I'm running for mayor to finally make City Hall work for you." Speaking directly into the camera, Lightfoot said she supports an elected school board and making all neighborhoods safe before ending, "Shady backroom deals haven't served us. It's time to bring in the light."

Fojtik was one of the unsung heroes of the Lightfoot campaign. In addition to pushing the ad spending, Fojtik helped pressure influential LGBTQ group Equality Illinois into supporting her campaign. Leaders with the organization had been supportive of Preckwinkle. Mendoza had a real base of support from gay Chicago. Some were skeptical of Lightfoot because she hadn't been involved enough with the community. Others were considering a double endorsement with Mendoza.

Fojtik, who is gay, pushed them to endorse Lightfoot alone and made clear where he stood. "Let me get this straight. The Black lesbian who put out the LGBT policy ahead of everybody isn't going to get the endorsement?" Fojtik asked one person, insinuating that passing on her would be racist. The orga-nization came through for Lightfoot, giving her an enormous boost along the white lakefront on the North Side.

The *Sun-Times* endorsed Lightfoot shortly afterward, giving her another big boost. "I was asleep and Amy woke me up and said, 'You got the *Sun-Times* endorsement.' You could've knocked me over with a feather, I was absolutely floored," Lightfoot said in the *City So Real* docuseries. "I frankly didn't believe her for the longest time."

Heading into the final stretch of the campaign, Lightfoot received a gift when state representative Robert Martwick made a fool of himself by crash-ing a press conference she had called to criticize a proposal he introduced to make the Cook County assessor an appointed position. Martwick, a property tax attorney himself and Preckwinkle ally, had been critical of recently elected assessor Fritz Kaegi, who had defeated Joe Berrios for the post after arguing that the system benefited insiders. He showed up halfway through and inexplicably chose to confront Lightfoot: "This sort of Trump-style, where you're trying to draw attention to yourself without assessing the facts of a situation, shows exactly why you're wholly unprepared to be mayor of the city of Chicago."

"You could have called him at any point. You could have called him during his transition period to have that discussion," Lightfoot retorted. "Instead, what you did is you dropped the bill on a Friday afternoon and you called him afterward. That smacks of cronyism. You're a Joe Berrios surrogate. You were a Joe Berrios surrogate through the entire campaign. You filed this bill to profit yourself. Who benefits from a system that's not changed?"

Martwick tried to cast the bill as a conversation starter and said it was just a way to figure out best practices. Other counties appoint assessors, he said. "Why are we not having that discussion?"

"Because you're not credible," Lightfoot responded.

"Neither are you, Lori. Neither are you," Martwick said. "If you intend to govern the city of Chicago like this, this is exactly why you're not prepared to be mayor of the city of Chicago."

"This is Rob Martwick, exhibit A of the broken and corrupt political system," Lightfoot said.

"Oh thank you. That's very nice," Martwick answered.

"Thank you for showing up," Lightfoot said, as she dominated the confrontation.

The confrontation has taken legendary status. In my view, it's overblown in significance—it isn't why Lightfoot made the runoff. But it helped show people the best of her, standing up for herself and diagnosing a problem, which the assessment system undoubtedly was. And it gave her significant free airtime. The only downside was the lesson it internalized for the candidate: that slapping rivals works. Fighting can often feel good, but you can't scrap with every clown who aggravates you in life or politics; the occasional beatdown is fine, particularly when someone else starts it, but nobody wants to be around someone who's in a daily brawl with a new opponent.

Lightfoot received a huge boost days before the election when Alderperson Scott Waguespack endorsed her, a move that put him at odds with Preckwinkle's team, which thought he would be on board. Later, a Waguespack political worker posted on Facebook, "Lori has confirmed Waguespack to be floor leader or Finance chair. Toni will not." That led to an angry denial from

Waguespack, who said they hadn't cut a deal. Waguespack was nevertheless the only sitting alderman to support Lightfoot.

Days before the election, Lightfoot received a text message from Alderperson Carlos Ramirez-Rosa's campaign asking if she'd support him. Ramirez-Rosa is a socialist who backed Preckwinkle but represented Lightfoot's ward in City Council. Lightfoot responded, "Carlos supports Toni Preckwinkle. Why would I support him? We need an alderman who actually wants to serve the people of the 35th Ward and can build conditions to get things done," Lightfoot wrote. "That's not Carlos. I support Amanda Yu Diet[e]rich. Please take me off your texting list." The exchange amused some people, but it blew their minds that she would engage with it while in the heat of battle.

Mendoza, meanwhile, was starting to find her voice—attacking Daley. She hammered him at a debate for an op-ed he wrote defending his brother's unpopular privatization of the city's parking meters as "good business." Her strong attacks against Daley hurt him, particularly with union members.

"It was good business for your family," Mendoza said to Daley. "It was terrible business for Chicagoans." She and Lightfoot also teamed up for a rare joint statement criticizing Preckwinkle after she held a Be Fair to Toni rally meant to rally women but that the two blitzed with criticism over the chief of staff's sexual harassment case.

Less than a week before the election, an independent union-affiliated political committee called Fight Back for a Better Tomorrow began airing an attack ad on Daley titled "The Real Bill Daley 2.0." It connected him to unpopular former Republican governor Bruce Rauner, who had just been defeated in November.

On Election Night, some Lightfoot team members bet that she would come in third place and miss the runoff, though others thought she might come in second. Lightfoot watched a Duke basketball game to distract herself. She came in first, stunning the city. At the campaign party, Klonsky cried over Alderperson John Arena's defeat at the hands of Jim Gardiner, a firefighter who had been accused of stalking a woman, but soon they turned their attention to second place. Klonsky and others wanted to face Daley, who would be a better matchup and allow Lightfoot to avoid an ugly battle with a fellow self-proclaimed Black woman progressive. As the results came in, Klonsky said, "Oh fuck, it's going to be Toni."

The surprise win kicked off a scramble for Lightfoot's team. Campaign advisor Dave Mellet was still editing her speech with the teleprompter operator while she was walking up the steps toward the podium. Mellet also had the foresight to bring the ad team to the election-night party to film her speech for a quickly produced new ad for the runoff. Lightfoot beamed in her victory speech. "So what do you think of us now?" she declared. "This, my friends, is what change looks like!"

6 | BRING IN THE LIGHT

THE MORNING AFTER LORI Lightfoot made the runoff, she went to a Chicago Transit Authority (CTA) station to greet voters. Immediately, she sought to distinguish herself from Preckwinkle. "I am an independent reform candidate. I do not represent the past. I am not tied to the broken political machine, and I did not aspire to climb the ranks of the Cook County Democratic Party to be the party boss," Lightfoot said. "I'm not affiliated with Ed Burke, Joe Berrios, or anyone else who represents the old, corrupt Chicago way. I am offering voters a complete break from that past and pushing us forward in a way that brings people together and makes government more inclusive."

Preckwinkle started her campaign with a defense around her political record: "I think I have the strongest progressive record of any of the candidates who were running, and that's still true. I'm the most progressive candidate in this race." It became a mantra: "I'm the progressive in the race." By making it about who's progressive, Preckwinkle made it harder to distinguish herself from Lightfoot, a fellow Black woman who also claimed the label. To sully Lightfoot's progressive credentials, Preckwinkle launched a negative campaign ad: "Lori Lightfoot talks a big game. But what's her real story?" the narrator said. "She defended a Wall Street bank being sued for racial discrimination and worked for Republican politicians trying to protect their power," it said, referencing Lightfoot's efforts to support a less gerrymandered map. "And after using her influence to gain a powerful appointment, she overruled investigators to justify police shootings."

Political campaigns are about drawing contrasts. But candidates also have to stand for something. Preckwinkle was glad to make the runoff, largely on the strength of her union support but without real momentum or strong voter affection for her candidacy—she came in limping. Her campaign began demonizing Lightfoot but often focused on the wrong items, and some of her political decisions were incredible. She ran a commercial featuring her own role in Laquan McDonald's death investigation—informing Jamie Kalven that the teenager had been shot sixteen times—but included footage from the shooting, drawing significant criticism from rival candidates and people with good taste that she was using a teen's killing for political gain. More critically, Preckwinkle needed to identify herself strongly with voters as something other than a soda-taxing schoolmarm. Her effort at redefining herself included a video in which different people came on screen with a series of descriptions of her. It started with "tough, no nonsense," highlighted her "strong sense of what's right," and continued with Preckwinkle herself appearing on screen and inexplicably yelping, "And very hip!" Preckwinkle is a lot of things, many of them good, but hip isn't one of them. Making matters worse, Preckwinkle's tendency to read responses from a binder left her cold. She often introduced herself as "a teacher by profession," when most people would say, "I was a teacher."

Preckwinkle's stiff campaign style left her vulnerable to Lightfoot counterattacks. During one forum, Preckwinkle said she had taken "the strongest position" against Burke. Lightfoot immediately butted in, "That's not true." "Everything you're talking about now, you only did after the scandal broke," Lightfoot added. Preckwinkle's campaign wheels started falling off right away.

A couple weeks before the election, the campaign dropped its commercials because it couldn't pay to be on the air. "We're making strategic decisions to put us in the best place to win this campaign," Preckwinkle said, in a ludicrous comment.

Lightfoot's campaign, meanwhile, pushed hard for change and presented a positive image. Her ad makers, Beacon Media, ran a series of crisp commercials that perfectly blended humor and seriousness. In one memorable ad, Lightfoot sat in a chair speaking out for public safety and against corruption while her daughter, Vivian, did the flossing dance in the background, played trumpet, and otherwise attempted to distract her as Lightfoot said she would remain focused on the city's issues.

Critics weren't able to get anything to stick against Lightfoot, who kept the worst elements of her personality under control, though she showed flashes of it off camera. Campaign staff found a Yelp review she had written in August 2017 and approached her about possibly taking it down. The review was astonishing:

> I would never use VIP Limo again. Driver Carlos showed up early for our pick up. A good sign, right? Turned out not be so [sic]. Carlos shows up and wants to use our bathroom. A little strange, but fine. Turns out, he pisses in our toilet and does not have the courtesy to put down the toilet seats. Beginning of the end. We were going to the United Center. Carlos clearly has no idea who [sic] to get there. He is totally reliant on a whacked GPS system that has him driving his huge Cadillac Escalade stretch down extremely narrow neighborhood streets going in a route that made no sense. I had to take over and give him clear directions to get to the expressway. Apparently that was totally emasculating to him, but how [sic] says, "my GPS says I should get off at Division" off the expressway when we are going much further south and west. We finally get there, and he says he needs two numbers for the return pick up. We had already given him one from my female spouse. I say I will just give him mine since I am the person paying. Carlos says "I need one from the gentlemen." I am totally confused, and question this. Carlos explains to this dumb female that he needs a number from a guy because "girls take too many pictures and run down the battery on their phone." My expression must have said something because he then said "trust me. I have been doing this 20 years." I am a middle aged women not some dumb kid from his misogynistic world view. I of course gave it to him and his response was to rudely close the window divider while I was still talking. This guy was a complete a-hole. Stupid, terrible driver and a complete jerk on top of it. Cannot believe he is employed and I would never use this service again while he is.

The review was vintage Lightfoot. So was her decision not to take it down, as she stood by every word.

Preckwinkle's constant missteps and bad luck were met with good fortune for Lightfoot. I followed her around the city for the *Tribune*, where I watched her deflect criticism and build support. Early in the runoff, Lightfoot beamed as she walked off stage at the Hideout. She had just done a public interview at one of the city's celebrated dive bars where she charmed the crowd of left-wing Pabst Blue Ribbon drinkers with a series of quips dissing Mayor Rahm Emanuel and Preckwinkle. In the interview with Chicago journalists Ben Joravsky and Mick Dumke, Lightfoot cast herself as an outsider, a fresh voice in a city where the status quo was failing. Seeking to draw a comparison between her and Preckwinkle, she beseeched the audience to remember "I was probably one of Rahm Emanuel's harshest critics, particularly around police reform and accountability."

"And unlike Toni, I ran against him," she said, drawing cheers and applause.

Lightfoot lounged around for a few minutes, soaking in the good cheer. She was headed for the door when a woman walked up to her with a question.

"I'm just wondering how you can call yourself independent when you were head of OPS between 2002 and 2004 when Ronald Watts was running wild," the woman said, referring to Lightfoot's time at the city's police over-sight agency and a disgraced former sergeant tied to more than two hundred wrongful convictions. As soon as the woman started her question, Lightfoot's staff tensed up. Like most aides to politicians, they hated unscripted encoun-ters with members of the public. They also feared what Lightfoot might say.

"Because of my body of work," Lightfoot responded. "Because of the things that I did to make sure we were making a difference at OPS and everything I've done throughout my professional life."

The woman was obviously unimpressed and said so, leading to a tense back and forth. "I just don't understand why your answer is always, 'I'm perfect, I did everything perfect,'" she responded.

"My answer isn't [that] 'I'm perfect.' I'm a human being. I'm fallible just like everybody else," Lightfoot said. "What I'd urge you to do is actually get the facts."

"I do have the facts," the woman said.

Lightfoot interjected, "I'm doubting that."

"I just feel like your answer is always either 'It's the system' or 'I did everything right,'" the woman said.

Lightfoot urged the woman to visit her campaign website, and when the woman said she'd been there, Lightfoot cut the conversation short. "Well, OK," Lightfoot replied as she walked away. "Nice to meet you."

As Lightfoot made her way to the exit, she was flagged down by bartender Marcelyn Cole, who wore a No Cop Academy button highlighting her opposition to a police training center on the West Side.

Cole asked if Lightfoot would support an elected Civilian Police Accountability Council, a proposed group that would have power to appoint and fire the police superintendent, investigate all police shootings and alleged misconduct, and overhaul the current disciplinary process.

"I support the GAPA proposal," Lightfoot said, referring to a competing plan pushed by the Grassroots Alliance for Police Accountability. She said she supports police oversight but thinks the GAPA plan would create a "more inclusive" board and is the ordinance "that's currently viable."

Cole thanked her for answering, then asked about "the ban on rent control." Lightfoot, who opposed rent control, said she thinks they need to focus on creating more affordable housing.

"Do you think those things are opposed though?" Cole replied. "Can we lift the ban on rent control and also support affordable housing? Can't we do both those things?"

Lightfoot again emphasized the need to build more units to accommodate, but as Cole interjected, she answered, "Alright, I've got to go, sorry."

At a debate, Preckwinkle said she admires Lightfoot for being an open lesbian. Lightfoot turned it around, suggesting that it was a dog whistle to hurt her, particularly with conservative Black voters. Around the same time, some Black supporters of Preckwinkle posted flyers around the city attacking Lightfoot for her sexuality, which Preckwinkle denounced. While on the West Side, I watched Lightfoot argue with a woman who asked her about promoting "an LGBTQ inclusive curriculum [in the schools]."

"What I'm asking you to do is educate yourself about the real issues," Lightfoot told the woman, in an incident I reported on for the *Tribune*. "That was stuff that was put out to inflame people that are conservative to get them to fear that this lesbian is somehow going to take over the world and corrupt their children." She ended the conversation abruptly. "It's offensive. It's homophobic. And it's completely inconsistent with my values. So, thank you, I've gotta go."

Lightfoot could do no wrong throughout the runoff. She had natural momentum and a favorable political climate. Manny Perez, who had been brought in as campaign manager in the runoff, worked to keep the campaign level and avoid unnecessary mistakes. It was working.

Near the end of the campaign, Preckwinkle started getting desperate. Her allies pushed a story to local media outlets over a 2004 house fire in which four children were killed. Lightfoot was briefly serving as chief of staff at the Office of Emergency Management and Communications. The family sued, alleging that 911 dispatchers ignored and hung up on calls about the fire and that the city violated a temporary restraining order when it destroyed records of calls after the fire, as we reported for the *Tribune.*

Lightfoot testified in a deposition that she received the temporary restraining order and directed her secretary to preserve the records, but somehow it fell through the cracks. Then Cook County Judge Lynn Egan described Lightfoot's approach to the restraining order as shockingly "lax" and "cavalier." Preckwinkle took the attack a step further with rhetoric that made it seem like Lightfoot had something to do with the deaths themselves.

"It's important to remember that in this 2004 fire, four young people died," Preckwinkle said during a debate. "Four young people died. It's profoundly disturbing to me. Four young people died."

"There was nothing cavalier about the way that we handled it," Lightfoot responded. "I directed the people who preserve the tapes to make sure that they preserved them, and they failed to do that. And the people who were responsible were disciplined accordingly."

The campaign launched a commercial about the incident, though, with high-ranking Preckwinkle campaign aide Jessey Neves releasing a statement accusing Lightfoot of leading "a troubling cover up." It burned Lightfoot to no end—she resented the scorched-earth tactics, as polling suggested she was going to win easily—and at the final debate between the candidates, Lightfoot brutalized Preckwinkle. "You've made the hallmark of your campaign since Feb. 26 to denigrate me, to challenge me, to portray me as something other than I am," Lightfoot said. "Our children are watching. You talk about your grandchildren all the time. I have to explain to my daughter what it means when adults lie. I have to explain to my daughter what it means when adults are bullies. I have to explain to my daughter what it means when an adult says something that's not true just to try to score political points."

A hapless Preckwinkle responded, "This is a person who is complaining now about the tenor of the campaign, but in the first debate called me a liar and has repeatedly said I'm a cockroach. I think it's a little bit hypocritical for her to complain now about the tenor of the campaign." (Lightfoot had compared the Burke candidates to cockroaches scurrying once the lights turned on.)

As the campaign started to reach its crescendo, Preckwinkle held a rally to get Chicago's Black political establishment on board. It got ugly. US Rep. Bobby Rush, a former Black Panther, referred to Lightfoot as "symbolic change," "counterfeit change," and "chump change." He falsely said she was representing the Fraternal Order of Police and said her voters would be responsible for the next person killed by a cop. "This election is really about what type of police force we're going to have in the city of Chicago, and everyone who votes for Lori, the blood of the next young Black man or Black woman who is killed by the police is on your hands," Rush said. "If you're against police brutality and murder, you ought to be for Toni Preckwinkle. She's the only one who is going to have the police under her control."

I'm the reporter who told Lightfoot what Rush had said. She dismissed it as desperation, then pulled up to me again. "So many of those people have been elected officials for decades and what has happened to Black and brown communities under their stewardship? Not a lot, and if anything, deterioration," Lightfoot told me outside the Wrightwood-Ashburn Branch of the Chicago Public Library. "I think what people want to hear is, what's our message for the future, what are we going to do in concrete terms to bring change." During one tour of a union training facility, I pulled Lightfoot to the side to ask her about a reception she had received from a Black audience at the DuSable Black History Museum. She whispered, "If I were Toni Preckwinkle, I'd be so fucking depressed."

Throughout the runoff, Lightfoot racked up endorsements. She earned support from almost all of her rivals except Bill Daley, who stayed out, and Amara Enyia, who stayed true to the sentiment she shared with Chance the Rapper. US Rep. Jesus "Chuy" García gave her his support and progressive credibility. Paul Vallas immediately endorsed her in his campaign concession speech on election night, but word got back to the Lightfoot team that he had been asking residents why they hadn't voted for him when he was supposed to be canvassing for Lightfoot. Southwest Side alderperson Matt O'Shea, whose ward sees the highest consistent turnout, also gave her his support. Even though she had been tough on police, O'Shea was impressed with her background as a former federal prosecutor and her straightforward demeanor. He thought she would be fair, and his propolice residents hated Preckwinkle for her tax policies and a belief she was antipolice—she had once called Garry McCarthy a "racist bully boy."

A key endorsement came from Willie Wilson, who had earned support from a large chunk of Black Chicago, winning several wards. To beat Preckwinkle with Black voters, Lightfoot had to contend with the fact that she wasn't really engaged in the city's South and West Sides. She was married to a white woman and lived in Logan Square. Wilson was central to that effort, though Lightfoot almost blew the endorsement. His team wanted her to visit him at his condo by the Chicago River, which she was reluctant to do out of concerns that there would be cameras in the lobby. She suggested meeting at a restaurant but was talked into going there. Lightfoot got him on board, and they began campaigning together, from a West Side club to a South Side steppers event where the three of us boogied together. I spent a lot of time with the two of them, to the point that Lightfoot teasingly asked me if I had become "a Willie Wilson groupie." In retrospect, I think Lightfoot would've beat Preckwinkle handily even without him, but no surrogate put more work into taking her around and campaigning on her behalf. He also gave me my favorite response to Rush's comments: "I think that he probably was drinking and smoking marijuana at the same time."

★ ★ ★ ★

In the end, Lightfoot stomped Preckwinkle, 74 percent to 26, the sort of lopsided margin Richard M. Daley used to rack up against total nobodies. Donald Trump called. "You're very special!" he said. Lightfoot grinned.

Lightfoot celebrated in her victory speech. "A lot of little boys and girls are out there watching us tonight, and they're seeing the beginning of something, well, a little bit different. They're seeing a city reborn, a city where it doesn't matter what color you are, where it surely doesn't matter how tall you are, and where it doesn't matter who you love, just as long as you love with all your heart." She added, "Together we can and will finally put the interests of our people, all of our people, ahead of the interests of a powerful few. Together we can and we will remake Chicago—thriving, prosperous, better, stronger, fairer for everyone."

7 | "I SUPPORT BOZO"

LEADING UP TO THE 2019 election, Mayor Rahm Emanuel brought his staff together to demand a smooth transition for his successor. Emanuel regularly invoked his time at the White House to hammer home points about a wide array of issues, and the transition was no different. In 1992, Emanuel told staffers, Bill Clinton defeated George H. W. Bush, and the Republican president was gracious in turning over power. Even before Donald Trump and January 6, it was important to Emanuel. He wanted his administration to give Lightfoot all the support she would need. And on a snarkier level, Emanuel believed she would need all the help she could get.

The morning after Election Day, Emanuel welcomed Lightfoot to City Hall for a meeting. Heading into the session, Emanuel planned to deliver a warning against an elected school board. Emanuel once told the media, "I don't believe what we need right now is more politics in school." Privately, Emanuel has a spiel about the five great jobs in American political life: president of the United States, governor of California or New York, and mayor of New York or Chicago, which made the list due to the level of control City Hall has over schools and trains. Emanuel bitterly fought the Chicago Teachers Union. Teachers went out on their first strike in decades against him. When Emanuel took office, Chicago Public Schools had the shortest school day and year, which he changed. He invoked all that in his last City Council meeting after Lightfoot was elected, as he asked alderpersons to "stand shoulder to shoulder with our mayor-elect."

"She will need your support to keep our students and our schools moving in the same right direction. Stand united with her in the defense of the hard-won gains," Emanuel said. "Do not allow those who stood in the way of progress before to reverse the progress we collectively have made over the last eight years."

In the meeting with Lightfoot, Emanuel launched into his spiel about the dangers of an elected school board. Lightfoot listened and assured him, "Oh, I don't want that." Emanuel's people were astounded by the comment, given that she had campaigned unequivocally on an elected school board. To them, it highlighted her untrustworthiness. Still, they were pleased by her stance and sent word to Illinois Senate president John Cullerton to put a brick on the bill. For years, House Speaker Michael Madigan had given support to the elected school board while Cullerton smothered it, and he was happy to keep that going.

Much more difficult was the decision on Lincoln Yards, a megadevelopment on the North Side that was seeking $1.3 billion in tax subsidies. Lightfoot had not taken a clear position on the project itself but had expressed reservations, particularly about process. In fall 2018 Lightfoot had demanded that the city "slow down" the project "to allow for transparency and community input." In March, during the runoff, Lightfoot said it should be delayed "until the next term and should not have moved one step forward without an explanation of the effects on population density, schools, traffic and other factors." But it was up for a vote that April, and Emanuel wanted her buy-in or wanted her to take ownership by blocking it.

The stakes were high. Lincoln Yards infuriated folks who believe the city only cares about the North Side. But it would be a major project that could grow the city if it developed to its projections. Lightfoot started taking pressure from trade labor groups, including big donors, who were concerned about jobs. Emanuel chief of staff Joe Deal told Planning Commissioner David Reifman, who had been the project's biggest champion, that it wasn't going to happen. Reifman was apoplectic. But Lightfoot couldn't stomach denying the project and let it pass after the developer agreed to a modest increase in construction contracts to more women- and minority-owned firms.

"Enjoy this moment in the sun, because you're never going to get a deal like this again out of the city of Chicago as long as I'm mayor," she told the developers, in a meeting she bragged about later.

Not long after the election, Lightfoot called a meeting in which she dressed down her team after a staffer showed up late for a meeting. "I want you guys to be here on time to take this shit seriously," she said, seeming giddy with power. Her campaign manager, Manny Perez, was taken aback because he hadn't seen her so angry. Her treatment of people started to change. There was a growing sense among some in her circle that she didn't think she needed anyone. After all, she had beaten Toni Preckwinkle, the head of the Cook County Democratic Party, a kingmaker who ran one of the largest counties in the country.

The victory went to her head. Some people on her team later joked that she was like a child star who had gotten too much, too fast. City Hall denizens worried she was buying the hype that she got elected by such a large margin due to intrinsic personal qualities. Without taking anything away from Lightfoot, one needs to realize that politics are often about a moment. This time, the moment was primed for an outsider, and Lightfoot faced a flawed candidate running an abysmal campaign.

While others enjoyed the victory, Perez worried about what it would mean for governing. When everyone is with you, who is with you? Who do you work most closely with? He wasn't the only one sharing the concerns about Lightfoot's base. Emanuel expressed his views to confidants another way: he scoffed that Lightfoot's support was a mile wide and an inch deep.

The relationship with alderpersons is the most important for a mayor. They are eyes and ears on the street who can help carry an agenda. She did little to build their individual support. Instead, Lightfoot made clear she was ready to scrap in a *New York Times* interview days after the election.

"The machine was built to last. And no one in that kind of context gives up power easily or willingly, and I know that. But what I said before and I'll repeat here is, we won in all 50 wards. We won with an almost 50-point spread. I am not going to allow a relic of the past to undermine the mandate of the people. And I would like to have a good, productive relationship with members of the City Council, but I'm not going to allow them to undermine what the people's choice was and what the people want, which is change," Lightfoot said. "And you know, I haven't gotten to where I've gotten in life by letting people walk all over me. And I'm not about to start now. And I would, as I said, would like people to recognize and respect the vote, and if they're not willing to, I'm ready to fight."

During the transition, Lightfoot traveled to Washington, DC, for meetings, including one with Ivanka Trump. That was one of the clearest signs of trouble at 121 North LaSalle: she had yet to meet with most alderpersons but was taking pictures with the president's daughter. She was also discarding allies. Very quickly, Lightfoot parted ways with Willie Wilson, who had devoted countless hours to campaigning on her behalf and escorting her around the city. Lightfoot complained he wanted her to hire unqualified people, but staff was stunned by how totally she shunned him.

When Lightfoot did sit down with members of City Council, she regularly brought up who had supported her and who hadn't. When she met with Walter Burnett, an affable, longtime alderperson who had gone to prison as a young man and turned his life around to be a popular politician, she asked him about supporting Preckwinkle. Burnett, who was closely aligned with Secretary of State Jesse White, a Preckwinkle ally, told her he did what White wanted him to do. "If Jesse White supports Preckwinkle, I support Preckwinkle," Burnett said. "Jesse White supports Bozo, I support Bozo."

Veteran alderpersons focused on committee chairmanships, which are theoretically supposed to be selected within City Council but have historically been chosen by the mayor. Burnett wanted to keep the post he had under Emanuel. Others wanted more power. Alderperson Anthony Beale felt frustrated by the administration's lack of feedback. He cautioned against elevating Alderperson Scott Waguespack, a reform darling who was expected to take over the powerful Finance Committee, and worked with Alderperson Tom Tunney to organize the council into picking their own chairmen. "What are we supposed to do, just sit back and wait?" he reasoned.

In a meeting with Lightfoot, he also complained that the administration had hired Cleopatra Watson, his opponent in the previous election. Perez had told him it was a mistake to bring Watson into the office and would be handled, but Beale raised it to Lightfoot. "I'll take care of it," she said, but the alderperson's tone rubbed her the wrong way. Alderperson Roderick Sawyer, whose father was mayor after Harold Washington died in the late 1980s, supported Preckwinkle. Joanna Klonsky had been a longtime friend of his and pushed for him to get a committee. He was angry that he got "health," which he called a "kiddy committee."

During her meeting with downtown alderperson Brendan Reilly, one of the sharpest political operators on the council and maybe the only one who truly understands the rule book, Lightfoot said she was looking at reducing the number of City Council committees as a good governance measure. He explained to her that she needed more. "You need votes, and chairmen will be loyal," Reilly said.

Alderperson Ariel Reboyras, who had served as Emanuel's public safety chairman, cried when Lightfoot told him he wouldn't get a committee, she told people afterward. He had been abandoned by many in the Latino Caucus for US Rep. Luis Gutierrez's daughter and unexpectedly beat her. All fall, Reboyras told his colleagues on City Council that he was only running to keep a chairmanship and make sure his staff remained employed. His sadness was a "How could you do this to me?" response. Lightfoot soon relented and gave him a committee on the census, then immigrants' rights. He almost always voted with her.

Lightfoot stalled on releasing names of chairmen as long as she could in an attempt to prevent them from successfully organizing by creating a sense of desperation, whereby they would accept whatever she gave them. It worked.

Meetings with alderpersons sometimes became exercises in senseless acts of self-harm. First-term socialist Rossana Rodriguez Sanchez, who had defeated the Mell political dynasty on the Northwest Side, recalled her first meeting with Lightfoot when she ended the conversation by asking if she could give feedback.

"There is a perception you do whatever Alderman Carlos Ramirez-Rosa tells you to do," Lightfoot said, referring to Rodriguez Sanchez's close ally. "And as a woman of color you should develop your own voice in politics. You should have your own voice. If you want to work on developing your own voice, I can help you." Rodriguez Sanchez took it as an insult. Lightfoot sat down later with Alderperson Raymond Lopez, but her team asked him to turn in his cell phone at the desk, which they claimed was standard. It was a lie because they were concerned about him recording the conversation.

Her choice for floor leader, Gilbert Villegas, went to work trying to help. He recommended Lightfoot meet with alderpersons for breakfast and with their state legislators to build coalitions. She didn't do it. Other relationships with Springfield, meanwhile, started badly. Billionaire J. B. Pritzker had been elected governor in November 2018 and was getting his feet under him. Lightfoot sent a crew, including Lisa Schneider Fabes and Paul Goodrich, to meet with his deputy, Dan Hynes, which became a real trainwreck. They used campaign slogans like "stronger together," which made them sound like rubes. The primary ask from Lightfoot was for Springfield to take over Chicago's pension liabilities, a total nonstarter. Hynes tried to be courteous, but he made clear that was not remotely possible. Pritzker's team was baffled: *Who are we dealing with?*

Lightfoot brought in Maurice Classen, a former prosecutor in King County, Washington, who had run for Seattle City Council and done work at the Chicago Police Department, to be her chief of staff. It troubled some people, who thought he'd be a better deputy mayor for public safety than top dog. Some people made fun of a 2011 interview he did as a candidate when he said, "People think you can't metricize public service but you can. But it should be results driven not metrics driven. Are we doing a better job as a government today than we did yesterday?" But Classen was a hard worker who was smart enough to understand his lack of experience at City Hall and brought in veterans of the Daley and Emanuel administrations to be top deputies and fill his blind spots. She brought in Dan Lurie, a former Biden staffer, to be policy chief and hired campaign manager Manny Perez to help run intergovernmental affairs. Michael Frisch, a former associate of hers at Mayer Brown, came in as a senior aide. But for the most part, she kept Emanuel's department heads.

Two days before the inauguration, Lightfoot bounded up the steps at Precious Blood Ministry of Reconciliation, a smile on her face as she walked past a church door propped open with a cinderblock. A group was waiting for her in a bright blue room with butterflies painted on the wall. As she prepared to become Chicago's fifty-sixth mayor, Lightfoot was returning to the church where she hoped to find answers to a crime problem that has tarred the country's third biggest city since the days of Al Capone.

Precious Blood helps anchor Back of the Yards, a Southwest Side neighborhood made infamous in Upton Sinclair's *The Jungle* for feeding the world with its cattle stockyards and the ugly underbelly of the meat industry. What once was a gateway for working people to make it into the middle class has faced challenges in recent decades as corporations took jobs overseas, leading to disinvestment, poverty, and crime. Gang violence is rampant in the neighborhood. The church works with recently released prison inmates, former gang leaders, and community residents to de-escalate conflict. It also participates in a yearly antiviolence march, started in 2007 after pregnant thirty-two-year-old Leticia Barrera was killed by a stray bullet while trick-or-treating with her two-year-old daughter and son, who were dressed as a dinosaur and firefighter.

Lightfoot had visited the church the year prior, alone, for the antiviolence march just after launching her long-shot campaign for mayor. Nobody knew who the short African American woman wearing extra-long slacks and her trademark fedora was, but she joined with mothers and community leaders for premarch exercises in the parking lot and listened as community members shared their stories. That march had a profound effect on Lightfoot, who called it "one of the most remarkable experiences I've had, really in my life." At one stop on the march, an activist talked about her son Ricky's murder and how she forgave the killer. Another man, who was convicted of participating in a murder when he was thirteen, shared his story and explained that there are "no bad children." He talked about his crime in the third person, Lightfoot recalled, because it was too emotional for him to relate his personal journey otherwise. Each of the people she met helped shape Lightfoot's view that crime can't be addressed solely by police, as she explained to reporters at a news conference when she returned for the march the following year.

"The short version is, this experience of this place, what they do here, what this march means, in this neighborhood, is really a story of people trying to find grace and peace and love," Lightfoot said. "I think they have done it in a way that has permanently touched me, and so it's my honor to be back here."

Pre-Burke raid, Lightfoot's campaign largely focused on public safety and police reform. "Nothing else matters," she often said, if city residents don't feel safe. Chicago crime had been declining through much of the 2010s, but it spiked after Jason Van Dyke murdered Laquan McDonald in 2014. The issue took center stage again as the transfer of power approached. In some ways, the city felt as though it was turning a corner. Lightfoot seemed to understand the need to change how Chicago handles violence so that crime reduction could be sustainable. That included, according to her, supporting law enforcement and prosecuting the gunmen who terrorize communities, but it also required investing in communities and developing relationships.

After the news conference at Precious Blood, Lightfoot walked down the stairs and waited just inside the front door of the church for her turn to address the marchers. Her body person, Kelsey Nulph, who went on to become one of her closest advisors, leaned over and pinned a peace pin on Lightfoot's T-shirt, which called for "peace and love." As the program started outside, however, Lightfoot's staff stirred. Alderperson Raymond Lopez, the City Council member who represents Back of the Yards, had arrived and was speaking.

Lopez had received death threats for his harsh antigang rhetoric and frequently took aggressive actions against criminals, like calling the Buildings Department about derelict landlords. A former skycap for Southwest Airlines who got into office by doing constituent services in his neighborhood as a private citizen, Lopez had been an outsize personality on the City Council, and he hit his familiar themes decrying Chicago's ongoing violence.

"Families should not have to grieve for the loss of their children, for the loss of their moms, for the loss of their family members. That is something we can do without because we can be a city that doesn't kill each other," Lopez said. "We can be a city that lets kids live in the city of Chicago, and today our moms continue that fight. Our moms continue to show the rest of the city that we will not be defined by violence, that our moms know best. They are here long after politicians like me have come and gone."

Prior to the speech, members of Lightfoot's team had conveyed that they didn't want Lopez on the steps with the mayor-elect as she spoke. They wanted him to make his comments, then leave. Lopez was confused. Although he had not endorsed Lightfoot, he had been a longtime critic of Preckwinkle, her runoff opponent. When he got word that she didn't want to be next to him, Lopez remembers thinking, *Who the fuck is she? You're in our neighborhood and this is how you're going to act?*

As he wrapped up his comments, Lightfoot staff grew restless. Lopez was clearly not going to leave the steps. After a pause, Lightfoot awkwardly came out—but did not acknowledge the alderperson, even though he was standing a foot away.

Speaking passionately and empathetically on a perfect sunny day, Lightfoot called for more economic investment and support for youth, saying many crimes are committed by people who "feel left out and disconnected from the legitimate economy, but also from themselves, their neighbors, and their community."

The crowd applauded and Lightfoot led the march through Back of the Yards, past memorials to innocent victims of street violence. She marched with a nine-year-old girl and Berto Aguayo, a former gang member turned peace activist who unsuccessfully ran for alderperson against Lopez. She appeared undaunted by Chicago's problems, optimistic for a more peaceful and equitable city. Everything seemed possible. But the conflict with Lopez hung like a cloud, an ominous sign of things to come.

8 | "TRAINED SEALS"

HALFWAY THROUGH HER INAUGURAL address at the Wintrust Arena, Lori Lightfoot turned to face the City Council members sitting on the stage behind her and invoked a Chicago legend. As Lightfoot gave her first speech to the city as mayor, she called out the memory of brash and wild Forty-Third Ward alderperson Paddy Bauler, who, according to a 1988 *Tribune* story, defeated a reformist rival in 1939 then declared, "Chicago ain't ready for reform."

"Putting Chicago government and integrity in the same sentence is, well, a little strange. But that's going to change. It's got to change," Lightfoot declared. "For years, they've said Chicago ain't ready for reform. Well, get ready because reform is here."

Lightfoot delivered a rousing denunciation of graft in politics, the sort of speech common in campaigns but unusual by a sitting elected. "When public officials cut shady backroom deals, they get rich, and the rest of us get the bill. When some people get their property taxes cut in exchange for campaign cash, they get the money and, sure enough, we get the bill," Lightfoot said. "The family with the bungalow, the lady who runs the hair salon, the guy who owns the store on the corner, they aren't big or powerful or well-connected, but they end up paying. These practices have gone on here for decades. This practice breeds corruption."

Then Lightfoot delivered the coup de grace, in a moment that defined her to her new colleagues when she declared, "Stopping it isn't just in the city's interest. It's in the City Council's own interest."

Her words were still reverberating through the arena when Lightfoot slowly turned to face everyone behind her and motioned with her arms for them to stand and applaud. Staffers compared it to a zookeeper training seals. The incident has taken on mythic proportions. Some people swear she turned and pointed at Edward Burke after delivering the lines about corruption. (She didn't.) But the resentment grabbed the colon of nearly every alderperson and refused to let go. That one act poisoned her relationship with City Council members who fumed at the implication they were all corrupt.

Some of them tried to put a positive spin on the comments afterward. Southwest Side alderperson Matt O'Shea noted that thirty alderpersons had gone to prison in his lifetime. West Side alderperson Michael Scott noted, "If you're not doing anything wrong, then it shouldn't really touch a nerve." But for most of the alderpersons, it was an insult that they returned to over and over, an offense that lingered inside their heads. Some of them hadn't even had a one-on-one meeting yet, adding another layer of umbrage.

Aldermen bickered with one another all the time, but they didn't like being criticized by outsiders. South Side alderperson Carrie Austin was once quoted by the *Chicago Reader* telling a group of activists who crashed a Black Caucus fundraiser to "take it outside 'cause I guarantee you ain't seen no gangsters like this city's aldermen."

Lightfoot's speech was otherwise a progressive tour de force on public safety and economic inequality. She built the speech around Chicago's flag and its four stars, reimagining them as representing safety, education, financial stability, and integrity. On crime, Lightfoot said there's "no higher calling than restoring safety and peace in our neighborhoods" and promised to develop a more proactive strategy against violence. "People cannot and should not live in neighborhoods that resemble a war zone. Enough of the shootings. Enough of the guns. Enough of the violence."

The focus returned to her aldermanic relationships days later when Lightfoot's first City Council meeting generated another moment that became legend. The intrigue going in was whether alderpersons would approve her plan to reorganize committee chairmanships. As Alderperson Ariel Reboyras walked into council chambers, he was asked if he supported the mayor's plan and responded, "Haven't you heard? I'm a rubberstamp!" But the alderpersons did not fight back against her committee structure. The only drama came when

Burke stood up to complain that Lightfoot's City Council rules used *his* instead of gender-neutral pronouns.

"In reviewing this, Madame President, I think that there's a serious flaw in the proposal on rules. For instance, Rule 2 provides as follows, 'The clerk, parenthesis, or someone appointed to fill his place.' It's not gender-neutral," Burke said. "In Rule 4: 'The presiding officer shall preserve order and decorum and may speak to points of order and preference to other members, rising from *his* seat. It's not gender-neutral. And clearly, the presiding officer of this body is a *her*. That should provide 'his or her.'"

Lightfoot clearly didn't think much of Burke's comments. Burke had been a fierce rival to Mayor Harold Washington in the 1980s, a power broker who aspired to the top job but remained on the periphery, assuming whatever power Daley and Emanuel allowed him to have while building a fiefdom that occupied its own space at City Hall, but as he complained about pronouns, he looked like an old man who had gotten lost on his way to the bathroom.

"Anything further, alderman?" the mayor said.

As a murmur ran through chambers, Burke cited five more "mistakes." Lightfoot quickly ran out of patience.

"Ald. Burke, you've been in the City Council for approximately 50 years. Is that correct?" the mayor asked in a manner of questioning honed by her years as a federal prosecutor.

"Yes, your honor," Burke replied.

"And you're a lawyer. Is that also correct?" she said.

"Yes, your honor," Burke said.

"You're aware that, under terms of the law and particularly as provided in the municipal code, that gender, whether it's designated as his or her, applies with equal force. So, if you're making an objection, please make it so we can move forward," Lightfoot said. "Is your general concern that the rules have a gender designation and not 'his or her'? Is that the gist of it? Is there any other thing that you want to call to the chair's attention?"

When Burke said he didn't have anything more to add, Lightfoot shut him down. "Alright. So, sir, we'll take your issue under advisement and we're gonna move forward."

Then Lightfoot called on Alderperson Michelle Harris, an old-time alderperson whom she retained as Rules Committee chair, a critical gatekeeping role that is used to kill legislation opposed by the mayor, and asked her to move forward after "we were interrupted by Ald. Burke's soliloquy."

The exchange marked the end of Burke's reputation as a master of City Council. For the next four years, Burke rarely spoke, a move that likely had as much to do with his federal corruption charges as it did fear. But the moment, again, angered alderpersons, who felt it was gratuitous on Lightfoot's part and resented the way she treated Burke. At a news conference afterward, Lightfoot kept mocking the alderperson. "The notion that Ed Burke, fill in the history, is somehow now concerned about gender equity is laughable. That was just a stunt." And she boasted, "Apparently, Alderman Burke has forgotten that I'm a thirty-year trial lawyer."

Early on, Lightfoot floor leader Gilbert Villegas started to become concerned about the dynamics. She wasn't taking meetings. Villegas attended a fundraiser where she was railing against the City Council and Burke, long after the election was over. He advised her to stop campaigning, that it was time to be mayor, not candidate. Alderpersons would complain to Villegas that she wouldn't call them back to talk about their issues. Lightfoot staff would tell Villegas, "She isn't a politician," and he would respond, "When you become mayor of the third largest city, you'd better become a politician." It was a common refrain for Lightfoot and a recurring theme worsened by staffers who indulged her feelings rather than explaining that she was, in fact, a politician the moment she put her name on the ballot and won.

Early in the Lightfoot administration, Alderperson Brendan Reilly joined Lightfoot and other elected officials for a meeting about Springfield. She was struggling with the real estate transfer tax, which she promised to hike on $1 million home sales and devote the proceeds to fighting homelessness. As mayor, Lightfoot wanted to use money on budget holes instead, drawing fierce pushback from progressive legislators who blocked its passage downstate. She also struggled to stop a proposal by Rob Martwick that would boost pension costs for the city. People who met with her thought she didn't understand her power.

"She thought having her name on the door on the fifth floor meant she got automatic respect in Springfield. She complained that Mayor Daley and Mayor Emanuel were treated with a certain amount of respect in Springfield," one alderperson said. "What she didn't acknowledge is that each of those individuals built relationships and grew them. She made no effort. She looks at Springfield dominated by white men, traditionally, 'and they're out to get me.'" This was critical: Some people who follow City Hall think Daley and Emanuel got things done through fear and force of will. But they were both legislators. Daley served in the state senate, and Emanuel had been in line to potentially be Speaker of the House. Emanuel's reputation as a prick missed that he would regularly ask alderpersons about their priorities and work to enact them.

Lightfoot struggled with another piece of the puzzle: the politics of hiring. Villegas kept sending her names of Latino job candidates, and she kept passing them up. Later on in the administration, Villegas recommended a candidate for buildings commissioner that he thought would be a strong leader, and she went with Matthew Beaudet, whom she touted as the city's first Native American commissioner. "Good luck with that caucus," Villegas told her. "This is bullshit."

One of the most shocking things to people new to Chicago politics is the force of race and how openly it is sometimes discussed by alderpersons. When I first started on the beat, I heard a story about Carrie Austin, a Black South Side staple of Emanuel and Daley's leadership teams, who once attended a contracting fair in white North Side Lakeview, where she pressed businesspeople to do minority set-asides. "And I ain't talking about no Koreans," Austin said. (She couldn't be reached for comment. Austin was indicted for corruption charges in 2021 and resigned in March 2023 after federal prosecutors accused her of faking sickness.)

While Lightfoot brushed off referrals from alderpersons, she did a disastrous early clout hire of defeated alderperson John Arena for a job in the Department of Planning and Development. Arena had been close with Joanna Klonsky, Lightfoot's top campaign advisor, and a constant thorn in Rahm Emanuel's side. He lost his reelection for two reasons. First, he bravely stood up for affordable housing developments in his ward, despite an at-times racist and classist backlash. But he could also be a real jerk. Arena was unpopular with police officers but went to a Cubs game and asked police if he could park in their lot, a violation of the rules. When they said no, he refused to accept the answer until they relented. It led to an embarrassing story in the *Sun-Times*. He later resigned his post after being accused of hassling Gardiner, a charge he denied.

When the rumors started that he would be getting a job in the Lightfoot administration, practically all the Northwest Side alderpersons beseeched her not to hire Arena, including Jim Gardiner, the man who defeated him. Lightfoot refused: "If we start a precedent of somebody who is a winner basically banning someone from employment, where does it end? And so, I think what Gardiner should focus on is what matters to his ward," Lightfoot said when it emerged publicly. "He doesn't have a say over my hiring decisions, nor does any other alderman. I respect the views that aldermen bring to the table, but at the end of the day I'm going to make the calls that I think are in the best interests of the city, and that's what I did in this instance." The whole situation was an unforced error.

One of the first fights was with alderpersons over a plan by Willie Wilson to give reparations to Black residents. Wilson's idea wasn't particularly well baked, but the idea was a talker, and she wanted no part of it. When Alderperson Roderick Sawyer was working with Wilson on some form of reparations, Lightfoot called him to complain. "I'm not voting for any Willie Wilson–sponsored bullshit that's not going to do anything," she said.

Early on, though, Lightfoot's biggest problem was the Black Caucus, headed by Jason Ervin, whose wife, Melissa Conyears-Ervin, was city treasurer. Lightfoot stripped Conyears-Ervin of her police security detail, saying it wasn't supported by a review by the department, and accused her of wanting special treatment. Lightfoot was likely correct on the merits of the argument, but the controversy infuriated Conyears-Ervin, who complained to the *Tribune*. "People truly associate me with money," she told me. "I've had people, when I walk in the room, they say"—here she burst into song—"'Money, money, money—money.'" Lightfoot was also concerned about the possibility of Conyears-Ervin, a charismatic South Sider who moved to the West Side, running against her for mayor. A bigger fight with the Black Caucus started with Ervin pushing to delay legalized marijuana sales in Chicago to protest the lack of Black dispensary ownership. Governor J. B. Pritzker had passed a law that was meant to be equitable to communities ravaged by the war on drugs, but the wealth was predictably going to white businesspeople. Lightfoot was personally disappointed in the lack of Black representation, but a delay wouldn't do anything other than harm Chicago's bottom line. Ervin vacillated between pressing the issue and letting it go, but he made a furious push at the December City Council meeting to stop the bill. At one point, as Lightfoot interrupted him, Ervin slammed the microphone down and added, "If you need it that bad, take it."

It was a moment of triumph for Lightfoot, who was able to avoid an embarrassing loss. Had Ervin succeeded, it would've emboldened the council, but it allowed her to flex muscle. A month later, alderpersons were discussing a study to look at possible set-asides for gay- and transgender-owned businesses.

Members of the Black Caucus were deeply uncomfortable with the potential of LGBTQ set-asides and said so. Walter Burnett, who had been a close Lightfoot ally, referenced the Adam Sandler movie *I Now Pronounce You Chuck & Larry* to express concerns about the idea.

"I think about that movie, the two firemen where they were faking like they were gay, right? I think about that, and they did all those things . . . to get benefits," he said. Lightfoot responded a day later during a City Council meeting, declaring she had listened to slurs as a young woman and wouldn't be quiet for them now that she is mayor of the city. "I will be silent no more on any issue where people say and do things that are offensive and racist. I feel like I have an obligation to speak, and so I am.

"As a Black gay woman proud on all fronts, I have to say I'm disturbed by the nature of the committee discussion and the nature of the discussion here today," she added. "We need not ask anyone's indulgence, patience, or forgiveness or acceptance to be who we are and who we love.

"It's also shameful for any member of a discriminated community to give indulgence to offensive words spoken by someone else," Lightfoot said. "In some ways, that's even worse. My friends, the pie is big enough to slice it in lots of other ways."

Burnett was bothered by the mayor's response, which was like using a sledgehammer to crack an egg. But he left it alone. "Sometimes you take a licking and keep on ticking," he figured. Colleagues noticed the way she treated a friend.

Other cracks started appearing publicly and behind the scenes. Lightfoot repeatedly talked about the need to curb aldermanic prerogative, the unofficial right to rule the ward that City Council members had enjoyed for decades. Her most powerful ally, Scott Waguespack, spoke out in the *Sun-Times*, telling the newspaper's beat reporter Fran Spielman she would lose if she forced the issue. "You should still have aldermanic prerogative until you have a Planning Department that works proactively for the residents and the businesses that are out there now—and it doesn't," Waguespack said. She sent him a text message: "Scott, not sure what you were hoping to accomplish with your comments today to Fran, but the statements and the results were supremely unhelpful." He did not text her back. For the rest of her term, Lightfoot repeatedly blustered that she would be proposing an overhaul of zoning to eliminate aldermanic prerogative, but she practically abandoned the issue.

9 | EARLY SUCCESSES

LORI LIGHTFOOT ACHIEVED SEVERAL successes early in her administration, most of which became signature victories. But they came with a caveat: many had been bottled up by Mayor Rahm Emanuel. She pushed a predictive scheduling ordinance—the Fair Workweek legislation—supported by unions. Lightfoot worked closely with Chicago Federation of Labor president Bob Reiter, who genuinely liked and admired the new mayor, to get it passed. Labor icon Susan Sadlowski Garza gave Lightfoot a bottle of Hienie's, the thick neon orange sauce famous on the Southeast Side, as a thank you. Lightfoot later attended an event where Reiter was speaking about the initiative and lashed out at him for not crediting the administration.

"Oh, that's right. No one from the mayor's office did a single thing to facilitate the passage of the Fair work week that was stuck for 2.5 years," Lightfoot texted him. "It makes perfect sense to me that you would give zero acknowledgement of me or my team. Guess you can do $15 (minimum wage) all by yourself too. Good luck."

"Lori, did not mean to trivialize your work or staff's work on workweek. I would hope you know I don't work like that and give me the benefit of the doubt," Reiter responded. "I've stood with you publicly on it all summer. If you want to talk, let's talk."

Politicians crave credit and get angry when denied the spotlight, but it highlighted Lightfoot's defensiveness even while celebrating a big win.

Most substantially, Lightfoot put her attention to the city's revenue and pension problems. In June Lightfoot leaked word that she would like the state to take over Chicago's pension debt, the possibility that had been laughed out of the room by deputy governor Dan Hynes. She then started to get serious and focused on getting Chicago its long-desired casino, which would increase tax revenue to fill pension holes. State legislators passed a bill giving Chicago a casino in 2012, but Democratic Illinois governor Pat Quinn vetoed it, citing concerns about a lack of oversight for the city gambling den.

Springfield lawmakers were already working on a gambling expansion that would finally authorize Chicago's long-sought casino when Lightfoot took office. Her role was including a feasibility study to make sure the tax structure would be workable for potential operators. That August, the study panned "very onerous" taxes and recommended a location for the casino away from the South and West Sides. She then worked to get the legislature's fall veto session to lower the taxes. The effort got close in November 2019, but the legislation didn't pass. State Representative Sara Feigenholtz texted Lightfoot, "This place is horseshit." Lightfoot responded, "Yep. Can't convince me otherwise."

Lightfoot kept working at it, however, and released a diplomatic statement: "After thirty years of only being talked about, our proposal has moved Chicago closer than ever to bringing much-needed relief for our police and fire pension funds, while unlocking significant economic opportunity for our communities and capital funding for our entire state," Lightfoot said. "From the beginning, the city's proposal for the gaming bill has always been about finding a workable tax structure for a casino development that is projected to fuel thousands of new jobs, create hundreds of millions in new gaming revenues for the City as well as the state, all while redirecting $260 million in additional funds annually that have otherwise been lost out to gambling across the border."

In May 2020 Lightfoot convinced the legislature to modify the tax structure, making it more attractive and clearing the way for a Chicago casino. The project is ongoing but was a major win—the only true major legislative victory for Lightfoot of her administration. A casino won't solve all of Chicago's financial problems, but it would be a big boost if it comes to fruition as planned.

On the flip side, Lightfoot's first budget befuddled alderpersons by not raising property taxes. Mayors typically raise taxes in their first year so they can blame it on the predecessor. She chose not to. She also kept the budget-deficit figure from Alderperson Pat Dowell, her handpicked budget chair, before announcing it during a big speech at the Harold Washington Library, preferring not to inform even key allies of her plans.

Her first budget raised the city's minimum wage to $15 per hour, another measure smothered by Emanuel. In an effort to raise more revenue and reduce congestion, Lightfoot raised the tax on solo ride-share users heading into and out of downtown. That came with a bizarre moment when she accused Uber of offering Black men of God comically large bribes.

"They offered up Black ministers $54 million—a one-time deal—if they would convince the mayor to do away with any other kind of regulation," Lightfoot said. "And as we walked these ministers through the realities of what's actually at stake here, I think they realized that, frankly, they'd been hoodwinked." She refused to name the ministers whom she had spoken to, however, and the *Tribune* tracked down at least one person who had been on her schedule and denied the claim.

The City Council Progressive Caucus was in a tough situation with Lightfoot's first budget. Alderperson Scott Waguespack told freshmen, who had ridden in on a progressive platform pushed by the CTU, that the new budget was far better than that under Emanuel and praised the process. Some of the freshmen alderpersons empathized with the fact that it was different—but as Alderperson Rossana Rodriguez Sanchez figured, "We didn't come here to do Rahm-lite." Waguespack encouraged the alderpersons to vote their conscience.

"Well, everybody will be able to vote however they want; there won't be repercussions because this is a new day in council, and this administration is different," Waguespack told colleagues. He delivered that message publicly on the City Council floor as he urged alderpersons to vote their conscience without fear. Lightfoot didn't share the sentiment. Behind the scenes, she was furious and demanded her political team send expensive mailers to constituents. They talked her down into launching a website highlighting *no* votes, which angered alderpersons who didn't think it was fair. "We have an absolute right to make sure that people really understand who voted, why they voted, what they voted for," Lightfoot said. She said the website was "providing an important service, and I stand by it." It was entirely unnecessary and highlighted the emerging issues.

She also went around badmouthing freshman alderperson Matt Martin, who had voted against the budget despite Lightfoot granting his request to raise the City Council's staff budget. For the next couple years, she regularly dismissed Martin as a "liar" when someone brought him up or asked about working with him on an initiative. Martin is mild-mannered and well liked.

ProPublica reporters Melissa Sanchez and Sandhya Kambhampati wrote an impressive series of stories detailing how Chicago ticket debt was sending Black motorists into bankruptcy and wreaking havoc on residents. Lightfoot said the city was balancing its budget on the backs of working people and promised to reduce its "addiction" to fines and fees. Lightfoot worked with City Clerk Anna Valencia on a package of fines and fees reform aimed at addressing the issue, which had also been bottled up by Emanuel. She created a six-month payment plan that reduced required down payments and allowed more time to pay, an important measure giving real relief to working people.

One of the top issues facing Lightfoot early on was the Obama Presidential Center, which had faced years of delays and challenges in its quest to open in Jackson Park. A key player was Alderperson Jeanette Taylor, a progressive icon who rose to prominence as a hunger striker protesting Emanuel's decision to close the South Side Dyett High School in 2015, an effort that got CPS to reopen the school. Taylor knew all the struggles of Chicago residents, particularly Black women. She understood what it's like to feed your kids and be hungry and had been on the Chicago Housing Authority's wait list for decades.

By 2019 Taylor was the heart and soul of Chicago's left-wing City Council slate, running to fill the Twentieth Ward seat vacated by Willie Cochran after he was imprisoned for stealing from his ward charity to pay for gambling trips, fat meals, and Mercedes accessories. Two of his predecessors in the ward, Clifford Kelley and Arenda Troutman, also went to prison. Troutman was famously recorded by the FBI declaring, "Most aldermen, most politicians, are hos." Taylor easily defeated her rival and entered office skeptical of Toni Preckwinkle and Lori Lightfoot. Preckwinkle was too close to developers and business. But she thought Lightfoot wasn't trustworthy either. "They're the same," Taylor later reflected. "The difference is, Toni will say, 'Bend over, I'm about to fuck you.' With Lori, you look up, and your ass is sore."

Taylor respected Obama and had nothing against the project. But she wanted to ensure there were protections for longtime residents who faced the possibility of getting priced out of their community due to Obama Center–related gentrification. "Just because he was the first Black president, he doesn't get to run amok in this community," she told me. Taylor was pleasantly surprised by the way Lightfoot approached the possibility of ensuring a Community Benefits Agreement (CBA) for the Obama Presidential Center. "This should have been done," Lightfoot told Taylor, blaming the previous administration for letting it linger. "You all are right to want to get an agreement and not want to be pushed out of your community."

Taylor brought fresh eyes to the issue. At a meeting on the Obama Center, Taylor brought a staff member who asked a question. Alderperson Michelle Harris cut in and said, "Staff do not talk in meetings with the mayor." Taylor interjected and Lightfoot demurred. "Let her speak," she said, impressing Taylor, who nevertheless saw the hierarchy as an example of why the city struggles to get things done.

The Obama Center's proponents promised to bring billions of dollars of economic transformation to the South Side. But activists wanted assurances that Woodlawn, the neighborhood that would be home to the former president's center, wouldn't be up for sale to the highest bidder as a wave of speculators and others moved into the neighborhood. From City Hall's perspective, President Obama's team isn't easy to deal with. They view themselves as emissaries for the man who once led the free world, a privileged position that made them hard negotiators. At times, that led to friction over logistical issues, which are common between politicians but really chafed Lightfoot's and Obama's teams. During an event with the Obama Foundation, an Obama staffer was disrespectful of Lightfoot aide Gaby Luurs, who was upset by the encounter. In the elevator, Lightfoot directly confronted the Obama aide. "I just want to let you know that you are in my city, and in my city we treat people with kindness and we treat people with respect," Lightfoot said. "How dare you speak to someone on my team the way that you did?"

Negotiations over the Obama Center went slowly, however, and tensions emerged. A group of pro-CBA demonstrators with young children sat down outside her office and protested. Word came down from Lightfoot that she wanted them cleared. Anel Ruiz, the press secretary, was alarmed by the message, so she grabbed Jim Smith, the head of security, to seek out another way to deal with the protest. A police official said they could cut off power and access to bathrooms and eventually they'd leave. "Fine," Lightfoot said, fuming. Ruiz was proud of herself for helping the protesters while avoiding a nasty scene for the mayor.

As Lightfoot negotiated with Taylor and the activists, Obama was frustrated with the project's pace. Lightfoot and the former president met during NBA All-Star Weekend 2020, where their heated discussion could be heard outside of a hotel conference room. "This is my city. I'm in charge of these people. If we displace these people, it's on me. You're not here. You're not the mayor of this city. It's my responsibility to figure out where these people are going to go," Lightfoot said. "I have a responsibility to them, and I understand you want to build your presidential center, but you're not here to deal with these people, and I am. They're trusting me to make sure they're taken care of." Obama told her he respected what she was saying.

Eventually, Lightfoot reached an agreement that would provide funding for affordable housing in Woodlawn and support for renters, a measure that fell short of initial demands but provided some satisfaction to Taylor and her allies.

One of Lightfoot's big announcements that first year was Invest South/West, a project aimed at generating development in disinvested communities that she counts as a signature achievement. The mayor and her team legitimately spurred development on the South and West Sides, and they deserve credit. But they also exaggerated the scope of the project's impact as well as its origin, because much of it originated under Rahm Emanuel. As we later wrote for the *Tribune*,

> Some of the largest investments were already on the launchpad when Lightfoot took office. Others were for standard repairs to existing buildings. And many of the projects are still in the conceptual phase and have not even begun to be built. Of the more than $750 million that the city counts as part of the public spend for Invest South/West, more than half has been allocated toward those kinds of expenditures rather than new or groundbreaking projects, the *Tribune* found. . . .
>
> In all, the *Tribune* examined every Invest South/West project that cost $1 million or more—108 out of 288 total projects—and found that of the $757 million the city and sister agencies have allocated for projects, at least $409 million was committed for projects that either launched before Invest South/West was unveiled, was for routine government projects such as maintaining field houses or replacing park turf, was for bureaucratic infrastructure such as fixing pipes in fire stations or the work at the horse stables, or was for broader city spending that wasn't limited to the South and West sides.

Despite some of the early successes, Lightfoot started to show strain behind the scenes. Early on, Lightfoot took to berating her staff in ways that made people uncomfortable. "A high school intern could have done this better," she told the intergovernmental affairs team, in a message that spread everywhere. Talking to an outside advisor, Lightfoot complained that she'd had access to the best and brightest while working at Mayer Brown but was restricted to lesser workers now. Aides struggled with her inconsistencies. Sometimes, the mayor would criticize people for things she had previously praised them for, creating more issues. Lightfoot had privately praised Ruiz for how she prepped her for a meeting. But during another session in a conference room, Lightfoot snapped, "I don't need this! This is foolish. Who do you think I am?" Maurice Classen, her chief of staff, later regaled associates about one particular incident where Lightfoot told him to "strap on your balls." She would tell her comms team, "Stop stepping on your own dicks." Staffers joked that Lightfoot would "banish" them from her presence for a day when she got angry.

Once, Lightfoot sent top staffers a photo of a torn piece of paper and wrote, "Here's my new practice for memos that come at the last minute. As I noted, I want decisions memos no later than 48 hours before the decision is needed and I have directed (staff) to reject all efforts to bring things to me directly that skirt these rules. I have asked nicely, now I am done."

Lightfoot did not care for her communications director, Marielle Sainvilus, who joined during the transition. They had little rapport. Unlike most comms chiefs, Sainvilus did not get walk-in access from Lightfoot, a key issue in a fast-paced environment. Her contempt for Sainvilus, a fellow Black woman, was well known. In early July, Sainvilus emailed Lightfoot the daily report on media coverage and plans. It included a line referencing "Mayor Emanuel." Lightfoot responded, "What is the reference to Mayor Emanuel conducting neighborhood conversations?" Sainvilus apologized, saying "this was copied and pasted and it should say Mayor Lightfoot." The mayor forwarded the exchange to Celia Meza, her friend, senior counsel, and senior ethics advisor, and wrote, "Read the two emails below."

Less than one hundred days into her term, Lightfoot sent staff to secure Sainvilus's resignation. The administration also had Lightfoot's security detail walk her out, escorting her from the premises. It immediately made the rounds within the administration and outside City Hall, angering some coworkers who felt the treatment was designed to embarrass her.

Meza, a former federal prosecutor, was hired by Lightfoot after Meza had worked a series of stints in government. In 2013 Meza worked at the CTA, where she was the subject of complaints. A former intern, Ashley Cannon, complained about the way Meza treated her during a conversation. "She put her fingers in my face while being verbally abusive and aggressive. Every piece of advice or commentary I made was attacked. I felt as if I was a target—and I wasn't quite sure why," the woman said. "When I asked if she wanted suggestions on how to make the process better, she raised her voice at me and told me, 'I am not asking you for any advice, I don't want any extra comments or suggestions; I just want you to answer the questions!!'" Cannon said Meza became more "hostile" and she "felt afraid." The woman complained that Meza said "she has little to no patience for people who do not answer her questions directly." The woman also said Meza told her it would help her out in life if she would answer the question being asked of her.

Another woman, Anita Brooks, sent an email saying she was "very uncomfortable and afraid to respond when working with the transitioning of Programs because of the way that Celia handles situations." Brooks said she asked if she could help, and Meza "rudely told me, and I quote, 'What did I tell you to do! Say it with me. . . . What were you told to do? PROCESS ONLY.' I found that to be very disrespectful."

Asked about it, the Lightfoot administration dismissed complaints. Meza "has no recollection of the individuals or the conversations" and said she "has conducted herself professionally throughout her career." These sorts of anecdotes percolated through City Hall about Lightfoot and her staff, creating friction with the workforce that is critical to implementing everything from a mayor's budget to her travel plans. Meza was seen by some as an enabler for Lightfoot's worst instincts.

Even her early successes illustrated problems. Chicago's Board of Ethics proposed increasing the maximum fine for an ethics violation to $20,000 in the early days of her administration, in an apparent attempt to curry favor with the reform-minded mayor. Lightfoot pushed an ethics overhaul through the City Council weeks later that was far weaker than what the Board of Ethics recommended. Steve Berlin, the board's executive director for decades, is not a bomb thrower, so her overhaul coming in softer than what he wanted sent a message. Lightfoot's ordinance gave Inspector General Joseph Ferguson the ability to audit the council's committees and increased fines for ethics violations, with a maximum $5,000 penalty, but fell far short of her reform promises.

Alderpersons Matt O'Shea and Michele Smith later introduced an ordinance before the city that banned elected officials from also being paid lobbyists. "We are surrounded by impropriety; at the state level, at the county level, and in this body. The feds are all around us. We need to send the message that this BS is over with," O'Shea said, when he introduced the measure. Behind the scenes, Lightfoot tried to slow it down but wasn't able to stop the measure. She later said she would push to overturn it, and the Board of Ethics acknowledged that it wouldn't enforce the law until her effort failed or succeeded.

The ordinance didn't affect many people because there aren't a ton of elected officials who are also lobbyists. But it did affect Gyata Kimmons, a south suburban village trustee who also lobbied on behalf of Walmart, McDonald's, Starbucks, and the United Center. He was one of the few prominent Black lobbyists and close with several Black alderpersons. The effort to weaken an ethics reform garnered headlines in the *Tribune*. Similarly, the *Tribune* reported on Lightfoot aide Lisa Schneider Fabes, who lived in the tony North Shore suburb Wilmette and was therefore ineligible to work for the city. But on Lightfoot's inauguration, she was hired by World Business Chicago, a body controlled by the mayor and apparently unbound by residency rules, and "detailed" to Lightfoot's office. She resigned in December while under inspector-general investigation. That drew hypocrisy charges from critics who said Lightfoot was being a do-as-I-say-not-as-I-do leader. An Emanuel aide called me around this time to express astonishment that she was fumbling around on ethics issues, her bread and butter. "She doesn't understand why she won," the aide said.

10 | ACCOUNTABILITY MONDAYS

THE CHICAGO POLICE DEPARTMENT Lori Lightfoot inherited was in bad shape despite good signs. Crime had been trending down in recent years. Officials were working to modernize the department. The consent decree, approved by US District Judge Robert Dow Jr. in January 2019, would force change, even if implementation is often slow. Superintendent Eddie Johnson, meanwhile, generated significant respect citywide. In December 2017 I visited the home of Jennell Cross, a South Chicago resident who was about to watch a movie in her daughter's home when police broke down the front door—a wrong raid after they had misread the numbers in front. While I was there, Cross shared a voicemail Johnson left her apologizing for the incident, a small gesture that he repeated all around the city, even though it wasn't always appreciated.

Still, the department was too parochial. Its professionalism and training lagged behind peer departments in New York and Los Angeles. Despite those cities having far more residents, their violent crime numbers were lower, while Chicago had more police officers per capita. As a former federal prosecutor and police oversight official, Lightfoot viewed herself as a subject-matter expert who could lead change in policing. Even before Lightfoot won the election, she was working to take control of the department. In March 2019 Lightfoot recounted a story about visiting a strip mall on the West Side while campaigning. As she pulled into the parking lot, Lightfoot said she "heard some guys yelling, 'Blow, blow' and selling dope out in the open." She picked up the phone and called Johnson. "You got to do something about this," she recalled. "This is nuts."

During the campaign, Johnson did everything he could to let people know that he supported Lightfoot in the runoff. He didn't exactly have a choice:

Preckwinkle had campaigned on a promise to fire him for testifying that he wasn't aware of a code of silence in the Police Department. But Johnson had gotten to know Lightfoot during the Laquan McDonald murder aftermath—she oversaw the Police Board, after all—and, despite her anger at his initial selection, they grew to respect one another.

Shortly after Lightfoot was elected, she went to police headquarters for a conversation with top brass. Beforehand, Lightfoot asked to speak with Johnson. "Supe, you know who I trust in CPD?" she asked.

"Who?" Johnson said.

"You, and that's it," Lightfoot responded.

The answer took Johnson aback and left him with a sinking feeling. He complained about it afterward to staff and friends. *How could she say that about a department with more than ten thousand members?* he wondered. That same meeting, Lightfoot told Johnson she had "sources" who were critical of Fred Waller, the chief of patrol. Lightfoot regularly dropped information like this to people and attributed it to sources, an exercise that frustrated officials who vacillated between anger at colleagues for gossiping with the mayor and concern that she was exaggerating.

In the meeting that followed, Johnson chief of staff Bob Boik presented the department's "summer strategy." Lightfoot was critical of CPD's longtime overreliance on overtime spending. As usual, the department planned canceling days off and redeploying officers for Memorial Day weekend, a regular show of force whereby police boost their presence around the city to keep the peace and put on security theater. In truth, her plan was a lot of the same. But Lightfoot later characterized her antiviolence plan as a new initiative with an all-hands-on-deck approach.

Not long after taking office, Lightfoot let slip to the press that she would have a regular meeting with the brass called Accountability Monday. The idea was to bring in police leaders for a review of recent trends and to drill down on issues facing the city. One of the central tenets Lightfoot chief of staff Maurice Classen believed in was the idea that more coordination was needed to work through issues and manage the department, and that CompStat meetings had been softened by Johnson after Garry McCarthy was fired. These are regular meetings where police review statistics to identify trends and hold each other accountable. Classen believed that the lack of focus after McCarthy's termination had contributed to 2016's crime spike. McCarthy's CompStat sessions were legendarily tough—a story circulated once through the department about an officer who faked a car crash to avoid the meeting.

As with other Lightfoot initiatives, the meetings weren't new. Mayor Rahm Emanuel already had a weekly briefing with police brass to talk about trends and problems. Lightfoot's meetings were bigger and sometimes included people outside the police department, but that didn't always mean they were better, as they sometimes got sidetracked. The Accountability Monday tag also alienated cops, who took it as an attack when they were supposed to be an opportunity to be more collaborative. Lightfoot and her team felt the meetings opened up lines of communication. In one session, West Side police leader Ernest Cato complained that the drug unit was in his district, but he didn't know why it was there. Narcotics chief William Bradley said he would tell him later. Lightfoot emphasized that commanders needed to know what's happening in their district to be effective, an exchange her team took as a good example of the meetings working, by forcing Cato and Bradley to communicate.

Police leaders, meanwhile, said they were only cagey during the meeting because of outsiders present in the room.

Lightfoot approached those meetings like a prosecutor would cross-examine a witness. She'd interrogate their word choices. After one early session, Lightfoot responded to a comment by Chief Jose Tirado saying officers had done a "wonderful job" over the weekend.

"Wonderful job, you gotta be fucking kidding me!" she responded, before ripping into problems from the weekend. Lightfoot was not the first mayor to be tough on police leaders, of course. People who also attended meetings under Emanuel noted he would chew them out too. But it became a staple of the approach, and eventually, the brass started to tune her out. Humiliating chiefs in front of their peers and subordinates had a predictably negative effect. *She's never put a handcuff on anybody*, they figured. Some Lightfoot staff members, meanwhile, started sarcastically referring to her as "Detective Lightfoot."

Early on, Lightfoot gave police leaders an edict that they couldn't take time off during the summer. Johnson's second in command, Anthony Riccio, had a previously approved vacation the first week of June. Reporters learned about the time off and asked Lightfoot about it. "That would be incredibly disappointing to me if that happened because I gave a very specific directive that no exempt should be taking vacation during the summer. If that happened, that'll be something that we have to have a serious conversation about." She added that police leaders "have to set the example. And the example of doing something that the mayor has directed them not to do is highly problematic." Johnson was frustrated by the incident, which undercut his authority and was an unnecessary attack on a well-respected leader. Officers, and especially brass, work long hours, and sometimes the summer is the only time they get to spend with families. Nothing really came from Lightfoot's public comments, which meant the incident didn't do anything other than piss people off and illustrate that her tough talk is often just bluster.

Other tensions boiled up early in the mayor's administration. Lightfoot wanted retired former deputy US marshal Jim Smith to be given control of her security detail. Johnson tried to push back, but Lightfoot said Smith was her guy and that was the end of the discussion. Officers took it as a major act of disrespect, with one cop scoffing, "You've got to bring in the feds to protect the mayor." The episode reflected Lightfoot's concern that the police department was too loose and unprofessional in protecting the mayor; the feds are generally paranoid about insulating those they protect. It also illustrated Lightfoot's mistrust of cops.

The detail is deeply political and always has been. Despite being wealthy men, Mayor Rahm Emanuel and Mayor Richard M. Daley continued to have taxpayer-funded police security details, a practice that my colleague Jeremy Gorner and I reported was an aberration among big cities. Alderperson Edward Burke got full-time protection long after the 1980s Council Wars, when he feuded with Mayor Harold Washington. But this was a new level of drama due to the frustration officers felt. The drama over Lightfoot's detail boiled over early in her term when the *Tribune*'s John Byrne and NBC reporter Mary Ann Ahern reported that she was hiring Smith, bringing the aggravation to light. Not long after the stories broke, Classen called over to Boik and said the mayor wanted to talk with Johnson's staff.

As they gathered to speak with the mayor, Johnson's team was excited to spend time with her. But their enthusiasm quickly dissipated when the mayor launched into a rant about media leaks and how they could affect the department.

"This man has given his fucking life to this city and this department, and I will not let you all fuck this up for me or this man right here," Lightfoot said, according to two people present.

Afterward, Johnson spoke to the mayor in private and told her none of his employees knew what she was talking about.

"Well, if they didn't, now they know to keep their motherfucking mouths shut," Lightfoot responded.

Early in her administration, Lightfoot said civilian oversight of police was a one hundred–day goal. As a candidate, Lightfoot supported the Grassroots Alliance for Police Accountability (GAPA) ordinance, which would've given a civilian board power to fire a police superintendent and set policy. She changed her position early on. "Now that I'm mayor, I don't want any commission picking the superintendent," one aide recalled her saying in private, as plans stalled.

The department faced a new challenge in October, when Johnson called Lightfoot to give her a warning that there had been an incident, and he had drinks with dinner. Johnson had fallen asleep at the wheel on his way home from a night out at Ceres Cafe, a legendary downtown bar known for boozy pours, though that detail didn't emerge immediately. ("That's where you go to get fucked up," a Lightfoot aide told me when I asked about it.) Publicly, Johnson blamed his failure to take blood pressure medication. But it set off a feeding frenzy. Who was he with? Why didn't his driver take him home? Where were they?

Common sense indicated problems with Johnson's story. But Lightfoot threw her support behind the superintendent. "This is a guy who has sacrificed a tremendous amount for the city over the last 3½ years. He stepped into a breach at a time when our city really could have come apart. Remember where we were in December of '15 and into '16, and the anger that was manifest itself all over the city," Lightfoot said. "That was a really scary time for us, and we didn't come apart in part because of the superintendent's leadership and stewardship. I want to look at the entirety of the man's body of work. I think he deserves that, I think he's earned that."

Her public words belied private concern. Lightfoot quickly arranged a meeting with Johnson and Maurice Classen at the Union League Club, where they plotted the way forward, including what his future would be with the city,

Johnson later testified. Near the end of the sit-down, Johnson later testified, Lightfoot told him that she wanted him to remove officer Cynthia Donald from his security detail.

"She told me that she had sources that had told her Officer Donald and I were having a sexual relationship," Johnson testified. Lightfoot said she wanted Donald sent to the city's first district and demanded, "I want that fucking shit done today. There will be no debate about it, no conversation. I want it done, and I want it done by the end of today."

"I told her, 'You're the mayor. You want her moved, I'll take care of that by close of business today,'" Johnson said. But he asked to check in with Donald about where she could get sent. Lightfoot said yes, "but I want this shit done by the end of today."

Johnson left the meeting and met with Boik, Riccio, Director of Communications Anthony Guglielmi, and Waller. Riccio told him to let him know where Donald wanted to go, "and I'll ensure that it happens."

Johnson also met with Guglielmi, whose advice was simple. "Basically he said to me, 'Supe, listen, the mayor is ordering you to get rid of Cynthia, so I wouldn't screw around with that,'" Johnson recalled. "'I would get that done as soon as possible.'"

Johnson denied having a sexual relationship with Officer Donald, telling Lightfoot that they weren't "sleeping together." Soon, they came up with a plan to announce his retirement, but that created a problem: who would be the interim superintendent? There was talk of reaching out to Chuck Ramsey, prominent former Philadelphia police chief; Kathleen O'Toole from Seattle; and Hiram Grau, a longtime Chicago Police leader whom Lightfoot initially wanted.

Lightfoot's deputy mayor for public safety, Susan Lee, set her sights higher and called Charlie Beck, one of the most respected men in policing from his time in Los Angeles. Beck was familiar with the Chicago Police Department and had lent his chief of staff, Sean Malinowski, to help Johnson. Beck didn't want the full-time job. He felt the salary was too small, and he was newly retired from Los Angeles. But Lee, a respected public safety expert, said that the department had a thin bench and the search might take a while. Beck agreed to come lead the department later in the year, with Johnson announcing his retirement but stepping away later.

"It's time for someone else to pin these four stars to their shoulders," Johnson said at a news conference, as Lightfoot proudly stood with the superintendent. "These stars sometimes feel like carrying the weight of the world." A reporter tried to ask Johnson tough questions about the investigation, but Lightfoot stepped in. "We're happy to take your questions, but let me say this: This is a day for celebration. It's a day for remembrance."

Mayor Lori Lightfoot's relationships with other officials had always been fragile. In the fall of 2019, they really started falling apart, with a particularly significant rift deepening between her and Inspector General Joe Ferguson. She had helped recommend Ferguson as city watchdog to Mayor Richard M. Daley when he was first appointed in the 2000s. The two had been colleagues at the US Attorney's Office, where they had developed reputations as pranksters. As a candidate, Lightfoot had campaigned on a promise to release Ferguson's full report into Laquan McDonald's murder as well as the slaying of David Koschman by a Daley nephew. Full IG reports have historically been kept hidden from the public, with the city asserting it can't legally release the documents. Lightfoot pushed City Council to pass a law allowing the city's top lawyer discretion to disclose full reports, which she only used to release documents that predated her administration.

The McDonald report had been obtained via leak in 2016 by *Tribune* reporter Jeremy Gorner, who worked with colleagues to publish a searing story on the findings. Ferguson's investigation exposed a cover-up by police officers and revealed that top brass reviewed the video and believed there was "no question whether the shooting was justified. Everyone agreed that Officer Van Dyke used the force necessary to eliminate the threat, and that's pretty much it." Johnson was present at the meeting, but through a spokesman said he "strongly disagrees" with the report's finding. The rest of the report documented the McDonald cover-up by other police officers and leaders who largely escaped punishment. Other media outlets weren't able to match the *Tribune*'s reporting because they couldn't get the report.

Lightfoot's top lawyer, Mark Flessner, released the McDonald report but added a note saying the city couldn't vouch for its accuracy. Ferguson went ballistic and sent Classen an email calling it "corporate lawyer ass-covering horseshit." He was right, but the email angered Lightfoot as the two became increasingly disillusioned with one another. Ferguson had been optimistic about her potential to be a great mayor but was worried she had "completed the transformation" into "politician who cares about the things politicians care about." In no small part, that meant loyalty.

Late in November Ferguson delivered investigative findings from the Johnson investigation to Lightfoot. It accused Johnson of lying about key events and revealed he had been out drinking with Cynthia Donald. Johnson was out of the office on time off but recalled being summoned to City Hall for a meeting with Lightfoot. Through staff, Johnson asked if it could be rescheduled, and the mayor's office said no, leading him to deduce that he was going to be fired. Johnson headed to CPD headquarters the night before his appointment and cleared out the office. When he arrived at City Hall, Lightfoot read off a letter to him telling him that he was done. As she informed Johnson that he couldn't go to police stations any longer, Johnson interjected that she could demote him from superintendent while he remained a lieutenant, leading to an awkward moment. When Lightfoot told him his office was being cleaned out by facilities workers, Johnson got salty.

"Mayor, if 2FM puts their fingers on anything of mine, they're going to get a bullet for their troubles," Johnson said, according to one account of the meeting I heard. "My property is at my house." Another person recalled Johnson making a tamer comment: "You're not going to have to do that. My office is already cleaned out."

After firing Johnson, Lightfoot walked into the City Hall briefing room for a hastily called news conference where she announced that the department needed a culture change and called him a liar. She declined to get into specifics, alluding to the notion he was having a sexual relationship with a subordinate. "While at some point the IG's report may become public and those details may be revealed, I don't feel like it's appropriate or fair to Mr. Johnson's wife or children to do so at this time," she said at the news conference.

"I saw things that were inconsistent with what Mr. Johnson had told me personally and what he revealed to members of the public," Lightfoot added. She then went to police headquarters, told command that she had their back but they can't lie to the inspector general or the public. In an email to the department, Lightfoot tried to calm police.

"While I recognize this news comes as a surprise to most of you, this was a decision I felt was absolutely necessary to preserve the legitimacy and honor of the Chicago Police Department," Lightfoot wrote. "I deeply respect the work that each of you undertake every day and you deserve a superintendent who lives up to the ideals that I expect each of you to exemplify."

Ferguson's investigation of the Johnson case led to conflict between Lightfoot and Cook County State's Attorney Kim Foxx. Prosecutors wanted to review the document for allegations of sexual misconduct. (Donald later accused him of rape.) Lightfoot's team didn't want to share the investigation with Foxx, forcing the prosecutor to obtain a grand jury subpoena demanding the team turn it over. Lightfoot privately complained to Foxx that Cynthia Donald was "a liar" and said she didn't believe her rape claims. Her anger over the issue shook Foxx, who didn't understand why Lightfoot felt so strongly about the allegation.

Beck took charge of the department immediately that afternoon. Johnson's firing left him in a precarious position, but he tried to reassure the department. In Beck's parlance, it was important not to scare the horses. "In order to not scare horses, you don't move suddenly," Beck said. "You don't do anything that's outside their experience." To show he wasn't there to play politics, Beck told the department that he would not be applying for superintendent. "While I'm here, I want to work on some things; I want to expose some of you to some of the things I've been exposed to," Beck said. "I want to make this place better. I'm not looking to publicly denigrate or crucify anybody. I'm going to be here to be a steady hand and keep this organization focused on the right things and maybe introduce some new things along the way."

Decades as a policeman taught Beck big lessons about cops. He said police departments need clear direction—otherwise, they will misinterpret orders "either by accident or on purpose." Beck didn't waste time making changes. He immediately demoted a police commander, Anthony Escamilla, who had improperly made officers babysit his special-needs child. Johnson had taken a softer approach. Beck got rid of merit promotions, which essentially gave career boosts to politically connected folks and discouraged officers by creating a perception of favoritism. Beck also reorganized the department so that the Office of Constitutional Policing and Reform was on the same level as the Office of Operations, a move aimed at fostering change, while trying to put more officers on the streets in local areas rather than citywide units.

While at the department, Beck was impressed by the personnel but felt they needed to be exposed to more policing. Earlier in Beck's career, LAPD chief Bill Bratton sent him to other places, like Charlotte, where he got more experience. "It's like if you stayed in the same school all your life," Beck figured. "All you know is your school. That doesn't give a broad enough experience." He brought much needed stability and professionalism to the department, giving Lightfoot plenty of space to hire the next superintendent. For his part, Beck liked the job and the city, which he contrasted with Los Angeles. "Chicago really wants to like its police department—really wants to," Beck recalled. "L.A. wants to dislike its police department no matter how good they are, and Chicago is the antithesis." Those notions would be hotly tested.

11 | "ALL IS NOT FORGOTTEN"

TWO DAYS INTO MAYOR Lori Lightfoot's time in office, the Chicago Teachers Union turned out in force for a downtown rally that sent a clear message on how they felt about her leadership. Hundreds of educators, clad in the union's trademark red, set up across the street from City Hall under a banner declaring, SCHOOLS CHICAGO'S STUDENTS DESERVE.

"Chicago's new mayor ran on a platform that mirrors what our union has been championing for nearly a decade—eliminating racial and economic inequities in school communities, increasing trauma services and wraparound supports, and supporting an elected, representative school board," the union declared. They named the rally "Keeping the Promise" and demanded "that City Hall make that promise for educational equity real!" In effect, the union said it created Lightfoot's political platform and didn't trust her to follow through. For her part, Lightfoot also made clear how she felt about the union when she was asked about the relationship in a news conference. "All is not forgotten, but the campaign's over," she said.

Since it became the official bargaining group for Chicago teachers in the mid-1960s, CTU has spent decades battling City Hall, most often over bread-and-butter contract items like salary and health insurance. The union went on strike several times in the 1980s, at a time when Reagan education secretary

William Bennett said Chicago schools were the worst in the country—including a nineteen-day strike in 1987 that was the longest in the city's history.

Mayor Richard M. Daley, who ruled Chicago from 1989 through 2011, didn't want the labor strife and pursued a policy of financial appeasement to keep teachers in the classroom. Under Daley, the school district gave out regular raises while trying not to rock the boat on classroom issues. Union presidents under his tenure were happy to work closely with Chicago Public Schools to keep the relationship stable. The most controversial items Daley pursued involved school privatization and charter schools, which the union didn't oppose with real vigor. In the end, Daley's policies helped weaken the district's finances and set them on a doomsday clock due to his mismanagement.

A *Tribune* investigation found the district knew enrollment was going to shrink dramatically but "issued billions of dollars in bonds to repair, expand or replace the vast majority of the district's schools regardless of future needs and without voter input." The district borrowed more than $10 billion and spent about $1.5 billion in schools that were less than 60 percent full, and $100 million in schools later closed under Rahm Emanuel, the *Tribune* found. The Daley years left Chicago with a major hole for Emanuel to handle at a time when the school district's relationship with the union was changing due in part to the emergence of Karen Lewis, a charismatic former chemistry teacher who led the Caucus of Rank and File Educators in an effort to shake up the system.

Lewis grew up on the South Side and graduated from Dartmouth College in 1974, two years after the school first admitted women—a hard time in her life. "Dartmouth was a really bad experience for me, but it made me stronger. I was the only black woman in my class, and it was clear that women weren't wanted," Lewis told the college's alumni magazine. "That did teach me that top-down decisions usually take a while for people to buy into." After graduating, Lewis attended medical school but dropped out and became a chemistry teacher. Lewis developed as an activist, she said, through a book club that only read nonfiction about education. She felt strongly that poverty was "the real cause of the achievement gap" and criticized approaches that didn't deal with the broader issue.

In 2010, Lewis ran for CTU president. Under Marilyn Stewart's tenure, Lewis argued, the teachers' union had failed to fight back against privatization and school closings, leading to greater inequality for Chicago Public Schools students and their families. In contrast to Stewart's more conciliatory and bridge-building approach, Lewis loved to quote Frederick Douglass: "Power concedes nothing without a demand."

Lewis prevailed in the election and chose as her vice president Jesse Sharkey, a wonky Brown University–educated history teacher who grew up in rural Maine. Sharkey got involved with CTU after the district announced plans to make Nicholas Senn High School, where he taught, share space with a military academy. He got to know Lewis during professional trainings at her school. Their odd-couple leadership team united Chicago teachers in a broader advocacy campaign for affordable housing, police reform, and other items that are outside the scope of a teacher contract but that they felt were crucial to changing the system.

To help implement their goals, Lewis and Sharkey turned to Stacy Davis Gates, the union's political director, whose firebrand style was closer to Lewis's. Originally from South Bend, Indiana, Davis Gates took a job in 2004 teaching history at a South Side high school. CPS shuttered the building in her second year due to low enrollment. "That was the moment I was radicalized," she told *Chicago* magazine. As the union's political director, Davis Gates fiercely advocated against the policies of Chicago's political class, arguing that poor Black students in particular had been poorly served by the city. She also objected to the total power the mayor's office held over Chicago schools.

One of the union's key goals under Lewis was to get Chicago an elected school board, as CPS was the only district in Illinois without an elected governing body. Chicago's board was appointed by the mayor. Proponents of the system said it ensured accountability, since the mayor would be blamed for problems, but CTU said it was undemocratic and disenfranchised poorer students and families with less political clout. Davis Gates's fierce advocacy on the issue helped make an elected school board part of the political mainstream.

The union's activism intensified in 2011, when voters elected Emanuel mayor. Emanuel privately criticized his predecessor's handling of the school district, saying Daley had treated the city's taxpayers like an ATM machine and didn't do enough to improve education. Soon after coming into office, Emanuel demanded a series of concessions from the union. CPS had the shortest school year and school day in the country; Emanuel immediately expanded the calendar. He also took away promised teacher bonuses. As CTU president, Lewis feuded with Emanuel, who in one meeting balked at one of her ideas by declaring, "Fuck you, Lewis." Lewis said Emanuel backed down after she fought back. "I know bad words too," she later recalled. "I can take my earrings off, put Vaseline on my face and go. I can do that!"

The union hadn't gone on strike since the 1980s, but, in response to Emanuel's aggressive changes, Lewis led CTU into the 2012 teachers' walkout, which lasted seven school days and helped kick off a string of ambitious walkouts across the country, including Los Angeles and Arizona. *Vox* called the 2012 teachers' walkout "the strike that brought teachers unions back from the dead." Having risen to national prominence, Lewis prepared to take it to another level with a run against Emanuel for mayor in 2015, but she was diagnosed with brain cancer, ending her campaign before it started. She stepped down from the union's leadership post in 2018 and ceded the presidency to Sharkey, who was succeeded in that role by Davis Gates.

In addition to her union duties, Davis Gates helped form a political organization in 2014, United Working Families (UWF), to support progressive candidates seeking citywide and state offices and to battle Emanuel allies. Though UWF's chosen standard bearer for the 2015 mayor's race, Cook County commissioner Jesús "Chuy" García, ultimately lost to Emanuel, Davis Gates wasn't disheartened. She insisted the city was moving to the left and doubled down on political advocacy.

"We planted seeds in 2015," Davis Gates would later tell me for a story about progressives eyeing veteran City Council members for defeat. It would take another election cycle for it to fully pay off, but ultimately, she would see those seeds come to fruition. More than a dozen candidates won in 2019 with some CTU support, and the political debate shifted in favor of an elected school board. At the highest level, Lightfoot and Preckwinkle, two Black women identifying as progressives, made the mayoral runoff, representing a stark contrast to the Daley and Emanuel eras of white Democrat centrism.

When Lightfoot triumphed over Preckwinkle, CTU took the view that, though its chosen candidate didn't win, it had succeeded in shifting Chicago's politics to the left; despite having actively campaigned against Lightfoot, some union leaders developed a theory that they had made her election possible. She had, after all, run on a platform that closely resembled CTU's goals of increasing affordable housing, implementing police reform, and providing a nurse in every school. Lightfoot understandably resented the notion that her success was due to a union that vociferously opposed her.

Not long after the election, Davis Gates spoke with Lightfoot advisor Ra Joy, who she later told people had been combative. Joy's basic attitude was, "We'll work with teachers," a comment that pointedly suggested ignoring union leadership. Davis Gates took offense and told him so.

"I don't know if you understand labor law," she said. "But you're not talking to my members about policy or contracts. You're talking to their elected representatives, and the last person who said that ended up with the first strike in Chicago history in twenty-five years, so I would tread lightly."

★ ★ ★ ★

Weeks earlier, as the runoff was starting in early March, left-wing journalist Ben Joravsky sat next to Lori Lightfoot onstage at the Hideout for a special edition of the First Tuesdays show. Lightfoot, who likes to unwind with craft beer and strong bourbon, appeared casual and relaxed as they talked city politics. She parried Joravsky's hard questions with charm and humor; when he asked if it was "possible to be a corporate lawyer and still be caring about working-class people, middle-class people," Lightfoot wryly responded, "I'm going to treat that as a serious question." When Joravsky asked if Lightfoot could work with the Chicago Teachers Union despite its support for Preckwinkle, or if she would be "Rahm-like" in seeking vengeance, Lightfoot gave the perfect answer for her audience. "You harm me mortally by comparing me to Rahm," Lightfoot said. "I'm not going to lead with my middle finger."

Joravsky had covered Chicago politics for four decades and wrote a longtime column for the *Reader*, the local alternative newspaper, where he advocated progressive policies. He had come to like Lightfoot, even though many of his left-wing friends looked skeptically at her record with the city and her career as a corporate lawyer. But he had been dismayed during the runoff by the discord between Lightfoot and the teachers' union. Joravsky thought it was counterproductive for the CTU, which would need a working relationship with Lightfoot if she won the race. And he didn't like to see Lightfoot alienate progressives, whom she had courted.

Joravsky had known Joanna Klonsky, a top Lightfoot political advisor, since she was five years old. Klonsky's father, Michael, was a longtime radical who had been a leader with Students for a Democratic Society and friends with Black Panthers chairman Fred Hampton. The Klonskys were Joravsky's type of people. After the election, Joravsky felt confident enough to make a suggestion to Joanna: get Lightfoot to sit down with Lewis and see if they can make peace.

By the time Lightfoot was elected, Lewis's brain cancer had progressed significantly. Though she was seriously ill and living in a nursing home, she agreed to meet with Lightfoot after the mayoral election. That meeting became a major flashpoint in the relationship. First, Lewis told people she had been stood up by Lightfoot during one scheduled appointment. (The Lightfoot camp disputes that and says they asked to reschedule due to snow.) When they finally got a date in May, word reached union leadership that Lightfoot would be meeting with Lewis while a CTU rally was going on. Sharkey scrambled to get someone to the nursing home, as the union was concerned about Lewis meeting with Lightfoot alone. Sharkey was incredulous that she would try and go around CTU leadership and also concerned that the mayor would come out of the meeting claiming Lewis's endorsement or mischaracterizing her comments. It was also a real act of disrespect to try to go around the current president.

Lewis did want to meet Lightfoot. She was proud of Lightfoot as a Black woman. Lewis also knew the meeting would be leaked. When Lightfoot walked into the room, she saw Davis Gates and was immediately hostile. She angled her seat so that she was facing away from Davis Gates and wouldn't have to look at her. Lewis told Lightfoot "how good her mom looked" on television and praised the pink suit she wore to the inauguration. "Lori, I want you to be successful. I want to help you be successful. Stacy and you can work together. You can work with Jesse. We can do well by the schools." Lightfoot expressed her admiration for Lewis.

After Lightfoot left, Lewis turned to Davis Gates and said, "You're going to have to strike on her."

Though the conversation was amicable, the aftermath worsened the dynamic between the mercurial mayor and the street-fighting union. Lightfoot complained to associates for months afterward that she felt "ambushed" by Davis Gates's presence at the meeting. One former aide recalled her angrily complaining, "That fucking bitch was in the room." The mayor's anger over the encounter got back to Joravsky, who was flabbergasted. Lewis could've been a go-between, helping make peace with the two sides and facilitating a conversation. Instead, it devolved. Lewis didn't understand why Lightfoot was upset. She later told Joravsky, "I'm the president emeritus, Stacy is my political director, and I'm not meeting any mayor without my political director."

Lightfoot's team had some regret about the whole encounter. They insisted they weren't trying to go around Sharkey and Davis Gates, just giving Lewis a show of respect. But the meeting morphed and took on a life of its own—which from City Hall's perspective characterized the way the CTU twisted anything Lightfoot did as malicious.

The meeting marked a missed opportunity for Lightfoot, who didn't do much to develop a relationship with Sharkey or Davis Gates. In the months that followed, Lightfoot regularly complained about Davis Gates, saying she was using her growing political power to harm the mayor. Lightfoot would get personal at times, criticizing Davis Gates as a political grandstander, a "fake," at one point even mocking her hair. Lightfoot also privately belittled Sharkey as weak and ineffective, lampooning him as a hypocrite living off his rich wife and driving a Tesla, while saying the district could avoid a future strike if not for Davis Gates. Though Davis Gates is an undeniably stronger personality than Sharkey, the idea that he was out of step with her underestimated Sharkey's own ultraliberal politics. It also misunderstands her background. Davis Gates spent years learning how to work with state legislators, reaching compromises, and had a high capacity for collaboration.

Throughout the coming weeks, however, Lightfoot made clear that she wanted to go around their leadership. She would call out "teachers" positively, but not the union. CTU contract negotiations are a long process in Chicago. They have to go to mediation, an independent arbiter who makes some determinations, and then they bargain. Early that summer, Lightfoot made what Sharkey considered a "classically unwise" move by offering the union a financial offer that was close to what they ended up agreeing on. It was insulting because the union was arguing about more than money, and she should've recognized that. He understood her reluctance to negotiate.

"If she meets with us, there's only one thing we're talking about at that point, what's going to go into our contract?" Sharkey said. "It's a conversation she doesn't want to have."

Lightfoot felt she was on higher ground due to her popularity and landslide victory. Lightfoot's team would defend her to people who didn't like her approach, saying she won the election by being demanding and prosecutorial. It fundamentally misunderstood the nature of the election win and the elusiveness of political popularity. As the union wound up for a strike, Lightfoot called people around the city to complain. Sometimes, that was Cook County

State's Attorney Kim Foxx, who knew Davis Gates and Toni Preckwinkle well and had relationships with both of them. Quickly, Foxx grew concerned about the mayor's griping sessions. She thought they were unwise and unproductive. She figured, *You've been here for eight days, and what you don't realize is that four years is a long time.*

12 | LA LA LAND

STANDING OUTSIDE MAYOR RAHM Emanuel's office on the fifth floor of City Hall after submitting their bargaining demands, Jesse Sharkey and Stacy Davis Gates submitted a comprehensive contract proposal to CPS in January 2019, but all sides knew it would fall to the next mayoral administration to renegotiate. The contract proposal was breathtakingly ambitious: a seventy-five-point document that demanded maximum classroom sizes with 20 to 24 students in early grades, counselors for every 250 students, and librarians and nurses staffed at every school. If approved, it would be quite expensive. Asked how the proposal would be funded, Davis Gates said, "Where will the money come from? Rich people."

"We have a governor who has committed to legalizing recreational marijuana and putting a tax on it. We can take that as well," Davis Gates said, launching into a spirited spiel. "They are also talking about sports betting. We can take that. They're talking about opening a new casino here in the city of Chicago. We can take that."

CTU's proposal, though aggressive, underscored a shocking reality about Chicago's schools. Many lacked social workers, even in neighborhoods where many students live with the daily trauma of gun violence. Others lack libraries and school nurses. Many of the things suburban parents and students at private schools take for granted are absent in Chicago. While many residents viewed CTU as asking for too much and exceeding the scope of the union's rightful concerns, others felt it was time Chicago's students and teachers received the resources they deserved.

The contract proposal set the stage for a battle between City Hall and the union—one that all sides knew might end in a strike and school shutdowns. The brewing battle also promised to test the limit of what's legal and what isn't in Chicago when it comes to a teachers strike. In the 1990s, Daley and his Springfield allies pushed a law through the state legislature making it illegal for CTU to strike over anything other than financial terms. Given the scope of the proposal, CTU clearly was preparing to walk out over broader issues than pay, and the question for Lightfoot was whether she would take them to court over it. To the CTU, the law restricting its strike rights was a clear sign of how the deck was stacked against teachers and their schools. Union leaders decided in internal meetings that they were willing to risk being called out for an illegal strike, though they bet Mayor Lori Lightfoot would refrain from taking them to court for fear of making Sharkey and Davis Gates into martyrs.

In the early months of the Lightfoot administration, union leaders complained City Hall wasn't negotiating and lacked urgency, a charge lobbed back by the mayor's office. Lightfoot kept Jim Franczek as the city's top labor lawyer, retaining the man who had negotiated previous deals under Daley and Emanuel. But she sent attorney Michael Frisch, a former associate of hers at Mayer Brown law firm, to be part of the team negotiating her contract, which drew scorn from union leaders. CTU thought he was there to spy on negotiations for Lightfoot and ridiculed him for not speaking much during meetings. Davis Gates thought of him as "the kid no one wanted to sit with." "What was he gonna say? 'Does anyone want coffee? Cream? Sugar?' He doesn't know anything about what's going on."

The Lightfoot team, meanwhile, thought Sharkey and Davis Gates were divided and hoped to exploit that perceived rift. The sides didn't substantively address the issues in the coming weeks, but in early July Lightfoot negotiators submitted a counterproposal that included a 14 percent overall cost-of-living pay increase for teachers. CTU leaders blasted the proposal for not addressing smaller class sizes, school nurses, and other staffing demands made by the union. CTU didn't formally respond to Lightfoot's full offer for weeks—a negotiation tactic aimed at bringing them closer to a potential strike date.

On September 4, the second day of class for Chicago's students, union leaders set a strike vote. If at least 75 percent of members voted in favor, the city could go on strike in October. The next day, CTU sent CPS a staffing proposal demanding that the school district hire 4,025 employees at a cost of over $800 million over three years.

Lightfoot officials were apoplectic. Even if the district could afford to make the hires, they responded, it would be impossible to do so due to lack of available candidates. Lightfoot officials were also reluctant to put commitments in writing about class sizes, saying the problem wasn't widespread.

On September 15 Lightfoot's top negotiator, Jim Franczek, sent a letter to CTU ripping their proposal and accusing them of dragging their feet. "We are committed to negotiating a fair contract that reflects our mutual belief in the importance of the work of your members and for the benefit of the students and the parents of CPS and the taxpayers of Chicago. We expect that the CTU would approach these negotiations with the same urgency," Franczek wrote. "We have not seen that sense of urgency from CTU." He went on to accuse CTU of ignoring "hours of discussions at the bargaining table" and presenting a proposal that they knew CPS could not agree to.

As the fall unfolded, CPS and Lightfoot officials grew increasingly frustrated with what they considered "pie in the sky proposals." Lightfoot staffers said the union was living in "la la land." One of them complained, "We have to be the adults." As bargaining sessions continued, the union repeatedly brought educators into the room to talk about circumstances in the district but did not present formal proposals. Lightfoot staffers often felt like they were negotiating against themselves, which they often were.

In mid-September, four months after Lightfoot was first sworn in, Lightfoot and Sharkey had their first meeting. The talk turned tense early on, when Lightfoot told Sharkey, "I don't bend to pressure." Afterward, Lightfoot publicly called it "a good start in getting to know each other better."

But Sharkey released a more combative statement: "It's unclear if [Lightfoot] is willing to listen to the needs of classroom educators and the families of our students," he said, adding that the new mayor "has yet to commit to being accountable for the commitments that she made as a candidate."

Though negotiations went slowly and tensions were rising, CTU was not sitting idly. On September 24, teachers began a three-day strike authorization vote. To mark the occasion, CTU held a rally at its headquarters headlined by Vermont senator Bernie Sanders, who was in the midst of his national campaign to become the Democratic Party's presidential nominee. CTU filled its labor hall with hundreds of teachers as Sanders praised them for "standing up and fighting for justice."

"Every problem in society—hunger, domestic violence, poverty—it walks into your doors, doesn't it?" Sanders said. "You see it every day and at a time when we, in the wealthiest country in the history of the world, have the highest rate of childhood poverty of almost any major country on earth. You are demanding and I am demanding a change in national priorities."

In a resounding victory for the union, more than 90 percent of voting members authorized a strike. Eager to avoid this outcome, Lightfoot's team continued talks, repeatedly dropping demands and sweetening its offers. In early October, the city dropped its attempt to raise health care costs for members by 1 percent over five years, as well as CPS's demand that teachers submit to principal-mandated prep time.

Bargaining-table frustrations began spilling out into the public sphere in early October, as a potential strike date neared. On October 7, Lightfoot stood by blue-and-white signs with a big number 141, because that's how many days it had been "since CTU has given CPS and the Lightfoot administration a comprehensive counterproposal."

A week before the October 17 strike date, city leaders met with Sharkey and Davis Gates once again and came away optimistic they could reach a deal. The next day, Frisch and Franczek waited for Sharkey and his crew at their office. They were expecting an early start but later complained CTU officials didn't show up for five hours. When Sharkey and Davis Gates finally returned, they rejected almost everything the city gave them on the big issues and said they would stand by their initial proposals from January, city officials said at the time. Some of Lightfoot's aides advocated walking out then and there.

"In English, this is a big 'Fuck you, we're going to strike,'" one Lightfoot staffer complained. "This is them saying we're not going to negotiate with you. We're going to stick a finger in your eye."

After reading through what the union was proposing, Franczek gave the union's leaders an impassioned speech. "Look, time is running out," he said. "You've told us we need a deal by Monday. We need to move things along. You've been dribbling and drabbling counters to us. We want to respond in a comprehensive way." Then he laid out the city's bottom line: "On duration, on compensation, on prep time, we're basically done. This is our last best final offer."

Instead of hurting CTU's resolve, however, Franczek's comments lit a flame. "What this offer represents is an invitation for us to strike," Sharkey said. "It seems like you're challenging us to strike. Your words here today about the pay and the term, you saying you have no more room to give, I'm interpreting this as a hostile act." Members of his bargaining team whooped and cheered. A Lightfoot official described it as a "Braveheart-esque" speech. One proud CTU member afterward described it this way: "Jesse told them to go to hell."

The teachers took advantage of October 14 being a day off due to Indigenous Peoples' Day and Columbus Day to hold a massive rally downtown, where American Federation of Teachers president Randi Weingarten said they were going to "teach the new mayor a lesson."

Sharkey also criticized Lightfoot for not moving on the union's proposals for lowering class sizes. "You'd think if that was really in her heart, if that were really in her soul, she would have offered educational justice first," Sharkey said. He raised the prospect of avoiding a strike, but made clear they weren't close.

"It was only today—today, sisters and brothers, today—that we had a meaningful conversation about class size and staffing," Sharkey said. "I'm going to stay negotiating. I'm going to try to avoid a strike. We want a fair settlement without a strike, to be clear. But if it requires a strike for us to win educational justice in this city, if it requires a strike to get the 'noes' at the bargaining table to turn to 'yeses,' if that's what it takes . . . then our union will show our unity and show our strength."

CTU had made concessions over the weekend. The union said it would accept phase-ins of smaller class sizes and social-worker staff increases, but specific numbers needed to be outlined in the contract. Lightfoot responded by highlighting concessions she had made and appealing directly to teachers—another attempt to circumvent the union. "I believe there's more that unites us than divides us," Lightfoot said. "And to all who will be taking part in today's rally, I want you to know that we hear you, and I respect what you stand for. My office is taking every step to ensure that you are safe and supported."

Though Lightfoot's office publicly acted as though the strike could be averted, behind the scenes the attitude was much different—and far more cynical. Michael Frisch, one of her top aides, sent her an email on October 15 with the subject line "Confirming our Agreement." In it, Frisch documented a "bet" on when the strike would start and end, with three cigars and a bottle of scotch for the winner. According to the email, Frisch and Maurice Classen, Lightfoot's chief of staff, bet that the strike would end before the following Wednesday. Lightfoot bet that it would extend past Wednesday; her response ended with "Now no one can back out."

Classen ripped Frisch for sending the email. When I got my hands on it through a public-records request, Frisch claimed it had been a bad joke and did not reflect an actual bet. Whether or not that was true, the bet reflected Lightfoot's belief that the union solely wanted to harm her politically.

Davis Gates meanwhile was frustrated when she attended a meeting with Lightfoot, Classen, and the mayor's CPS team. As the meeting dragged on, Davis Gates felt the administration had gotten repetitive and disparaging, then stood up. "It's time to go," she said.

On Thursday, October 17, the teachers went on strike—and it lasted well past the following Wednesday. Lightfoot later said the union was going to strike "no matter what." For the next thirteen days, three hundred thousand students missed school as adults battled over their future. Parents expressed support, but some complained that the city's most vulnerable children were being hurt by the shutdown. Several politicians reached out to Lightfoot with condolences—or to soothe the mayor's feelings as they showed support for the union.

US Rep. Jesús "Chuy" García, who had won a congressional seat in 2018 after challenging Emanuel in the 2015 election with CTU support, texted a heads-up to Lightfoot early that morning, stating he would be "issuing brief statement saying I stand with CTU as I have stood with striking workers for decades. It's my labor tradition. Good luck in negotiations."

Eight minutes later, Lightfoot responded. "Well, I would strongly urge that you say you stand with teachers and urge both sides to continue negotiating. Anything else would be highly problematic from my perspective. You can certainly express your solidarity without giving the CTU a talking point which they will use to pit you and I against each other. I don't want to be in a position to be fighting with you in the media. Not sure how that's helpful to either of us. I take a pretty dim view of that, Chuy." García apparently tried to find a middle ground, issuing a statement that he stood with the unions "as I have always advocated for workers to organize for better wages and working conditions. As the teachers initiate their strike, I encourage all parties to continue negotiating for a fair contract that addresses wages and working conditions."

Democratic Governor J. B. Pritzker similarly texted Lightfoot to say he would be speaking at the Illinois Federation of Teachers Convention over the weekend but hadn't expected the union to be on strike when he accepted the invitation. "I was endorsed by IFT, and they have been good allies. I cannot cancel. I plan not to take questions and I plan [to] not opine about the strike during my remarks. I have also respected the bargaining process overall," Pritzker said. "Just wanted you to know so you don't conclude that there's any challenge intended toward you."

Lightfoot's one-word response was curt: "Ok." Karen Lewis addressed that convention and told them, "You're at it again with another lying mayor."

The next day, Lightfoot staff and union leaders had a heated meeting. One person in the room recalled the teachers' union leaders saying they needed to put more in the contract. CPS chief financial officer Arnie Rivera responded, "This is all we have." Davis Gates responded, "There's always more money from Springfield." City officials summed up the exchange after: "They're still in la la land."

Again and again, Lightfoot's prosecutorial arguments backfired, Sharkey felt, because there wasn't a third party serving as the judge. She had to persuade the union, not put them behind bars. But her arguments only angered the union's rank and file.

Lightfoot would draw lines in the sand, repeatedly, then move off them. "I will never do this, then do it," Sharkey said. "There won't be another penny going into the contract, then the next day there's more pennies going into the contract. It teaches us that her public pronouncements aren't the bottom line."

Nationally, the 2020 presidential race was heating up, with more than a dozen Democrats still vying for the nomination. Like Sanders, many viewed the situation in Chicago as an opportunity to show their commitment to unions and working families more broadly. On October 22, Massachusetts senator Elizabeth Warren attended a rally with teachers where she threw her support behind the union. "Everyone in America should support you in this strike, and the reason is because when you go out and fight, you don't just fight for yourselves—you fight for the children of this city and the children of this country." Months later, when Lightfoot was asked if Warren had called to seek her endorsement, she harkened back to the event and took a shot at Sanders too. "They haven't reached out. They've been to Chicago. They were very supportive of the Chicago Teachers Union strike, but didn't feel it was necessary to talk to the new Black LGBTQ mayor," she said.

Throughout the process, Lightfoot complained about the union's big bargaining table and wanted them to make it smaller. For Sharkey, a big negotiating team was a critical component. "Karen used to say, if I did that, our members would shave my head and parade me through the street," Sharkey recalled.

After two weeks of teachers and students out of the classroom, CTU and Lightfoot finally came together and settled most of the outstanding issues. Under the deal, there would be a full-time nurse and social worker in every school by July 2023, as well as limits on class sizes. Tensions rose again, however, when Sharkey said the union wanted to make up days lost to the strike. Lightfoot fumed and privately told people she wouldn't "reward" the union for going on strike, even though it was common to make up lost days. (In 2012 the school district canceled some holidays to make up for them.) Lightfoot angrily summoned Sharkey to City Hall for a meeting. Her chief of security, former deputy US marshal Jim Smith, was under strict orders not to let Davis Gates upstairs.

"Sharkey, you go up," Smith said. "Stacy can't."

In her office, Lightfoot glared at Sharkey contemptuously and said, "Sharkey, you looked me in the fucking face, and you told me if I got you these things, we'd have a deal, and now you're coming back and telling me we don't have a deal?"

Sharkey tried to explain the situation, he recalled, but she accused him of holding students hostage. "She said we were extending the strike because we wanted to hurt kids, and we wanted to get Brandon and Stacy elected and take her job, and she wasn't going to let me bend her over the table and fuck her up the ass," Sharkey recalled. "I was speechless at that point."

It was a line she had privately used to characterize the union's position during internal meetings. But the heated meeting belied a key fact: both sides had lost resolve and lacked appetite for an ugly fight extending into November and costing teachers their health care. Neither was happy, but it was over—for now.

In some ways, the 2019 strike was a "mirror opposite of 2012," as Sharkey put it, when Emanuel came into office with a radical set of demands for change and the union was reacting. It was CTU leading the disruption this time, he said, a notion Lightfoot later called nonsense.

After they reached the agreement, Lightfoot asked Sharkey to stand with her at a news conference to announce the labor peace. He refused, figuring his members didn't want to see him "smiling with the mayor" after the bitter ending. Right before Lightfoot left her office to face the press waiting outside, an aide asked about Sharkey's whereabouts.

"He's looking for his balls," Lightfoot responded, before heading out to make the announcement on her own.

13 | "STAY HOME, SAVE LIVES"

THE SECOND CONFIRMED CASE of coronavirus in the United States was diagnosed in Chicago. It was detected in a woman in her sixties who visited her aging father and returned to the city. On January 31 President Donald Trump declared a public health emergency and temporarily barred most visitors from China. Concern started rising about this disease, though the city's leadership was still largely unalarmed. Lightfoot, especially, suggested it was overblown. She was particularly concerned about street violence, as the year started off on a wrong note with the city's homicide total increasing. The *Tribune* reported homicides jumped by 50 percent to thirty-three, up from twenty-two a year earlier, while shooting incidents rose 36 percent to 132, up from 97 a year earlier. "I talked to the superintendent about it this morning," Lightfoot said. "We cannot afford to take our foot off the gas."

The first weekend in February, while Lightfoot attended Chinatown's Lunar New Year parade, she said the federal government needed to provide US cities with clear guidance for dealing with the coronavirus and asked for assurances it will pay for costs related to dealing with the emergency, as I reported for the *Tribune*. She downplayed the issue. Underscoring her "everything's fine" message, Lightfoot noted she wasn't wearing a mask and didn't see a reason to before marching through the neighborhood parade flanked by Mickey and Minnie Mouse. "Chinatown, as you can see, remains open for business," Lightfoot said.

The earliest days of the pandemic everywhere were marked by confusion and attempts to tamp down panic. Health officials constantly warn about diseases, most of which don't become anything that changes the world. Lightfoot was fundamentally a believer in the status quo and not disrupting the system too abruptly, and she managed the crisis accordingly. Even as cases began rising and officials raised further concerns, Lightfoot urged caution. As the federal government started issuing sterner warnings, Lightfoot said she was "very disappointed" with comments from the Centers for Disease Control, which said people should prepare for significant disruption to their lives. "So far in Chicago, we've had two cases," Lightfoot said. "Now am I going to sit here and say with absolute certainty that we won't have any other cases? No, I will not, but I want to make sure that people understand as they continue to go about their normal lives, we have extremely well thought-out, well-planned responses in the event that the virus appears again in anyone else in Chicago."

In truth, that was bluster, and the city was not prepared for a pandemic. Over the next few weeks, the problem worsened. *Crain's Chicago Business* reported at the beginning of March that the International Housewares Association called off a show that would've brought nearly sixty thousand people to town. Not long after, there was a slew of further cancellations to trade shows that were the lifeblood of Chicago's vibrant trade-show industry. Paul Vallas, the failed 2019 candidate who had run Chicago's budget office under Mayor Richard M. Daley, predicted problems ahead. "The city and state have done little to address the long-term debt crisis other than to continue to base pension fund investment earning forecasts on totally unrealistic growth rates," Vallas told *Crain's*. "Illinois is a state whose economy is heavily dependent on exports. Anything that slows or disrupts the world's economy has a greater impact (here)." Later, when Vallas wrote a commentary piece in the *Chicago Tribune* that stated the city "needs a wartime financial plan, now," Lightfoot snapped. "Over the course of this crisis, you see a lot in people," she told reporters. "Unfortunately, some people are desperate to be relevant. Mr. Vallas, from my estimation, probably hasn't touched a city budget, doesn't know the nuances, in two decades."

A pivotal moment in the pandemic came March 6, when South by Southwest canceled its show in Texas, highlighting the deep and ongoing fractures to civil society by the pandemic. That and the NBA season suspension were the moments when I knew this would stick with us. The next day, students and staff at Portage Park's Vaughn Occupational High School on the Northwest Side were asked to self-quarantine after one of their employees tested positive from a trip on the *Grand Princess* cruise ship. All of it led to escalating panic. Illinois governor J. B. Pritzker came to City Hall for a news conference with

Lightfoot about Vaughn and sat in her conference room. The mayor afterward cracked to staff that he didn't fit in his chair, a comment that struck people as insensitive, though some on her staff had heard her mock him and other heavy politicos like Alderperson Jason Ervin as "fat fucks." The case was the sixth in Illinois, and Lightfoot publicly tried to "reassure all of our CPS students and families that our city's been working relentlessly to protect the safety and security of our students, faculty, and staff, along with their friends and loved ones."

Lightfoot continued to tread lightly, not wanting to freak residents out, but her partners in state government became concerned that she wasn't taking it as seriously as they were. The first big test of COVID came in the form of the St. Patrick's Day parade, which was scheduled for March 15. Chicago traditionally has two big events to celebrate the Irish: a dyeing of the river and parade downtown, as well as a giant neighborhood event in Beverly on the Southwest Side. The South Side Irish Parade has historically been a bawdy time. For three years in the late 2000s, it was canceled due to giant mobs of drunks urinating on people's homes and destroying the community. It returned in 2012 with private security and a heavier police presence to tamp down on craziness and has gone off more smoothly in recent years. Even in its milder version, however, the South Side Irish Parade brings hundreds of thousands of people to the community from all over the country for a day of heavy drinking.

As COVID continued spreading throughout the world and the region, some officials became nervous about Chicago's gathering. The 1918 flu pandemic was popularly believed to have been exacerbated by a Liberty Loan Drive parade in Philadelphia, leading some to advocate for shutting down the St. Patrick's Day festivities. Lightfoot, however, was slow to act, leading to her first series of conflicts with the governor. As the days ticked by, the governor had a feeling of dread; in good conscience, he believed allowing such a large crowd to congregate as COVID numbers continued rising was wrong. Complicating matters was the Lightfoot administration's personal connection to the parade. Lightfoot security chief Jim Smith was cochair of the local committee overseeing the parade and, in an interview with *EP Podcast*, joked that his role requires him to "drink a lot of Paddy's Irish whiskey."

"We're not canceling any parade for some crazy virus," Smith said. "We'll make sure we'll be careful of the kissin' and huggin', but we'll be fine."

Alderperson Matt O'Shea, who grew up in the ward and had been its alderperson since 2011, was caught in the middle. He went to the city to ask what was going to happen and was assured it was still going on. In a text message, he told *Tribune* reporter John Byrne, "The 42nd annual South Side Irish St. Patrick's Day Parade will step off on Sunday March 15th at 12 p.m. #WashYourHands." Privately, though, he was concerned about the ongoing toll.

The next day, O'Shea voiced a more concerned tone. "This is the mayor's decision, but I think we should be taking advisement from medical professionals like the Illinois Department of Public Health and Chicago Department of Public Health," O'Shea said. Pritzker also went public with his concern about the parades happening. "My own view, I'll just say, is I want to keep people safe, and I think we've got to follow the guidance that medical experts give us," Pritzker said. "The CDC is talking about avoiding mass gatherings. They aren't giving a number to what is a mass gathering, and I think that's not helpful, frankly."

Lightfoot had taken a trip out of town, slowing the process. Mid-week, she returned and canceled the parade. She asked O'Shea to stand with her for the announcement, and he did, but he wondered whether Pritzker put his foot down. Had Lightfoot not agreed to cancel the parade, Pritzker would've done it for her.

The next few weeks escalated dramatically. Pritzker ordered the shutdown of public events with more than a thousand people. On March 13 Pritzker closed all schools in the state, a move he announced hours after Lightfoot had publicly suggested she didn't want to shut down CPS due to the "significant secondary effect" of childcare problems, kids going hungry who depend on school meals, and potential street violence. She had also privately dismissed Alderperson Andre Vasquez when he came to her with the idea: "We will be guided by the science and we see no basis to close the schools at this time. We cannot do 'monkey see, monkey do' because a lot of stuff is happening completely untethered from any scientific basis which just leads to panic and confusion."

On March 19, as cases continued rising, Lightfoot gave a somber speech where she declared, "We may get bent, but we will never be broken." A day later, Pritzker issued a stay-at-home order at a news conference, highlighted by Dr. Emily Landon, who gave a viral speech. "It's really hard to feel like you're saving the world when you're watching Netflix from your couch. But if we do this right, nothing happens," Landon said. "A successful shelter-in-place means you're going to feel like it was all for nothing, and you'd be right—because *nothing* means that nothing happened to your family. And that's what we're going for here." Lightfoot watched the remarks with anger, though, as she felt they were alarmist. Privately, Lightfoot's staff began calling Landon "Dr. Doom."

Those early days were marked by constant frustration from the governor's office that Lightfoot was always steps behind the governor. Lightfoot and her team always wanted a day or two more to roll something out. Pritzker's people were concerned with the possibility of exponential growth and the idea that every day matters. As the constant push and pull continued, Pritzker called a confidant and voiced his frustration. "I really want to bring her along, but she's two steps behind me on everything. This is a crisis," Pritzker said.

Lightfoot, for her part, privately complained that Pritzker was playing presidential politics and trying to keep up with New York and California governors seen as potential candidates. "He's running for president," she said, summing up her views on his motivation. But to her credit and his, they saw the public conflict between New York's governor and New York City's mayor and consciously tried not to replicate it by avoiding too much public bickering.

Ironically, Lightfoot disapproved of almost all his closures, but she was proud to have shut down the city's lakefront, the only major closure ordered by her. Keeping the lakefront closed for months was a good snapshot of Lightfoot's leadership. She made a decision and stuck with it, even after it became clear that the virus was less likely to spread outdoors. Leadership requires resolution, but unwillingness to adapt to new facts is death.

As Chicago residents settled into their new normal, the Internet started creating memes depicting a stern Lightfoot blocking the Lakefront Trail and other popular spots, including Georges Seurat's *A Sunday Afternoon on the Island of La Grande Jatte* painting at the Art Institute of Chicago and the Superdawg drive-in eatery. It followed viral videos of Italian mayors yelling at citizens for not obeying public health orders. The images had a certain irony to them, given Lightfoot's reluctance to close down, but they took on a life of their own and boosted her popularity with a weary public looking for the bright side.

Lightfoot aide Michael Fassnacht, a German-born communications professional who joined her administration as a one-dollar-per-year "chief marketing officer," paid special notice. He took a lesson from the memes: people liked Lightfoot and wanted to see her in authentic situations, and City Hall could bypass the media with mass-produced clips. He took the idea behind the memes and added a "Stay Home, Save Lives" tagline for a series of clever videos. In one, she sang the phrase while strumming a guitar. In another, she scolded someone for going to the hair salon: "Getting your roots done is not essential!" Others were sarcastic. "Your dog doesn't need to see its friends," she said in one. "You can work on your jump shot inside," she said in another. Lightfoot got into trouble after media found out that she'd gotten her own hair cut during the pandemic, when it was against the rules, which she justified by saying she needs to look good on national television—one of the first clear public stumbles of her administration's COVID campaign.

Lightfoot's PSAs were a hit, but she took the wrong lesson. People didn't want to see her face everywhere. The memes happened organically and were not a substitute for regular engagement with the press or a license to market her like a new Pokémon video game. But Fassnacht felt empowered to continue promoting other videos, which eventually became an embarrassment. The administration hired a man on a horse and called him "the Census Cowboy," while Lightfoot wore a hideous green cowboy hat. It was widely panned, but Fassnacht told the press team, "I will never apologize for taking risks." (He argued to me it was a success because it provoked conversation. "Have you ever talked about a census campaign ever?")

Later in the year, City Hall dressed Lightfoot and public health commissioner Dr. Allison Arwady up as the Rona Destroyers for Halloween, which made for a cartoonish series of photos. Fassnacht was also prone to hyperbole: in a *Sun-Times* interview, he promised to launch a campaign rebranding Chicago and said it would change the public's perception of key holidays. "You will never look at Black Friday the same way. I promise you that," he said, before breaking the promise. His approach—to create videos—alienated some members of the Lightfoot press team who thought it was the beginning of a broader move away from real relationships with reporters. Fassnacht thought his strategy was sound—it's important for politicians to distribute their own message, and his advice wasn't to cut out media, even if that's what Lightfoot ended up doing.

As the pandemic started, Lightfoot announced the city would "limit ticketing, towing, and impounding and focus its efforts on public safety-related issues." In plain English, that meant the city would no longer issue tickets for people who don't pay their meters, a promise the mayor isn't able to make due to the hated parking meter deal. But she wanted to give off the appearance of doing something to help residents, and that's what she announced. City Hall tried to gently walk it back later, but a *Tribune* report later noted that thousands received fines anyway and resented her mixed message. She responded by demanding staff publish a screed canceling her *Tribune* subscription. Staff ignored that part of her message, but the angry email later leaked. It was a classic example of governing by press release instead of doing the work.

Lightfoot went before the City Council to push the Emergency Powers Ordinance—a measure allowing her to move money within the city budget and sign COVID-related contracts under $1 million without aldermanic approval. Alderperson Jason Ervin tried to use his power as head of the Black Caucus to fight her, but like the marijuana battle, he lost. "You can't let expediency totally wreck us because that way you'd be killing us in two ways: physically dying and economically dying," Ervin said. Lightfoot texted Reilly: "It would be helpful if some(one) said that the vast majority of the funds will be brought before the Council as specific appropriations. Jason is full of crap—again."

In early May, Lightfoot went to the West Side for a news conference decrying residents who were throwing house parties. She then walked across the street to a playground where several young Black men—teens—mingled and told them the playground was closed and to move on.

"Let's move on, move on, move on," Lightfoot said, surrounded by cops. "You want to take this virus back to your house, get your momma sick?"

The kids mostly ignored her, but as she turned to walk away, one of them responded, "Ya'll overdoing it. Ya'll need to find a cure, talking about go home. You go home." For years afterward, Lightfoot faced criticism that she should've tried to engage the children, rather than scolding them with police and walking away.

By late May, Lightfoot was itching to reopen the city and did so for many businesses, though not the lakefront, sports teams, or schools, a later source of tension with the teachers' union when she did try to reopen schools.

She spent the next several months casually threatening to shut down the city if cases spiked, while keeping things open. In early October, Lightfoot warned that the city was experiencing a "second surge" and said she would take action with shutdowns if necessary. "I won't hesitate to reimpose restrictions," Lightfoot said. There was real whiplash around this: Lightfoot and Arwady held a news conference and blamed spikes on private get-togethers in people's homes, not restaurants or any other locations. Days later, Pritzker had seen enough of the spike and shut down indoor dining and bars statewide as a means of stopping the spread. Lightfoot hotly criticized the move and said she hoped he would reconsider, and then they had a meeting, where she dropped her opposition. "We had a very frank and productive conversation with the governor and his team and my team as well. We explored a lot of issues and we came out of that discussion really committed to making sure that we work hard together. Obviously, we've got to work and make sure that we communicate effectively to the businesses across Chicago that are going to be affected."

Watching closely was the Chicago Teachers Union, which was concerned about how she was handling COVID-19 in the schools and was anxious about possibly returning to the classroom in the winter. The union was not impressed with the mixed messages.

Lightfoot and her aides feel she deserves credit for how she handled the pandemic. During her reelection campaign, they tried to rekindle the affection residents felt for her that was best typified by the memes. I've always thought Lightfoot's role responding to COVID was misunderstood: much of her leadership was reactive to Pritzker, who was the one making nearly every hard decision because the state had authority over Chicago. Her early waffling about shutdowns and false threats to close businesses if cases spread in the fall highlight the indecision and lack of vision that plagued her administration. But her handling of vaccines merits respect.

In late 2020 the feds approved vaccines for COVID-19. Lightfoot was adamant that her administration would try to ensure that Black and brown residents got priority. Statistically, those communities needed it most. They were generally the sickest and therefore most prone to serious infection from COVID, and they had died disproportionately during the pandemic. This was a challenge for a multitude of reasons, not least of which was resistance within the Black community to vaccines based on unfounded conspiracy theories and lies.

When Lightfoot got her shot, she tried to spread the message: "If we do not reverse this trend, we will continue to see more Black and brown [residents] die of this virus when a vaccine is right here, right now, for free, for all," she said. "To those of you who are hesitant, we are here to tell you the vaccine is safe. We want you to take it because it is safe and because it will save your life." In typical political fashion, Lightfoot and her team exaggerated their successes. But there's no doubt their attempts to be equitable about vaccines and focus on Black and brown residents saved lives.

14 | POP THE WEASEL

AS CHICAGO POLICE BOARD president Ghian Foreman led the search for a new police superintendent, Mayor Lori Lightfoot wanted to avoid the same sort of fiasco she experienced under Rahm Emanuel when her recommendations for police superintendent were ignored. Lightfoot said the process needed to have legitimacy and independence. "I led it four years ago," she reflected, according to the *Sun-Times*. "It was very important for me that they do their job with independence so the process had integrity. I would check in from time-to-time about the cadence but not the substance because, by law, that's up to them."

Although the process was supposed to be independent of the mayor's office, it wasn't. Lightfoot and her team conducted in-depth interviews with candidates long before they had received recommendations from the board. Behind the scenes, the jockeying began. Four names emerged as serious potential contenders: West Side police leader Ernest Cato, suburban chief Kristen Ziman, former Dallas top cop David Brown, and Sean Malinowski, Charlie Beck's chief of staff in Los Angeles who had been working with CPD since before Johnson got fired. Malinowski was an intriguing option, having come from a better police department while being familiar with Chicago. Beck tried to stay out of the process. He figured Malinowski didn't need any further endorsement from him than being his chief of staff. But Lightfoot was hostile to his candidacy. She complained that Malinowski had canceled an invitation to speak at an event last minute and that he didn't personally tell her. She also referred to Malinowski derisively as "the great white hope." Some at City Hall felt Lightfoot couldn't pick a white man for that post.

On April 1, 2020, the police board announced three finalists: Cato, Ziman, and Brown. A day later, Lightfoot appointed Brown. For his part, Beck was disappointed that Malinowski wasn't even a finalist. He understood that the mayor is entitled to a pick—"there's no marriage in any city government like the marriage between a chief and mayor in big cities," he understood. But to keep Malinowski off the short list entirely was a shock.

When reporters caught on that the process wasn't independent, Lightfoot deflected. "I've never been mayor before," she said, according to the *Sun-Times*. "So I can't tell you what the normal protocol is. But obviously I wanted to make sure that we were ahead of the game." She said she had "a sense of who the finalists were, particularly from the media reports. I wanted to get ahead of that to make sure that we started to do our due diligence and had enough time to do it to our satisfaction. And we did that. I'm grateful David Brown has said yes, and we move on from here."

★ ★ ★ ★

Brown came to Chicago with an astonishing life story. The fifty-nine-year-old former Dallas police chief had been with the department for more than three decades when he retired in 2016. His life repeatedly intersected with the criminal justice system, as people close to him emerged as both victim and perpetrator. One of his former police partners was killed in the line of duty in 1988. Brown's brother was murdered in 1991. His son, D. J., was bipolar and murdered two people, including a police officer, and was himself killed by the cops in a 2010 incident. Most famously, Brown authorized his police force to use a robot and a bomb to blow up a former-veteran suspect in 2016 who, angry over officers killing Black men, had murdered five cops in a mass shooting. He rose to national prominence over the incident and wrote a memoir, *Called to Rise: A Life in Faithful Service to the Community That Made Me.*

Brown's debut news conference went awkwardly. He was earnest. "My life and career has taken place in the city of Dallas, but the call to service and to rise is one that is heard across the nation. As Mayor Lightfoot mentioned, it's that call that has driven everything that I've done in my career as an officer and public servant. And, yes, it's a fire in my bones. All of us are at our best when we serve others. And to all the great residents of this city, I would only say: David Brown, reporting to duty. I'm at your service," he said.

But some of his comments came off like he was trying too hard. He referred to the city as "Chi-Town" and "that Windy City," two monikers more closely associated with suburbanites and outsiders than real residents. Asked why he wanted to come to Chicago, for instance, Brown responded, "Are you kidding me? The city that produced Michelle Obama and elected Mayor Lightfoot? Sign me up for that." He also made a reference to Chicago barbecue, a confusing comment as that isn't really what the city is known for.

The problems started immediately behind the scenes. Brown was upset with Bob Boik for bringing a captain onto his staff without getting his formal approval. Looking at his schedule on the first day, Brown dismissed the plans and said, "I'm not going to get controlled." He also made a comment Boik took as being critical of civilians serving at high levels of the department. Boik thought about quitting, but kept in there to help keep the department stable. As first deputy superintendent, Brown chose Eric Carter, an intense police leader who wore a block of medals on his chest, earning him the nickname "Qaddafi" from Lightfoot chief of staff Maurice Classen.

During a meeting with public-safety advocates, Brown was shown a slide-show detailing racial disparities in the city's violence statistics. "Stop," Brown said suddenly. "This is why I'm here." It left people with a feeling of hope. But the good signs slowly turned to concern. Susan Lee, the mayor's deputy for public safety who had coaxed Beck into being Chicago's interim superintendent, commented to Brown, "You weren't my first pick, but I'm behind you 100 percent," which he repeatedly brought up afterward. She meant it to convey support, but Brown did not take the comment well.

Early in his tenure, Brown raised eyebrows by talking about his "moonshot" goal of fewer than three hundred homicides for the city of Chicago, an admirable idea that nevertheless made him sound like a starstruck tourist. Chicago hadn't had fewer than three hundred homicides in the city since 1957. He also talked behind the scenes about calling a gang summit to organize peace treaties and smooth out the violence. The idea sounded good, but it was a relic of the past. There are still traditional gangs with hierarchies and discipline that run like violent Fortune 500 companies in Chicago, and law enforcement could theoretically talk to those groups to ask them to watch the violence when things get hot. But the vast majority of Chicago shootings today are driven on a block-to-block level by disorganized youth usually fighting over petty disputes.

In another early meeting, Brown called officers together and told them he wanted saturation policing, a surge of police showing their presence in tough areas. He told the brass they could come up with their own names for different saturation formations, like "pop the weasel." Within the department, it later became known as "the okeydoke." Combined, the sequence started to raise questions among staff about his leadership abilities. One member of command, Randy Darlin, turned to another and said, "I'm leaving." He followed through, taking a job in Colorado.

In Chicago, Memorial Day weekend typically marks the start of summer—the bloodiest time of year. The holiday, just a few weeks into Brown's tenure, saw the predictable wave of shootings. Afterward, Lightfoot held an extraordinary news conference where she panned "out of control" violence and criticized the planning by her department. "We have to do better. We cannot have weekends in the summer turn into a bloodbath. And this weekend's violence was out of control," Lightfoot said, according to the *Sun-Times*. "While I know that there was a lot of energy and coordination among a variety of groups, what I said to the superintendent this morning is, 'This was a fail. Whatever the strategy is, it didn't work.'"

After Lightfoot criticized Brown's performance, he was getting ready to speak to the press for a regularly scheduled news conference, and an aide shared her comments. Brown was hotter than a Texas barbecue. "If this is how it's going to be, I'm going back to Dallas," Brown said. Cook County State's Attorney Kim Foxx checked in on him afterward and he complained, "I've never been talked to like that in my life. She needs me more than I need her." He understood the dynamics. "If she loses her police chief after a month, it will look bad for her," Brown said. Not long after, Brown and Lightfoot are believed to have talked through the incident. She never publicly criticized him again.

Worries started growing in City Hall. Classen tried to reassure members of his staff that Brown would get more comfortable in the role once he completed the training necessary to wear a sworn police uniform, a notion that was ridiculed. Unlike other superintendents, Brown wasn't particularly visible at police roll calls or city events. Later, during a City Council meeting, Alderperson Tom Tunney told Brown he'd been "aloof" and asked him to be more visible.

"I have been aloof in a global pandemic," Brown said, though that excuse didn't fly with anyone. Beyond the faux pas, Brown started making concerning decisions. He undid Beck's plan to undo merit promotions, reinjecting political considerations into the process. He also undid Beck's moves to put cops in districts, saying he wanted to create large units that could rove across the city. "I just try not to do stuff that doesn't work," Brown said, according to the *Sun-Times*. "That structure wasn't working."

Those comments led to a rare public rebuke from Beck, who critiqued Brown's plans as "a more militaristic, shock-and-awe style of policing." "It has a major drawback. That is, it tends to alienate the community that's involved. You just cannot saturate neighborhoods with police and expect that to be a long-term strategy," Beck told the *Sun-Times*. "It'll work in the short-term. But it can't be your go-to. It has to be something for emergencies." Within City Hall, Lightfoot staffers were watching with ever-growing concern because they thought the strategies had been going in the right direction, but Brown's moves were considered regressive. Classen in particular was horrified and started to question, "Who did we hire?"

15 | "THE CITY IS UP FOR GRABS"

GEORGE FLOYD'S MURDER BY Minneapolis police officers on May 25, 2020, angered the world. Like the police killing of Laquan McDonald, Floyd's murder came in a city with highly institutionalized racism and ongoing segregation. The protests first started peacefully, then became violent. As tensions turned destructive, the city's mayor, Jacob Frey, ordered cops to abandon the third precinct police station, which was then burned down. Chicago Mayor Lori Lightfoot watched the unfolding events with disgust. During a planning meeting with her City Hall staff, Lightfoot declared, "They won't burn my city down."

As protests enveloped the country, Chicago Police leaders felt they were in good shape for expected demonstrations. Department chief of staff Bob Boik, however, had some concerns and proposed the idea of raising bridges to limit downtown access. Chicago has eighteen drawbridges over the river around the central business district. The brass and Lightfoot aides thought raising the bridges would be overkill and didn't like the optics of cutting downtown from the rest of the city. They also felt they were best in the country at handling protests, a reputation Chicago Police feels it earned after successfully handling left-wing demonstrations against NATO in 2012 and every action since. The lack of widespread violence over McDonald's murder also inspired a sense that the city would be OK.

Early in the week after Floyd's murder, city officials thought the administration was handling the mostly peaceful protests well. But the mood started shifting as the week went on. Boik's concern escalated as he was standing under the El tracks downtown and saw people on the platform throw rocks and bricks at police. There was some small-scale looting too, though Boik called City Hall and asked the Department of Streets and Sanitation to sweep up the glass. The idea was to put on a brave face and hold the city together.

The next morning, Chicago cops and Lightfoot held a meeting and decided to raise the bridges. It took longer than expected, as only a small number of city workers are trained to take on the task. They had also been expecting a protest at 2:30 PM, but the demonstrators arrived much earlier than intelligence indicated and subsequently overwhelmed police in an increasingly violent series of encounters. There were also car protests that complicated logistics and planning, as the officers hadn't started staging yet, and it was a challenge to handle both at once.

Lightfoot spent much of the day at the Office of Emergency Management and Communications (OEMC), which has a control center with walls of screens tied to the city's camera system, allowing for a panopticon view of Chicago. It's like a scene out of Batman. Her presence was appreciated and expected at first, but it started to become a distraction. Lightfoot watched the screens intently. She would look up, see someone committing a crime or other act of vandalism, and shout it out for action. Boik and any other police official with a radio nearby would then rush to the air and ask, "Is that addressed?" Some of it was relatively minor, however, and the mayor's orders put the already stressed command staff on edge. It was also taking away focus from bigger issues. Eventually, deputy chief Randy Darlin walked up to her and said, "Ma'am, with all due respect, I'm in command here." She backed off.

Later that night, Lightfoot called a news conference and instituted a city-wide curfew of 9:00 PM—a move she announced just after 8:20, giving the public a short window of time to get home. "What started out as a peaceful protest has now evolved into criminal conduct," Lightfoot said, denouncing people she said came downtown "armed for all-out battle" and promising, "I will not let criminals take over our city and shame the majority of us." Lightfoot also said she wasn't considering asking Illinois governor J. B. Pritzker to call in the National Guard for further assistance.

The morning after, Lightfoot emailed OEMC director Rich Guidice and asked him to "make sure ALL camera feeds from yesterday from Roosevelt to and including Oak Street, from the Lake to the Expressway are preserved from noon until 5:00 AM. I know that is a huge volume, but we need to make sure that if there are any accusations of misconduct by CPD, we have the video to disprove it, and also if we need evidence for any of the arrests made or TBD, we have video support."

Lightfoot wasn't really concerned about anyone's civil rights. She later told the inspector general's office that the protests had been "a concerted effort to bring chaos to our cities." It was, Lightfoot said, "a conspiracy, sophisticated, paid for and promoted by someone in multiple cities across the country at the same time. That's not a coincidence." She made the same point in calls to congresspeople and staff. Nobody could figure out whom she was talking about, and one staffer quipped it was "the Russians."

Raising the bridges and implementing a curfew did not stop the chaos. Sunday, the riots spread to Chicago's neighborhoods, mostly on the South and West Sides. I had been on a furlough for the past week, monitoring the national crisis and keeping up on Chicago, but I was back to work that Sunday—and I spent it driving around the South Side with my colleague, Jessica Villagomez, where we watched every major intersection with a store get looted. Police and security often stood nearby, helpless and overwhelmed by the numbers.

Throughout the crisis, Lightfoot stayed in touch with alderpersons. Through the Freedom of Information Act, I've obtained what the city purports to be all of her texts with the city's fifty individual alderpersons, and this period is the closest she came to treating the council like a real partner. As protests escalated, Lightfoot texted North Side alderperson Scott Waguespack, "This has been an unbelievable day. I am so angry and saddened by how vicious and nasty some of these young people acted today. It was so painful to watch."

West Side alderperson Chris Taliaferro texted her, "Mayor, the wards are experiencing heavy looting and large crowds gathering. Will the National Guard or police redeploy to the south and west sides before we [lose] control of them?"

Ever defensive, Lightfoot replied with photos of cops on the West Side and said, "This problem is all over the area, not just in Chicago. And if the caucus wanted to be helpful, activate your faith, community and other stakeholders to be in the streets to help calm it down and call people out."

When Taliaferro suggested a "sunset to sunrise curfew," Lightfoot replied, "Man, I'm getting shit for even daring to implement anything!"

Northwest Side alderperson Rossana Rodriguez Sanchez texted the mayor with alarm about the curfew. "I'm getting reports of CPD running over protestors, bridges up and CTA down and People trying to leave downtown and not being able to," Rodriguez Sanchez said. "I'm really concerned about the safety of the protestors. It seems like 35 minutes is not enough to allow people to get home safe."

"Your info is incorrect. The people that remain downtown are looters, not protesters," Lightfoot responded. "I am watching this unfold. Happy to discuss, but we are trying to protect lives and property."

The two then exchanged a flurry of messages:

> RODRIGUEZ SANCHEZ: I know people downtown, they are not looting. Can we get (CTA) back up in the loop for people to leave?
> LIGHTFOOT: Rossana, I am watching it real time from the OEMC. People can go west to the blue line or catch the brown line north.
> RODRIGUEZ SANCHEZ: I understand that. I'm also getting messages from scared young black People who don't know where to go. I don't think they are looters. They just want to go home and are confused about how to do that.
> LIGHTFOOT: Go west and then north. Rossana, the city is up for grabs.

She also texted South Side alderperson Michelle Harris, "You awake?"

"Yes," Harris texted back. "I'm up [watching] our resident[s] going crazy."

Alderperson Greg Mitchell texted Lightfoot a picture of a fire at 95th and Clyde. "Current fire?" Lightfoot asked.

"Yes," Mitchell responded. "I'm here now watching it burn."

That Sunday, Lightfoot held a painful conference call with alderpersons, an incident best reported by WTTW-TV reporter Heather Cherone and Paris Schutz. While some people dismissed the looting and riots as crime covered by insurance or argued that it was a sign of righteous anger, it destroyed businesses, particularly on the South and West Sides, where bigger companies were reluctant to set up shop and smaller businesses sometimes struggled. On the call, Harris worried about Walmart and CVS not reopening. "What are we going to have left in our community?" she asked. "Nothing." Alderperson Pat Dowell, whose ward spans some of the city's wealthier areas in the South Loop and tougher stretches on the South Side, lamented the riots. "I've worked really hard over the last seven years, and now I feel like I am five feet back."

Already, a narrative was forming that Lightfoot chose to protect downtown at the expense of the neighborhoods, which Lightfoot countered head-on by saying it "offends me deeply, personally, in part because it is simply not so. We've been working our ass off. It is all over the city." She recounted some of the craziest scenes: A "dude with a sledgehammer" breaking into a clothing store so a crowd of several dozen people could loot. A crowd at Madison and Pulaski being gassed with pepper spray twice but "they didn't give a shit." "I don't know about you, but I haven't seen shit like this before, not in Chicago," she said.

Alderperson Susan Sadlowski Garza cried. Alderperson Edward Burke put it into historical perspective: "This is far worse than it was in 1968." Lightfoot's frequent critic, Raymond Lopez, complained about a "virtual war zone" in his ward. She blew him off and said he was "100 percent full of shit." "Well, fuck you then," Lopez responded. The city blocking off downtown gave way to neighborhood looting, but that wasn't the strategy. It was a wildfire that couldn't be controlled. Lightfoot shared her reaction with me in a text: "Utterly depressing."

After the riots cooled in the first week of June, other political matters bubbled. City Hall worried about the unrest harming Chicago's reopening plan, a concern about which she texted downtown alderperson Brendan Reilly. "We should have a conversation about what tomorrow could look like for the downtown," Reilly said. "Very worried about protests, then violence, then looting returning if we end the lockdown."

There was enormous anxiety about COVID and the possibility of more violence, but Lightfoot decided the city needed to reopen, a tougher call than it looked but the right one. "Everywhere I went I asked a question: Should we open or should we delay?" Lightfoot asked at a news conference. "And to universal acclaim, emphatically, what I heard from people is 'Mayor, we have to step forward. We have to open.'"

★ ★ ★ ★

The next few days after the riots focused on damage control. A *Tribune* investigation later found that estimated harm to 710 impacted businesses was more than $165 million, far more than the estimated $77 million in damages (in 2023 dollars) that occurred during the April 1968 riots sparked by the assassination of the Reverend Martin Luther King Jr. Lightfoot held a news conference at a Jewel-Osco food store on the South Side during which she promised $10 million for businesses that had been ransacked. Later, Alice Yin and I dug in and found the actual payout for looting was $232,760, a number that still astonishes and disappoints me. It was a classic example of governing by press release: hyping something up for attention, then quietly not delivering.

Police felt they were able to shut down the bad conduct much quicker than did other cities, a sentiment that failed to reassure a shaken public. But in the aftermath, police leaders worked with city department heads to implement what they called a corridor protection plan—or what one garbage truck driver called a "blockade on wheels," to ensure that the city would be able to quickly mobilize vehicles that would block access to lootable areas in a pinch.

Seeking to address the public's anger, Lightfoot held a news conference to announce community groups would be reviewing the city's use-of-force policy. Standing in City Hall alongside Lightfoot, Arewa Winters, whose nephew was killed by Chicago cops, gave a speech in which she called officers "psychopaths with guns" and flexed her biceps. Lightfoot was livid and immediately called a big group of staffers into her conference room to shout, "Who the fuck brought this lunatic to the press conference?" Michael Milstein, a reform analyst at CPD, took ownership of the decision and apologized. He had built a good relationship with Winters, whom he respected, as did other people within the Police Department who had gotten to know her in the aftermath of her nephew's death and found her to be a thoughtful critic.

Conservative Northwest Side alderperson Nick Sposato texted Lori, "You have really lost it!"

"That was absolutely not my choice," Lightfoot texted back, falsely blaming Maggie Hickey, the independent monitor for the consent decree.

In those early days, Lightfoot attempted to address police misconduct by calling for an officer who was photographed flipping off protesters to be fired. While the cop was likely wrong, the notion that he should've been fired for a bad moment shook police confidence in the idea that she would have their back. She also held an extraordinary news conference with US Rep. Bobby Rush, who approached the city to complain that his office had been broken into and responding officers lounged around amid looting. Rush also ripped officers for having "the unmitigated gall" to pop his popcorn while there was looting going on around the city. Conservative alderperson Anthony Napolitano, a former cop, did an interview with WGN during which he mockingly had popcorn. Lightfoot texted him, "Supremely unhelpful. And really it will ultimately undermine the things that you believe are important and you give fodder for those whose views you oppose."

The Fraternal Order of Police escalated calls for President Donald Trump to send in agents who would help combat crime and handle protesters, a move that drew concerns around the city. From the first days of his presidency in 2017, Trump had threatened to "send in the feds!" to address Chicago violence. My colleague Jeremy Gorner and I reported in July 2020 that the Department of Homeland Security was planning to send 150 federal agents to the city, sparking widespread concern and national attention. Lightfoot was angry at us for our reporting, which she felt was "alarmist."

After news broke, Trump called Lightfoot and tried to defuse the situation by saying Ivanka speaks highly of her. Lightfoot's office released a statement saying Trump confirmed "that he plans to send federal resources to Chicago to supplement ongoing federal investigations pertaining to violent crime. The conversation was brief and straightforward. Mayor Lightfoot maintains that all resources will be investigatory in nature and be coordinated through the US Attorney's office. The Mayor has made clear that if there is any deviation from what has been announced, we will pursue all available legal options to protect Chicagoans." The feds did bring extra resources, but nothing meaningful came of the hullabaloo. Lightfoot canceled a roundtable appearance with *Crain's Chicago Business* and David Axelrod because she didn't want to share the stage with Minneapolis mayor Jacob Frey, whom she viewed as weak.

Early in the day on August 10, 2020, a rumor spread that Chicago Police had killed a fifteen-year-old boy. In truth, officers chased a twenty-year-old man after a report that he had a gun, leading to an exchange of gunfire. The suspect was hospitalized, but the incident didn't set off major alarms within City Hall or CPD because it wasn't a particularly provocative incident. But police believe that the criminal element in Chicago and Northwest Indiana took the opportunity to plan a wave of looting, which started that night.

Chief of Staff Maurice Classen was staying downtown in a hotel for the weekend because his wife and daughter were quarantining ahead of a trip to see their in-laws. He smoked a cigar on the roof and enjoyed a drink before turning in for the night. He woke up to a call telling him downtown was being looted. It started with a caravan at 87th Street and the Dan Ryan Expressway looting a shopping center there, but masses soon descended downtown and started ransacking the suddenly not-so-Magnificent Mile. Classen ran out of his hotel and across the Loop district to reach his car near City Hall, dodging looters along the way. Classen tried to call Lightfoot but couldn't reach her, so he worked with top police leadership to address the crisis, shut down expressway and CTA access to downtown, and raise the bridges once again. The ensuing damage that most residents woke up to the next morning was a big blow to the city's psyche.

Alderperson Brian Hopkins started getting phone calls from friends who live in high-rises downtown telling him that groups of looters were playing cat and mouse with overwhelmed police. The cops were constantly outnumbered. Hopkins felt it was important to bear witness and traveled around, watching the chaos. At one point, a man pointed a gun at him while he was in front of Water Tower Place. The next morning, Hopkins looked at his phone and saw it was Lightfoot. "I thought she was calling to check on me and see if I was OK, and instead she engaged in a very angry profane tirade and just screamed at me and dropped f-bombs," Hopkins recalled. "I hung up." Word went around City Hall that she asked, "Are you trying to fuck me?"

Later that day, Lightfoot and Brown held a news conference during which they blamed State's Attorney Kim Foxx, claiming that looters knew there would be no consequences due to her office's lack of action in June. "Put your best people on this," Lightfoot said. "We have made the case, we have the video, we have the officer testimony. These people need to be held accountable and not cycled through the system."

Foxx, who lives in the south suburbs, was heart-attack mad. She called a news conference of her own. On the way downtown, Foxx called Joanna Klonsky and pollster Jason McGrath, close Lightfoot advisors who had also worked with her, and cussed them out from 147th Street to 35th, angry over the mayor's attempt to use Foxx as a political scapegoat. "It does not serve us to have dishonest blame games when all of our hearts are breaking," she said at the news conference. Foxx's office noted they had been brought 325 felony arrests after the June unrest—90 percent of cases were approved, while another 6 percent were still pending investigation.

The ugly back and forth signaled a new break between Chicago institutions at a critical time. One aide later reflected on the mayor's early bluster with sad hyperbole. "They did burn the city down."

16 | BIGGER THAN THE ITALIANS

AS A BIG-CITY MAYOR, Lori Lightfoot faced a tough balancing act on a number of issues: policing, schools, finance. Public monuments weren't a big priority for her, and top advisors shrugged them off as "culture wars bullshit." But ongoing social shifts and a national debate over public figures and history put them right on her plate. Few things were as convoluted as her handling of Chicago's Christopher Columbus statues, particularly a massive monument at Grant Park downtown. Early on, Lightfoot made clear she wouldn't support efforts to remove public tributes to Columbus when she opposed renaming the holiday to Indigenous Peoples' Day. Her handpicked school board bucked her, however, and renamed the district's holiday.

"I absolutely have no plans to support any elimination of Columbus Day at the city level," Lightfoot said. "For a number of years, CPS essentially celebrated both Columbus Day and Indigenous People's Day. I thought that that made sense." The issue continued percolating. Columbus statues were vandalized with the words *killer*, *BLM*, and *genocide*. Lightfoot came out against taking down statues, citing ongoing tributes to Civil War confederates.

"I have been watching with great interest on the debate that's been going on around Confederate monuments, and there was a Black historian—and I don't remember his name—but he said, and I think he's right, that we can use this moment as an opportunity to not try to erase history, but embrace it full on," Lightfoot said, according to CBS News. "There was a lot of harm that happened over the arc of the history of this country, beginning with the original sin of slavery, and it's way past time that we have a reckoning on that.

But I think we also have to recognize that our history, both in this country and our city, is rich and diverse and the thing that we need to do is do what I think the organizers of the Columbus Day Parade have done, which is invite many people of different backgrounds, different perspectives, to participate in what is really a people's celebration."

The comments reflected Lightfoot's desire to avoid alienating Italian Chicago political leaders but also a misunderstanding of monuments. Statues are not history. They're tributes. And people were becoming tired of seeing monuments to white men who had engaged in various acts of barbarism. The social tide had shifted against Columbus.

On July 18, 2020, the conflict came to a head as more than one thousand people "swarmed the Christopher Columbus statue in Grant Park on Friday evening in a failed attempt to topple it after a march turned tense and chaotic when some people began throwing fireworks and cans at the police, who in turn struck members of the crowd with batons," as my colleague Alice Yin reported. It was a wild scene. Teenage Miracle Boyd had her teeth knocked out by a cop. One man scaled the top of the statue to try to tie a rope around it so people could pull it down, a dangerous stunt.

In the immediate aftermath, Lightfoot was furious. She called alderpersons, including Matt O'Shea, in a conversation he remembered as "shot out of a cannon." "These fucking animals attacked our police," Lightfoot said. Her staff immediately started to compile video of protesters using umbrellas to shield themselves as they prepared to attack officers, footage she wanted released as soon as possible. Soon, Lightfoot released a Twitter thread condemning the activists but also adding, "If you believe you have been mistreated by the police, then I urge you to file a complaint through COPA or by dialing 311." O'Shea was livid over what he considered double talk.

While Lightfoot's first priority was proving that the protesters started the violence, others expressed concerns about the provocation Columbus's statue would continue to pose. The next morning, Rogers Park alderperson Maria Hadden texted Lightfoot: "The Columbus statue needs to come down. Can we talk about making that happen?"

Lightfoot said she'd be happy to talk, "but I don't take kindly to demands."

Less than a week later, I got a phone call from a source: Lightfoot was going to remove the Columbus statue late at night without public notice. I called a few trusted Chicagoans and was able to determine it was true. I called it in to my editors, who felt good enough about the information to break the news. Soon, a crowd of people, including Alderperson Rossana Rodriguez Sanchez had assembled at Grant Park to watch. Fraternal Order of Police president John Catanzara arrived and debated Columbus critics, including a man wearing a vulva costume. Around 1:00 AM, workers arrived to gently take it down and move it into storage.

That morning, I got a phone call from Lightfoot chief of staff Maurice Classen, who joked that I had ruined his Meigs Field moment. (Richard M. Daley had ordered workers to destroy the runway at Meigs Field in the dead of night, leaving the city shocked the next morning.) For her part, Lightfoot insisted the statue's removal would be "temporary," a promise that stunned even close allies. Even if some believe Columbus was a hero worthy of such a statue, there's no realistic scenario where that monument could go back up in Grant Park.

Former Chicago Park District general counsel Timothy King and his deputy, George Smyrniotis, entered into negotiations with the Joint Civic Committee of Italian Americans over a Columbus statue in Little Italy's Arrigo Park that Lightfoot had taken down. The committee sued the Park District in July 2021, alleging it had violated a 1973 contract to display the Columbus statue in Little Italy. King and Smyrniotis tried to make a deal allowing the committee to display a Columbus statue in a parade, according to the lawsuit. But Lightfoot learned of the plan, called the lawyers into a Zoom meeting, and berated them. The filing made Lightfoot sound like Joe Pesci in *Casino*: "You dicks, what the fuck were you thinking? You make some kind of secret agreement with Italians, what you are doing, you are out there measuring your dicks with the Italians seeing [who's] got the biggest dick. You are out there stroking your dicks over the Columbus statue. I am trying to keep Chicago Police officers from being shot, and you are trying to get them shot. My dick is bigger than yours and the Italians; I have the biggest dick in Chicago. Where did you go to law school? Did you even go to law school? Do you even have a law license? You have to submit any pleadings to John Hendricks for approval before filing. John told you not to do a fucking thing with that statute without my approval. Get that fucking statue back before noon tomorrow or I am going to have you fired." After I reported this story, a Chicago Public Schools official let me know Lightfoot had made similar comments to CPS lawyers belittling their legal credentials.

Lightfoot released a lawyerly comment that mostly denied making the dick comments, but it was a big black eye. As her staff oddly denied she talks that way, I obtained a text message she sent Alderperson Gilbert Villegas accusing another lawyer of "stroking himself in public and claiming he is ready to file suit." The phallic comments, which we broke in the *Tribune*, followed her. When she later went to the Wieners Circle, a North Side hot dog temple, she was roasted. "She got a big dick, all right," the cashier said, as another employee added, "biggest dick in the city."

★ ★ ★ ★

That July, O'Shea received an email about Cork and Kerry, a popular bar in his ward, alleging its management didn't take COVID seriously and that workers were being exposed to dangerous conditions. "They have been shamed/ questioned by co-workers when they wear their masks (Western location)," the email said. "'Why are you wearing your mask? You don't need it.'" He forwarded the email to city business and health officials on July 22 with a note: "Please see the below urgent message from a resident of my community who is COVID positive, please let me know if there is a time today that we can discuss next steps."

The next morning, O'Shea looked down at his phone and saw a text message from Bill Guide, the bar's owner, that sent him into a rage: "Good afternoon. The word is we will be getting a visit from the COVID City Hall task force. Have you heard anything?" O'Shea immediately suspected that the tip-off had come from Lightfoot security chief Jim Smith, a friend of Guide's, and called City Hall to express his concern and anger.

As the days went on and Smith remained Lightfoot's chief of security, O'Shea felt that the mayor's office was trying to sweep it under the rug. I got wind of the incident and called over to the mayor's office to talk it through. Aides wouldn't substantively address the matter or answer questions. Their statement wouldn't address the accusation, and they tried to sidestep the issue by noting that City Hall shut down Cork and Kerry days after O'Shea forwarded the constituent complaint. That was true, but it didn't negate whether someone had tipped off the bar.

I thought the whole situation was outrageous, particularly the effort by Lightfoot officials to stonewall my attempt to get more information, and I told them so. The public had a right to know if someone in the mayor's office was tipping off businesses to safety visits. For his part, Smith denied leaking anything to the bar, and the bar owner denied receiving any heads up from Smith. "I talk to Jim all the time but he did not tip me off of anything," Guide said.

As I was getting ready to report about the behind-the-scenes brouhaha, Lightfoot's office announced Smith would be resigning, allegedly to spend more time with his family. But Lightfoot was furious with me over the episode. She sent a mocking email to her staff that led off, "I read the 'blockbuster' Pratt story." Days later, a still-angry Lightfoot emailed her team on the same thread: "I am just reminding this group—for the foreseeable future, there will be nothing given as placed stories or friendly background to Greg Pratt. If he makes an inquiry, answer it as briefly as possible, but under no circumstances is anyone to give him anything proactively. Are we clear?" When I obtained that email, I tweeted it and pinned it to my profile, where it's gotten 2 million impressions. If you've ever wondered what I did to really piss her off, now you know. Other stories made her angry, but this one was the breaking point.

Lightfoot's 2020 budget included a $94 million property tax hike, a relative drop in the bucket. It also included a measure to raise property taxes annually by an amount tied to the consumer price index. It was a reasonable, responsible measure. At the same time, Lightfoot asked for City Council approval to lower the threshold on the city's speed cameras so that they could ticket motorists going 6 mph over the limit—a significant reduction that seemed to many like an obvious cash grab.

As she negotiated her budget deal, Lightfoot also struggled with her mother's health in Ohio. Her nerves were shot, and she complained to alderpersons that she was losing hair. During a meeting with the Black Caucus, Lightfoot warned that people wouldn't get support from her administration if they didn't vote for her spending plan. "Don't come to me for shit for the next three years" if you don't support the budget, she said, a comment we scooped.

I think the meeting was still going on when alderpersons started reaching out to me, astonished by the remark.

Similarly, Lightfoot ended up in a nasty fight with City Clerk Anna Valencia after the mayor hired away Valencia's chief communications officer, Kate LeFurgy, for her own press team. Valencia, who had recently given birth to her first child, emailed Lightfoot to complain about a lack of heads up. "I shared my fines and fees platform with you, that my team built and had been working on since November of 2018, which handed you your first win with community groups," Valencia complained. "I've kept community group relationships healthy for you in the Fines and Fees Collaborative, smoothed over ruffled feathers when they felt as if your office was stonewalling them or ignoring them."

Lightfoot responded with a screed about LeFurgy's "decision to leave your employ." "Anna," Lightfoot wrote, "don't send me again an unhinged screed, dredging up every petty grievance, real or imagined. If you have an issue, pick up the phone and call me, instead of writing a bunch of accusatory nonsense where you got everything wrong except she accepted a job. Be a professional." The exchange quickly spread among women in government, who were simply astonished.

Weeks later, she kicked off comments during a meeting to the Latino Caucus by declaring, "I don't consent to being recorded." It gave off the impression of a mayor skidding out of control. In the end, she was able to narrowly get her budget approved. But the worst was on its way.

17 | "MY NAME IS ANJANETTE YOUNG"

CAROLYN GRISKO COULDN'T BELIEVE what she was watching. She had helped Lori Lightfoot with the Police Accountability Task Force. Its first major policy enacted was the timely release of police video evidence, a critical measure that Lightfoot had touted. But here was her Law Department, fighting to suppress video of a Black woman abused by the Chicago Police Department. A former journalist and longtime public affairs professional, Grisko didn't understand how her friend "fell into the same trap that tripped up Rahm."

In truth, the Anjanette Young scandal that played out in December 2020 was years in the making. It reflected a system aimed at protecting police, even when they're wrong, that existed before Lightfoot took over as Chicago's head of police oversight, while she led the troubled Office of Professional Standards, and when she was tasked with scrutinizing the system for reform. The same governing structure that turned a blind eye for decades to police torture, false confessions, and a code of silence continued in full force while she was in charge.

Anjanette Young wanted the world to know what happened to her on February 21, 2019. The Black social worker had been home, enjoying her Thursday night self-care routine, and had just gotten undressed to change into something more comfortable. Suddenly, Chicago Police burst through the door looking for a suspect, guns drawn.

"What is going on?!" Young yelled. "There's nobody else here, I live alone. I mean, what is going on here? You've got the wrong house. I live alone." They bound her hands behind her back. A cop wrapped a coat around her bare shoulders, but it left her front completely exposed. At least a dozen cops milled around as she begged for information. "You've got the wrong house, you've got the wrong house, you've got the wrong house," Young shouted. CBS Chicago, which broke the story and covered it in depth, noted Young told police at least forty-three times they were in the wrong home. Yet the police continued their search undeterred, while Young stood there in agony.

The cops did, in fact, have the wrong home. A cop had shown a photo of a man with a felon to a confidential informant, who showed the officer where the man allegedly lived. But they got the wrong unit—he was actually next door. The cops apparently hadn't done their due diligence to collect more information and get the right address before seeking a warrant.

One of the remarkable things about the Anjanette Young case is that she shared her story with the public. In November 2019 CBS Chicago ran a report headlined INNOCENT WOMAN: CHICAGO POLICE HANDCUFFED ME WHILE I WAS NAKED DURING WRONG RAID. She told Dave Savini, Samah Assad, and Michele Youngerman everything: the feeling of humiliation, officers milling around, her crying and yelling, "You have the wrong place." A pastor at her church talked about visiting with her shortly after the incident and being struck by "the total dehumanization of a person."

Before the report aired, CBS contacted Lightfoot's office, and Deputy Mayor for Public Safety Susan Lee forwarded a summary of the case to the mayor. "Please see below for a pretty bad wrongful raid coming out tomorrow," Lee wrote in the November 11, 2019, note. Lightfoot wrote back shortly after. "I have a lot of questions about this one," Lightfoot said. "Can we do a quick call about it?" Later, she emailed her team, "We need to escalate the training for the 2+ search warrant affiants. We cannot afford any additional hits." But when the story aired, nobody in the administration really seemed to care. The Civilian Office of Police Accountability contacted Young to open an investigation, and then nothing happened. Without video, it was just a story.

That wasn't an accident. The Lightfoot administration did not want the world to see what happened to Young. It didn't even want her to see the footage. Young's lawyer, Keenan Saulter, filed a federal lawsuit. In court, he complained that they were entitled to see it. "A particular concern for me is getting access to the body cam footage of the officers who entered my client's home," Saulter said in Judge John Tharp's courtroom. "My client's naked body was depicted on these body-worn cameras. Their office, police officers have seen this. My client has been denied access to it. She's filed several FOIA requests and appealed those. That's one. Two, there is no circumstance that I can imagine that the plaintiff in a case of this nature would not be entitled to body-worn camera footage of her own home and her own body that was filmed by these officers. I can't fathom a valid argument as to why she shouldn't be entitled to her own images. It seems as if they're trying to hide something. And obviously they say, well, we're concerned about snippets being played in the media."

City lawyer Marques Berrington argued that it was premature to disclose the footage now, as the case faced potential dismissal. "Our understanding of why counsel wants this video now as opposed to down the road is because there's already been a lot of plays in the media and, you know, things of that nature," Berrington said. "It's gotten a lot of media attention. And we would think it would be unfair at this point to present snippets of videos that present things in an unfavorable fashion when, you know, editing in a certain way just so, you know, the case would then be presented in a mischaracterized light." Later, the city acknowledged, it opposed release of the videos to Young because they believed it was "an attempt to provide the media with the body worn camera to paint an inaccurate picture of what happened during the subject search warrant."

Another city attorney, Elizabeth Kathryn Hanford, requested a confidentiality order "because of the sensitive nature of the videos." Tharp granted the request. It was a wild illustration of the city's ongoing culture of covering up misconduct and minimizing problems, an ethos that exists as a malignant animating force in the bureaucracy. Over the next few months, the case fizzled. Saulter motioned to dismiss the federal case so he could pursue it in state court and it remained under the radar.

On Saturday, December 12, city lawyers saw a promo for a story about Young's case by CBS. They started calling all the officers and emailing one another on a thread that dripped with contempt under the subject line: "Anjanette Young – 'Naked' Raid." City lawyer Marques Berrington wrote to colleagues: "I probably should have mentioned that the 'full story' is set to air on Monday at 10 PM. As far as we can tell from Keenan Saulter and CBS's pages, there's only a promo out there right now with the BWC [body-worn camera], and it looks like it's coming from the footage we gave to Keenan Saulter pursuant to the CO [court order]."

On Monday, Berrington emailed Saulter and CBS: "Please contact me immediately. It has come to my attention that Mr. Saulter has potentially provided CBS with body worn camera video in violation of Judge Tharp's confidentiality order. See Young, 19 CV 5312, ECF Nos. 35, 34. I understand this footage is to be aired tonight. We have conferred with our clients and have no reason to believe that either Ms. Young or CBS obtained this video through FOIA or any other appropriate legal process. Please contact me immediately regarding this. We intend to seek emergency relief as soon as possible if the above is correct."

It was a remarkable escalation, and the city prepared an emergency request for an injunction to prevent CBS from airing the video and sanction the plaintiff. At 3:37 PM, city attorney Caroline Fronczak emailed Caryn Jacobs, a top aide to corporation counsel Mark Flessner, asking for permission to file an emergency motion to stop publication. At 5:11 PM, Fronczak emailed the Law Department's spokeswoman, "Just a 'heads up' FYI that we filed this motion. CBS is airing a story after Plaintiff's counsel improperly gave it to CBS in violation of our confidentiality order." Flessner later recalled being in his office that evening when Jacobs entered "and told him that a lawyer had violated the judge's protective order in the case," as I reported for the *Tribune*.

The deputy said "they wanted to go in and make the judge aware that the protective order or the confidentiality order has been violated and I said yes," Flessner said at the time. The story aired, this time with explosive video footage. Tharp denied the motion to prevent CBS from airing it—after the story had already been broadcast.

That night, I tweeted a link to the report, which took my breath away: "Wow: Mayor Lori Lightfoot's law department went to court to try and stop @cbschicago from airing video of Chicago police raiding a social worker's home. She was changing and naked; police refused to give her the video until a judge ordered them to."

The next morning, as Lightfoot's daily 8:00 AM phone call was wrapping up, Joanna Klonsky asked about the CBS video. "What video?" Lightfoot responded.

Mark Flessner, the city's top lawyer, downplayed it and said, "What's the big deal?" and suggested she was naked only for a moment, which I previously reported in the *Tribune*. Very quickly, the meeting shut down as the administration struggled to answer incoming media queries, including from me.

As the morning unfolded, City Hall staff began frantically emailing one another, including Chief of Staff Maurice Classen and Communications Deputy Director Kate LeFurgy. Soon, LeFurgy forwarded the thread to Celia Meza, who eventually sent out an email: "Please no one else comment on this thread. I am shutting it down. I will reach out to the people I need to touch base with on this matter."

The city's lawyers didn't think they'd done anything wrong. That morning, Fronczak emailed colleagues: "We'll never get CBS to stop airing this garbage . . . but maybe this will send a message to Plaintiff's attorneys to stop giving them videos." The goal was to prevent lawyers from sharing unflattering footage with the media, a measure aimed at minimizing litigation risk and hiding misconduct.

Lightfoot's first comments on the scandal downplayed the significance of what was happening and the role her administration played in pushing for sanctions against Young. Asked about the attempt to sanction Young, Lightfoot responded, "I can't comment on that. A federal judge put rules in place. It's for that judge to determine whether or not that was appropriate." It was a disingenuous dodge since her lawyers were the ones seeking the sanctions.

Lightfoot also noted the raid happened in the waning days of Emanuel's administration, though it was her Law Department that fought Young in her subsequent lawsuit. To Lightfoot, that was key. "The important point is the raid happened while Rahm was mayor," Lightfoot texted former Cook County circuit court clerk Dorothy Brown. "3 months before I took office. Rahm Raid."

As the day dragged on, Lightfoot released a statement saying she "had no knowledge" of the matter before Tuesday. "I had a very emotional reaction to what was depicted on the video as I imagine that many people did," Lightfoot said. I felt it was important to push her and sharpened the edges when I reported her quote for the *Tribune*, writing that the statement "did not address why her administration was trying to punish the woman for allegedly sharing the video." After I'd reported on the case, Berrington celebrated. "I made it to the *Tribune*!" he wrote in an email. "That's gotta get me in the [Federal Civil Rights Litigation] hall of fame, right?"

The next day there was a previously scheduled City Council meeting. Alderperson Byron Sigcho-Lopez repeatedly pressured Lightfoot over the incident, and she shouted at him to "get the facts." Her team still wasn't allowing the broader press corps to cover news conferences because of pandemic protocols. Instead, Lightfoot would take questions from a rotating pool reporter. Through that reporter, I asked Lightfoot why her administration had refused to give Young the video from her own incident. She angrily lashed back: "Mr. Pratt's reporting has been reckless and irresponsible—unfortunately, now, a pattern of his stretching back many months." She insisted she had learned about the incident "yesterday morning."

Almost immediately, CBS backed up the accuracy of my premise: Lightfoot's administration had refused to give Young the videos in response to FOIA. Amid the controversy over the case, Cook County State's Attorney Kim Foxx released a statement: "The audacity that the city calculated its embarrassment over the release of the video is a clear violation of Ms. Young's body and autonomy. This was a complete and utter dismissal of her humanity. Her humanity was, literally, stripped from her. This disturbing video explicitly illustrates who the victim is, who deserves justice, and who holds the power."

By the next day, Lightfoot totally changed her tack. She apologized to me, publicly, after privately acknowledging that she had been wrong about the FOIA request. She also apologized to Young. She acknowledged that she had, in fact, been told in 2019 about the email, which she later said she'd simply forgotten about. It was time for full-on damage control. She also sent a letter to the Law Department: "Damage has been done, confidence shattered and the disclosures over the week have caused anger, confusion, and hurt. This goes way beyond any single case because important trust has been lost. People are hurting."

Even as the administration shifted into damage control, the city realized it hadn't released all the videos. Lightfoot privately exhorted the Law Department to turn them over, shouting, "I am fighting for my political life!" as one aide recalled. Earlier in the week, Lightfoot was asked about potential firings in the Law Department and gave a noncommittal answer. A *Sun-Times* reporter tweeted her comments, and Flessner sent them to Lightfoot in an email with a question mark in the subject line. Not long after, she personally asked Flessner to resign, a move she made with much regret. He signed his resignation letter "Your friend."

★ ★ ★ ★

Young was prepared for the video's release. She had worked closely with the CBS reporters, who aired a special on her story: "My Name Is Anjanette Young." And she was disappointed with Lightfoot's reaction. "How dare you take my story and say that you and your Black friends are now angry?" Young wondered. "You knew about this way before it hit the news." Young had seen Lightfoot at Progressive Baptist Church, Anjanette's home parish, during the campaign, when the candidate came to seek church members' support. She had given Lightfoot her vote and felt betrayed.

Now with the scandal unfolding, Young invited Lightfoot to talk with her directly about the incident. There was some public back-and-forth over whether the meeting would be private or alderpersons could attend, and for a moment it seemed to have been called off. But ultimately, the two sides agreed to meet on New Year's Eve—a day before the Lightfoot administration released the emails showing that she had known about these events in 2019.

Young and Saulter were angry before Lightfoot walked into the room. Saulter said he wouldn't have agreed to the meeting had they been aware of the additional videos and the mayor's prior knowledge. At one point, Lightfoot shut her notebook, wordlessly got up from the table, and walked out. Eventually, she returned to continue the conversation. Saulter credited her for firing Flessner, and she responded, "It was the right thing to do." But what was clear to Saulter in the meeting was that Lightfoot can't acknowledge fault.

Young, meanwhile, had written out a statement about what she felt and experienced. Young read the statement to Lightfoot. She remembers Lightfoot crying. They left on good enough terms that they exchanged a friendly farewell. Due to COVID, they didn't hug, but they leaned back-to-back and rubbed their shoulders together as a way of embracing one another, an affectionate gesture Young used with friends during the pandemic.

But in the coming weeks, the city nevertheless kept downplaying Young's suffering in legal filings. It also fought an ordinance Young wanted to place restrictions on raids. She was disappointed in Lightfoot. "It is part of a pattern of them sweeping things under the rug and hoping enough time will pass that people will forget about it," she told me.

★ ★ ★ ★

The Anjanette Young saga had three postscripts. In December 2021 the city settled with Young for $2.9 million. But it didn't give Young what she wanted: the officers fired and broader policy changes.

That January, after forcing Flessner to resign, Lightfoot met with him near his South Loop home, where they sat in his car and spoke. He later claimed that she said he could do city work as retained outside counsel, if the Board of Ethics gave its OK. Flessner then went to the Board of Ethics with the question and received an opinion that it would be OK, which he emailed to her that April. The opinion, which Lightfoot received, noted Flessner's recollection that the mayor didn't object to him getting city work. After receiving Flessner's email with the opinion attached, Lightfoot didn't dispute his version of events—she just forwarded it to his replacement as corporation counsel, Celia Meza, and the chief of staff, Maurice Classen, with an "FYI."

When I received the email exchange via Freedom of Information Act request that September, however, Lightfoot wrote to the Board of Ethics that she was "recently made aware" of his statements that she had no objections to him receiving city work and said, "Please be advised that I made no such comment to Mr. Flessner. I have never indicated to him that I would approve of his engagement as outside counsel to the city on any matter."

Flessner was astonished by her denial, as he told me for a *Tribune* report: "Why would I have sought the ethics opinion, if the Mayor had said that I would not be hired? She is not being truthful." I wasn't in the car with Flessner and Lightfoot, but Lightfoot's denial didn't make sense and highlighted my ongoing concerns about her candor.

Several months after the Young scandal died down, Lightfoot engaged in a feud with Foxx over a shooting on the West Side after which prosecutors declined to bring charges and the mayor criticized the state's attorney. After a public exchange of criticism, Foxx and Lightfoot met to discuss the matter. Near the end of the meeting, Foxx asked for the room so they could talk one-on-one; then, Lightfoot, unprompted, brought up her critical statement. "I don't like that you came after me on Anjanette Young," Lightfoot said, accusing Foxx of "piling on."

"What are you talking about?" Foxx asked.

Lightfoot responded, "You didn't have to say anything, and you said the city should've released the records, but you shouldn't have said anything."

Foxx said, "That wasn't about you. I said, 'The city.'"

Lightfoot responded, "I am the city."

Foxx said no, "This happened before you came in. You had an opportunity to do something about it." She added, "It was never about you. It was about Anjanette Young."

Lightfoot didn't understand.

18 | A CITY IN CRISIS

DESPITE THE CHALLENGES OF 2020, the Anjanette Young scandal presented an opportunity for Mayor Lightfoot to reset. Successful politicians rocked by crisis use it to chart a new path forward and rebuild relationships. For Lightfoot, though, the problems started to come in a field that was somewhat in her control but largely out of her hands: crime. The year 2020 saw a more than 50 percent increase in homicides in Chicago. The year 2019 saw 491 people slain, while 2020 recorded more than 760 homicides. Crime is a challenge for all mayors. But like US presidents and the economy, blame and credit go to the top. Lightfoot knew the city couldn't afford another year with such high violence and sent a conciliatory email to police brass on New Year's Day.

"I think we all know that we must do exponentially better in this new year, and I am confident we will. My confidence is grounded in many things, but fundamentally it is grounded in my confidence in all of you. You now have many months under your belt as a senior leadership team at CPD. And your bond will only grow," Lightfoot wrote in the email, which I reported on for the *Tribune*. The message marked an attaboy, an attempt to reset with a kinder note, as Lightfoot pointed out that "despite all the challenges of 2020, and there were many, a lot of very good work was accomplished. We and you need to build on that in 2021, every day, step by step."

But other relationships continued to spiral. In late January Lightfoot sent her scheduler Taylor Lewis an email complaining that she didn't get enough of what she called "office time." That's typically a less structured part of the day when the mayor can think, write, or just take a breather. (President Trump was often ridiculed for "executive time.") At about 1:00 PM, Lightfoot sent a note to Lewis and her chief of staff that dropped jaws:

Since my prior requests for office time are routinely ignored, I am now resorting to this:

I need office time everyday! I need office time everyday! I need office time everyday! I need office time everyday! I need office time everyday! I need office time everyday! I need office time everyday! I need office time everyday! I need office time everyday! I need office time everyday! I need office time everyday! I need office time every-day! I need office time everyday! I need office time everyday! I need office time everyday! I need office time everyday!

Not just once a week or some days, everyday! Not just once a week or some days, everyday! Not just once a week or some days, everyday! Not just once a week or some days, everyday! Not just once a week or some days, everyday! Not just once a week or some days, everyday! Not just once a week or some days, everyday! Not just once a week or some days, everyday! Not just once a week or some days, everyday! Not just once a week or some days, everyday!

Breaks or transition times between meetings are not office time. Breaks or transition times between meetings are not office time. Breaks or transition times between meetings are not office time. Breaks or transition times between meetings are not office time. Breaks or transition times between meetings are not office time. Breaks or transition times between meetings are not office time. Breaks or transition times between meetings are not office time.

If this doesn't change immediately, I will just start unilaterally cancelling things every day. If this doesn't change immediately, I will just start unilaterally cancelling things every day. If this doesn't change immediately, I will just start unilaterally cancelling things every day. If this doesn't change immediately, I will just start unilaterally cancelling things every day. If this doesn't change immediately, I will just start unilaterally cancelling things every day.

Have I made myself clear, finally?! Have I made myself clear, finally?! Have I made myself clear, finally?! Have I made myself clear, finally?! Have I made myself clear, finally?! Have I made myself clear, finally?! Have I made myself clear, finally?! Have I made myself clear, finally?! Have I made myself clear, finally?! Have I made myself clear, finally?! Have I made myself clear, finally?! Have I made myself clear, finally?! Have I made myself clear, finally?!

That same day, I got a phone call from a source who told me to file for the email she sent her scheduler today. "It's the most childish goddamn thing I've ever seen," the source said. Morale plummeted. There had been a noticeable shift in Lightfoot's outlook, one she expressed that February to Alderperson Michelle Harris, who was running for state Democratic Party chair. "Be careful out there," Lightfoot said in a morning text message. "Treachery is everywhere."

In April 2021 I covered one of the silliest "scandals" of all time. A rumor spread midweek that Lightfoot had been beaten up by her wife, who had allegedly found out that the mayor was having threesomes. It morphed into a variety of different outlandish scenarios, including one allegation that Lightfoot had trysts at a city-owned apartment in Elmhurst, Illinois.

Where it started is unclear, but it probably has some roots within the police department, as cops are some of the gnarliest gossips. (Lightfoot privately blamed it on Alderperson Edward Burke.) By Saturday night, however, the rumor began to spread like wildfire. Before you knew it, people who should know better started to float the rumors publicly. Activist Ja'Mal Green tweeted, "Lori Lightfoot is resigning tomorrow in a stunning end to her mayorship. WOW." Former US education secretary Arne Duncan posted cryptically, "Chicago, will see what tomorrow brings." Lightfoot eventually tweeted a vague denial and called the unreported rumors "homophobic."

While the nonsense was going on, another rumor spread: Alderperson Gilbert Villegas was calling around trying to generate support from his colleagues to be appointed mayor once Lightfoot resigned. The mayor got wind of the rumor and called Villegas, who had recently resigned as her floor leader. "I heard you're calling around looking to get votes because I'm going to resign and you want to be voted in as mayor," Lightfoot told Villegas. "Well, that's not going to happen. I'm not resigning."

Villegas was astounded. He had not been calling around, and he told her so. Villegas angrily demanded a meeting with the mayor and his accusers on the City Council, which Lightfoot ignored. Over the coming days, Villegas repeatedly texted Lightfoot requesting a sit-down to clear the air. "Gil, you are not the center of my universe," she texted back. "When we all have a minute from this weekend it will happen."

After a few days, Villegas was granted his meeting and walked into her office at City Hall. He looked around and said, "Where's everybody at?"

"Gil, I apologize," Lightfoot said. "I was vulnerable, and I said some things I shouldn't have said."

Villegas, who had brought a printout of his cell phone log, tossed his phone records on the desk and said he had only spoken with Alderperson Felix Cardona over the weekend—and it had been about a tax increment financing (TIF) project.

The whole episode was idiotic, but it angered her to no end with the media and expanded her growing contempt for Chicago politics. Weeks later, as Lightfoot's two-year mayoral anniversary approached, she implemented a policy saying she would only talk with reporters of color to mark the occasion. As a Latino, I qualified, but I canceled my interview because we didn't believe she gets to dictate to media outlets whom they send to cover her. It was a controversial move, largely praised by my fellow journalists, though some thought my position was wrong. I just didn't want to be a pawn in her game—I believed the move had more to do with avoiding *Crain's*, Fran Spielman, and Mary Ann Ahern than a good-faith belief in diverse media. It backfired on Lightfoot, too, when she gave an interview to The TRiiBE, a site focused on Black Chicago, but couldn't name a single Black restaurant on the West Side. For my part, I declined an invitation to discuss the situation with Tucker Carlson, who suggested Lightfoot was a Nazi. It was a real shit show.

As the year went on, crime remained high. City Hall people tried to assure the media that the numbers wouldn't be as bad as 2020, due largely to the riots, which they said had inflated 2020's totals. But the city was experiencing consistently high numbers that weren't going down, and people were becoming less enamored with police superintendent David Brown by the day.

Lightfoot's problems, meanwhile, started springing up from unpredictable locations. That spring, Alderperson David Moore teamed with Alderperson Sophia King to rename Lake Shore Drive for Jean Baptiste Point DuSable, who's generally considered the first non-Indigenous settler of Chicago. Lightfoot resisted the measure. First, she noted DuSable had a bridge, a museum, and a harbor named after him, among other honors. Behind the scenes, she stalled on calling Transportation Committee chairman Howard Brookins, which drove her staff nuts. As an alternative to renaming Lake Shore Drive, Lightfoot proposed spending a combined $40 million in public and private money "for the full development of DuSable Park, commissioning of new public art projects, and programming to create the DuSable Riverwalk, as well as the establishment of the annual 'DuSable Festival.'"

Half the City Council was bewildered that they were spending their time fighting over a street renaming. May's City Council meeting went off the rails when two alderpersons moved to delay a vote on the measure using a parliamentary maneuver called "defer and publish" that stops consideration until another meeting. Moore angrily retaliated by sending a number of proposals from his colleagues to the rules committee by using a parliamentary maneuver that allows the banishment of ordinances if they are called to conflicting committees. Moore's move was so over the top it blew people's minds. (I was cackling in the press box—the absurdity of the scene had broken even me.)

In the end, she wasn't able to stop a motley crew of alderpersons from renaming the city's most iconic street, so she dropped her opposition to the measure and adopted the plan. The failure was nearly unfathomable for previous mayors and reflected her inability to make allies. (Moore started a trend by sending items to Committee on Committees and Rules: later in the year, Alderperson Anthony Beale "pulled a Moore" by sending a bunch of new legislation to Rules because he was upset about Alderperson Brendan Reilly deferring a vote on his speed-camera ordinance.)

In June Lightfoot truly lost control at City Council. Her appointment of Meza as the city's top lawyer was scheduled for a vote. But Alderperson Raymond Lopez teamed up with Alderperson Jeanette Taylor to defer and publish the motion "in light of everything going on with Ms. Anjanette Young."

Lightfoot was furious and walked off the dais in hopes of persuading Taylor to drop the hold. It did not go well. The encounter started badly, with Lightfoot telling Taylor she was "cutting out a woman of color" and putting her hands up near Taylor's face. One alderperson who was present recalled Lightfoot shouting, "What the fuck are you doing?" as she gestured.

Taylor responded, "Get your damn hand up out my face, and stop screaming at me. I'm not your child." Later, Taylor said she thought Lightfoot "had lost her fucking mind."

"This was not about this appointment. This was about their mistreatment of Ms. Young. I've said to her, and I'll say to you all, ever since we've been in a global pandemic and she got this ultimate power, she doesn't feel like she has to work with us, and that is not how this is going to work," Taylor told the media afterward. "I'm not for it. I'm going to stand up for Ms. Young."

"You saw me telling her to put her hands down. I'm a grown woman like she is," she later told the press. "We are coworkers, and clearly she doesn't understand that, and I'll make her understand that."

Later, Taylor half-joked that the scene could've gotten violent. "I could hear my mother saying, 'I ain't gonna get you out of jail; don't hit her,'" she said.

The next time they saw each other, Lightfoot walked up to Taylor and gave her a hug. Taylor didn't hold a grudge. But the scene highlighted a growing sense of chaos. It was quite an unhinged moment. To me, the scene highlighted how Lightfoot didn't fully understand her power. The mayor presides over City Council from an elevated dais. To speak with her, alderpersons must get her permission to walk past security. It is, simply, a throne. And the king or queen never vacates the throne for a fight, particularly not one they then lose.

★ ★ ★ ★

While Lightfoot continued to struggle with rising crime, an unexpected controversy emerged that summer when the Chicago Bears announced their interest in possibly moving to the northwesten suburb of Arlington Heights and out of government-owned Soldier Field.

Lightfoot's first response was to ridicule the team, tweeting, "Like most Bears fans, we want the organization to focus on putting a winning team on the field, beating the Packers finally and being relevant past October. Everything else is just noise."

Behind the scenes, Lightfoot had a somewhat contentious relationship with the team. Early in her tenure, Lightfoot's staff negotiated unsuccessfully on her behalf to move her season ticket location, citing security concerns. The mayor at one point bristled over the negotiations, telling an associate, "They'd better remember who holds their lease." She followed her tough words about the Bears' on-field failures with a series of announcements aimed at deflecting blame if the team moved by offering to build a $1 billion dome over Soldier Field. In truth, there was little she could do to stop the Bears from leaving—the issue was whether they could finance a deal for a modern stadium, not anything Lightfoot and her team did or didn't do. But the tweet came to be seen as another clear example of Lightfoot blustering her way into unnecessary conflict.

Also that summer, Joe Ferguson announced he would be stepping down as inspector general when his term ended. Citing statutory search requirements, he called on Lightfoot to make sure City Hall completed the hiring process before his term ended, to ensure continuity. For her part, Lightfoot didn't want Ferguson and wouldn't have reappointed him had he stayed. She was angry with him for launching several probes into her administration and privately alleged that he leaked to the media, which she thought was evidenced by a large number of reporters who attended his wife's funeral.

Ferguson's departure left Lightfoot with a problem: deputy inspector general for public safety Deborah Witzburg, a gutsy former county prosecutor, wanted the job. But Lightfoot didn't want Witzburg either, whom she had criticized as unqualified to discuss public safety issues. Despite receiving ample time to run the search, Lightfoot started late. Her process failed to produce strong alternatives to Witzburg, so Lightfoot dragged her feet on making a final decision until it was no longer feasible to stall. But, she said, the new inspector general should "stay in their lane." The episode highlighted Lightfoot's ongoing inability to organize her efforts strategically. How was it that, in all her years as a federal prosecutor and big-law attorney, she couldn't signal to one qualified person that they should apply so she didn't have to appoint someone she didn't like? Witzburg, meanwhile, took the last word in a *Sun-Times* interview: "I learned to drive in Boston, and I have always understood lane markers to just be suggestions."

Lightfoot replaced Susan Lee as deputy mayor for public safety with John O'Malley, a personal friend of Lightfoot's who had been a deputy US marshal and served on the Police Board with her. Lee remained an advisor on a contract that stipulated that she'd keep working on consent-decree issues. That summer, Maurice Classen left the administration and was replaced by Sybil Madison, a bookish friend of Lightfoot. A few months before Classen left City Hall, Brown proposed a series of promotions and a new organizational chart. The promotions included first superintendent Eric Carter's wife, and the new chart would've placed Bob Boik as head of reform under Carter, when a previous plan by Charlie Beck had put the head of reform on the same level as the first deputy, which he thought was best practices from his time leading Los

Angeles. Classen objected to the organizational chart and said he wanted the title of "deputy superintendent" for Boik, a measure he thought was important to instill a culture of reform within the department.

Brown pushed back. "Reform isn't titles. It's not org charts," he said. "It's me and the first deputy living it."

An incredulous Classen mocked the line for months after. In the end, Lightfoot sided with Classen on the org chart but allowed Carter's wife to be promoted, which disgusted Classen, who had become increasingly disillusioned with Brown's leadership. By this point, crime had continued spiking to levels not seen since the 1990s, and concerns were growing around Brown's leadership, but the mayor dismissed them, alienating key supporters, like Classen. In Brown's defense, Lightfoot argued that there were only a small handful of people capable of being the city's police superintendent, and they might not be available. To others, that seemed like a dodge from a person who couldn't admit mistakes.

Through it all, the city was struggling to implement the consent decree. A civilian staffer at the Police Department, Chad Williams, quit his job and sent out an email that made front-page news when I obtained it for the problems it exposed with the city's consent-decree implementation. Williams wrote:

> Unfortunately, my disappointment with the inability of this Department's top leadership to even feign interest in pursuing reform in a meaningful manner has made it impossible for me to remain involved. Even more unfortunate is that my experience is far from unique. Many well-meaning and talented civilians have signed up to help improve the nation's second largest police department, only to find themselves steadily thwarted by its perverse incentive structures until they inevitably depart due to demoralization. I spent much of the past three years attempting to convince senior leadership that it is critical to (1) understand the impact of each policy change on the Department's training portfolio, and (2) plan for data collection to allow for reliable assessments of compliance. Despite my efforts, both the Office of the Superintendent and the Office of Constitutional Policing & Reform continue to insist upon employing a "check the boxes" strategy that focuses on getting credit for "preliminary compliance" based primarily on policy edits that lack operational considerations. Over time,

the optimism I brought to this role withered in an incessant stream of discussions with the singular intent of identifying ways to "move the needle" by "getting the percentages up" to improve portrayals in local media coverage. Reality is at odds with public pronouncements that the consent decree is "a floor, not a ceiling" and the rank-and-file deserve better.

Further aggravating the situation, Lee sent Madison and O'Malley an email on August 2 seeking to "clarify" her role as senior adviser. In the email, on which she also copied Lightfoot, Lee said she'd been trying to "connect" with the mayor "for weeks" but had been unsuccessful. Lee also noted that she was being blocked from attending consent-decree meetings by O'Malley, despite it being a key item in the contract she signed after leaving the mayor's office.

"I have been told by Public Safety staff who was directed by John that I should no longer attend weekly reform meetings between mayor's office and CPD," Lee wrote.

Lightfoot replied two minutes later that she would call Lee. A day later, Lee submitted a resignation letter to corporation counsel Celia Meza in which Lee noted several initiatives she'd spent time on, including a violence-reduction program in West Garfield Park and the consent decree. Lightfoot didn't call.

"As I leave these streams of work behind, I worry that mayor's public safety team does not have enough capacity to keep moving the ball forward," Lee wrote in the email, which the *Tribune* obtained through a public-records request.

In early August twenty-nine-year-old police officer Ella French was shot and killed in West Englewood. Her partner, Officer Carlos Yanez, was hospitalized with severe injuries. He couldn't walk or talk, and there was concern he'd be paralyzed. Lightfoot arrived at the hospital, where she was scolded by Yanez's father, and a group of officers were photographed turning their backs on her. First Deputy Superintendent Eric Carter later infuriated officers by cutting short a traditional playing of bagpipes en route to the medical examiner's office. "We don't have twenty minutes for this shit," Carter shouted. Lightfoot then defended Carter, saying the critics were angry because he "wasn't part of the friends-and-family program. He did his job and came up through the ranks and worked his tail off and, now he's the first deputy."

In September, Lee and Alderperson Matt O'Shea wrote an op-ed calling Chicago "a city in crisis." The column itself was measured and suggested measures to improve public safety. But it was a brutal rebuke to Lightfoot. Days later, O'Shea sent an email to state officials about delays installing license plate readers on the expressway, which he said needed to be dealt with expeditiously due to high crime. Lightfoot responded with a message that was clearly more about the op-ed than the license plate readers.

"Dear Alderman O'Shea: I feel compelled to respond to your latest missive. In the City of Chicago, when we work with our partners in other governments like the state, we have found that the best way to move things forward is to collaborate and approach these opportunities with good faith. Sending poison pen missives, especially with an audience, which you seem to favor, is not the best way to move things forward," Lightfoot wrote. "Obviously, you have a method and history of dealing and you will carry on as you see fit, but we value our relationships with other governmental actors and nastygrams are not the best strategy. But of course carry on as you like. Happy to discuss in more detail at your Convenience."

O'Shea and Lightfoot continued clashing over public safety. He was pushing for more police helicopters to help with chases involving carjackers and fleeing suspects. But the city was stuck in bureaucratic spending limbo, and Lightfoot held out hope that a local rich man would just buy a helicopter for the department. The issue came to a head in a meeting with O'Shea where Lightfoot claimed, "We have a donor who is providing a fully funded helicopter," which O'Shea later learned was a reference to philanthropist Jim Crown. No deal materialized, and people in the department later came to believe that was a City Hall exaggeration.

O'Malley, the deputy mayor for public safety, later emailed O'Shea and claimed Lightfoot was supportive of more helicopters in addition to the one the city had and another that was "being serviced in California to the tune of 1 million dollars or something along those lines"—before listing a series of reasons why the city might not need one. "If this can somehow be worked out and we are actually in need of another helicopter and can properly staff and maintain an additional helicopter along with the ones we have, this is something that should be pursued," O'Malley wrote. "If we are going to receive a 6–7 million dollar piece of equipment that sits in storage because we can't afford to fuel it, maintain it and don't have authorized/FAA certified personnel to operate it, it makes zero sense." To O'Shea, it was classic double-talk from the administration on an issue that could address serious crime.

That September, Lightfoot fought another ally over Brown. Alderperson Brendan Reilly and Lightfoot exchanged a series of heated texts about crime after he called the superintendent a "moron" who "won't listen," reportedly in a tweet.

"Brendan, shameful and unhelpful. How about pickup the phone instead falsely creating the appearance of doing someone at everyone else's expense?" Lightfoot texted Reilly. "Really bush league."

"I used those words because I have lost confidence in the police superintendent. He's a fine cop, but I'm looking at my crime stats & can honestly say that, in my 26 years living downtown, I've never seen lawlessness to this degree. It's sickening," Reilly wrote back. "So I'll apologize for using the word 'moron.' And I am anything but 'Bush League.' I want you to be successful, Mayor & I support you. But his has to change ASAP. We are losing downtown."

"I don't disagree with the levels of concern. I share it. And the 18th district has tons of resources so there is no excuse for what is happening. I will push back and say that it was not that long ago that River North was not a nice safe neighborhood and that is recent enough that I remember it," Lightfoot texted back. "But Brendan, you know there are far more constructive ways to get stuff done. Pandering to the crowd is never the best answer, even when you are frustrated. I am committed to working with you to immediately address this issue, but public name calling makes it that much more challenging. It cannot be open season on cops."

She kept racking up embarrassing incidents. Not long before Christmas, luxury car dealer Joe Perillo experienced a smash and grab at his showroom in which robbers took $1 million in luxury watches. Perillo and Lightfoot got into a heated argument and she left, which later generated news stories first broken by the Wrigleyville crime blog *CWBChicago* about her calling him an "idiot."

Despite Lightfoot's January message, Chicago ended 2021 with its bloodiest year in a quarter century. It was much worse than 2020. As Classen watched from his perch out of government, he marveled at the irony of unfolding events. It was a fascinating turn for Lightfoot, the so-called accountability mayor who wasn't holding her police superintendent accountable.

Instead, Lightfoot started trotting out plans to fine gang members and seize their property. Civil rights lawyers came out against it, as did the Fraternal Order of Police, which considered it political spin. My colleague Rex Huppke wrote a column summarizing the issue: "Mayor Lori Lightfoot's plan to fix Chicago's violence crisis seems to involve trotting out ideas that didn't work before and won't work now."

19 | "ADULTS IN THE ROOM"

IN JULY 2020 FEDERAL prosecutors released what's known as a deferred prosecution agreement (DPA) with ComEd, the powerful electric utility. ComEd agreed to pay a $200 million fine and acknowledged engaging in a "years-long bribery scheme" for "Public Official A." That official was Illinois House Speaker Michael Madigan, the state party chairman and longest-serving Speaker in the nation's history. A disciplined old-school politician who didn't use email or cell phones and only kept notes for a short period, Madigan had ruled state politics for decades as the Democratic Party's top legislator but was known to be under federal investigation.

Lori Lightfoot punted when she was asked about the charges and Madigan. "Well, that's not really for me to say, and as mayor what I'm really focused on is the conduct of ComEd," Lightfoot said, later explaining to the *Tribune* that she bit her tongue because she lives "in a world where Springfield matters."

The DPA wasn't Madigan's first brush with trouble, but it was the biggest. Madigan had faced scrutiny for years. The *Tribune* had reported extensively on potential conflicts of interest between his private business as a tax appeal lawyer and his elected position. It also reported on hundreds of patronage jobs given to his allies. In 2018 Ray Long broke a story about campaign worker Alaina Hampton, who was sexually harassed by Kevin Quinn, a Madigan goon and brother of the Thirteenth Ward alderperson, Marty Quinn. The scandal was a huge embarrassment for Madigan, who fired Kevin Quinn, but he withstood that too, like he hoped to push past controversy of the ComEd agreement by noting he hadn't been charged with any crimes. The DPA, however, pushed

Democrats, who were already thinking about life without the Speaker, to give the possibility even more consideration.

Madigan was clearly in trouble as the legislative term ended late that year. Lightfoot went down to Springfield and ran into State Representative Emanuel "Chris" Welch, a prominent Black leader who was considered an obvious potential successor to Madigan when the next legislature was sworn in. "Madigan is done. We need to get behind Jehan," Lightfoot burst out, referring to Peoria legislator Jehan Gordon-Booth, a fellow Black lawmaker and rising star.

Welch's answer was noncommittal. But the story spread over the coming months as an example of Lightfoot's clumsiness dealing with Springfield lawmakers who had the power to help or hurt a mayor. A month after Lightfoot made the comment, Welch was voted in as Illinois House Speaker.

★ ★ ★ ★

At the start of the pandemic, Chicago Teachers Union president Jesse Sharkey thought being out of school would be temporary. Then the new reality of COVID-19 sunk in. Over the summer, as Lightfoot started pushing for the city to reopen every other facet of civil society, Sharkey was concerned about the district's processes for handling coronavirus cases within the schools. In the months that followed, as Lightfoot boasted about being the largest "open" city in America, it became clear to him that the mayor's motivations were political and economic, without enough regard for the concerns of educators and families.

Sharkey and the union clashed with Dr. Allison Arwady, the city's public health commissioner, a political mouthpiece for the mayor. Heading into fall 2020 and the start of a new school year, CTU was worried that the administration would try to force teachers back into buildings while the pandemic raged, so they scheduled a strike vote. That same day, Lightfoot's team announced that the 2020–2021 school year would start remotely. "They don't stop to listen until you threaten to strike," Sharkey said for a *Tribune* report. "This is an old story in Chicago Public Schools."

For the union, the struggle was two pronged: it carried the responsibility of bringing other people's children back to school safely and also their own members. Leading into January after the holiday break, the school district insisted that teachers and students could return safely and released a plan to bring them back in waves. Lightfoot wanted some staffers to return by January 4, others January 11, and the rest of K–8 grades on January 25. It was controversial within the union as some viewed it as an attempt to pit workers against one another. As educators started returning in early January, the Lightfoot administration started locking out employees who declined to come back from their Google Classroom and email accounts.

CPS CEO Janice Jackson couldn't hide her frustration as the conflict played out. "They took a strike for the contract that we are asking them to honor, that says they must educate our students where we ask them to do that," Jackson said. Privately, she was hopping mad with the union and wanted Lightfoot to take a harder stance. Before January 25, the union asked members to vote on a resolution to work remotely. About 71 percent of its voters said they would continue working remotely, setting up a showdown as the teachers' union went on what was practically a strike. The union noted that the overwhelming majority of parents were still keeping their kids at home, creating questions about the administration's urgency.

Lightfoot rebutted, "What do we tell those parents about the teachers who are refusing to show up to class? That's really the question."

Union vice president Stacy Davis Gates countered, "This discussion is not about if we return but how we return. And how we return is with the maximum amount of safety that we can obtain in an agreement."

As the standoff continued, Jackson and Lightfoot became increasingly frustrated. "Tomorrow will be the fourth consecutive day where teachers have been directed to remain home, and that makes 15 days in the past year and a half where CTU leadership has disrupted student learning," Jackson said, according to the *Tribune*. "No one should be OK with that."

On Sunday, January 31, Lightfoot held a news conference where she insisted, "We expect all of our teachers who have not received a specific accommodation to come to school tomorrow." Those who didn't, she suggested, would be locked out of their accounts and lose pay. It was a bright red line in the sand. And like her 2019 handling of the teachers strike, Lightfoot backed off the next day at a news conference where she called for a "cooling off period" that would lead to a final resolution. She also backed off the threat to lock them all out, "as a gesture of good faith" and to mark "good progress."

In truth, Lightfoot blinked, and it was a bad misplay. If you threaten someone with consequences, you must carry them out, or else you are known as a bluffer. And empty threats are pure death in political negotiations. As the week dragged on, Lightfoot continued to struggle to make headway. "My patience with delays from the CTU leadership is over," Lightfoot said, claiming her team made their "last, best, and final offer." That Friday, CPS said it would order teachers and students again to return over the course of several weeks but would start locking out people at the end of day Monday. Lightfoot also accused the union of wanting to take vaccine priority, a charge that incensed the union. "They want to prioritize teachers over every other resident in our city," she said.

An angry Sharkey shot back that the city was "literally trying to pit us against elderly people in the city of Chicago."

That weekend was one of the tensest I covered. Both sides held out hope early on that they would be able to make an agreement to bring students back. That Saturday morning, Lightfoot texted Chicago Federation of Labor president Bob Reiter, a friend of hers and the union's: "Hey, if we get this done today, I think it is really important that Jesse and I stand together. I know that is a tough ask for him because of the politics on his side, but this is important for the city."

Reiter said, "I'll try and ask him when the time is right. What's the current status?"

"Jesse and I agreed last night that we were all spent and could benefit from a night of rest. My team met last night and started to analyze the staffing impact of some of their proposals. We are meeting again internally shortly," Lightfoot responded. "My hope is to turn around a response as quickly as possible this morning and get a deal by mid day. The gap is very narrow at this point."

Later that afternoon, however, Lightfoot became pessimistic and texted Reiter again: "Sorry to say, I just don't think we will get there. They added new elements today and have effectively told us take it or leave it. I just don't see the path at this this point. I know you worked hard on this which I really appreciate."

"Well unfortunately I don't see it the same way," Reiter responded. "When you are working out the details, maybe it appears that some new elements are new, but that's not accurate. The flexibility is on your side. If there's a lockout and then a strike, it won't be because of the union in these final moments. You have the ability to set this right."

That set off a remarkable exchange that highlighted the situation and provided a window into high stakes negotiations:

LIGHTFOOT: Well, I am not surprised you see it that way. These folks
have not been good actors and I was willing to swallow a lot
but the constant moving targets, and never being able to rely on
their [word] is an impossible place to be. I know where you have
to be and you'll do what you do.

REITER: I've been witness to everything all week. You're letting this
deal go. If it's bc of CPS leadership, so be it. Jesse has been an
honest broker to get this deal done.

LIGHTFOOT: I was giving you a courtesy heads up. You should surely
know by now that I don't cave to bullying or pressure. CTU's actions and demands are causing labor strife as I am hearing every
day from more and more folks who say "They treat you like
shit, we support you, but you are giving more to these people
who work every day to destroy you than you are doing for your
allies." That is very compelling to me. A deal at gunpoint that
requires us to ignore all science, all data and shred our integrity
and values is not much of a deal.

REITER: And I'm giving you my point of view as a courtesy. You don't
have to agree with me. But I also want you to know, that I'm no
[sic] just supporting Jesse, not just bc he's an affiliate and my
Board member. I'm supporting him bc I believe he did the work
to get this deal done. I hope you don't see my thoughts as bullying. They are my thoughts.

Despite the drama, both sides were able to reach a deal that Sunday morning, though Lightfoot began panicking as the union was slow to provide them
with the formal agreement. She texted Sharkey, "Jesse, we need the signed TA
asap. Please don't slow roll us. We are seeing that you are going out in the
press at noon."

He responded, "In five minutes," and added, "Not slow rolling, just trying
to get [executive board] in the right place. Didn't want to send before we met."

By the time Lightfoot went out to announce their deal, she had a huge
smile on her face as she announced "the very good news that our children
will be returning to in-person learning this week." Lightfoot didn't earn style
points, and she had fumbled the approach, but CTU was returning and got
safety measures it could also tout.

Lightfoot told alderpersons during a briefing that Jackson was disappointed and felt she had given away the house, which the mayor denied to me in an interview. "I'm not going to get into what was suppose to be a private conversation but that's not correct," Lightfoot said. "If you report that, you're going to look very foolish, because it is not correct." She sounded like Trump.

As the crisis wound down, Karen Lewis died. It was a sad occasion for her family and the city. Lightfoot texted Sharkey her condolences. "I have a sense of how important she was to you. I spoke with her once and felt lucky to have been in her presence. I hope you will give yourself the space to grieve this loss," Lightfoot wrote. "With your mom's passing, I know you have had a tough year of personal losses." It was a nice personal touch, the sort of gesture that effective humans demonstrate in times of sorrow, but one Lightfoot rarely used.

In February Lightfoot did an interview with the *New York Times* that made waves and provided a clear window into her thinking. "I think, ultimately, they'd like to take over not only Chicago Public Schools, but take over running the city government," she said, referring to the teachers' union. "That'll play itself out over time. I don't really spend time, and certainly not in the middle of a pandemic, worrying about the politics. But politics intrudes, always."

She also told the *New York Times* that Chicago schools wouldn't have reopened if the city had an elected school board. "The fact that L.A. and San Francisco had to sue to force the conversation about reopening? Look, what's easy, the path of least resistance, the political expediency, would have been to do nothing and just let the unions dictate what the state of play was going to be in education," Lightfoot said. "That's never, ever going to be the path that I take."

Later, I asked Sharkey about the mayor's concerns. "I think when this mayor is at her worst, that's at the forefront of her mind," Sharkey said. "I think when she's at her best, I think she's willing to listen and trying to solve problems."

★ ★ ★ ★

Rahm Emanuel's 2018 declaration that the next mayor wasn't in the race yet was a backhanded attack on the people who dared to challenge him. But his statement foreshadowed future events when he said the next mayor needs to "fill that office." "And what I mean by that is, you're not going to shrink the mayoralty, and there's got to be a mayor that actually fills this job." In 2021 Lightfoot lost the schools, for herself and future mayors, effectively shrinking the mayor's office. After the school reopening fight, attention turned to the elected school board Lightfoot had campaigned on but abandoned. Internally, the team and mayor struggled hard with the notion. It was a master class in how to not deal with an issue. First, Lightfoot argued that she supported an elected school board—just not the one put forward by the union, which would have created a twenty-one-member model that would be the biggest in the country. Internally, Lightfoot staffers wanted her to argue for a hybrid board model, where the majority was appointed while others were elected, but Lightfoot rejected a push to give a speech laying that out explicitly.

Lightfoot's struggles to stop the elected school board followed Illinois Senate president John Cullerton's resignation. Cullerton had long put a brick on the bill for Emanuel and continued to kill it for Lightfoot. When he announced his departure, state senators Kimberly Lightford and Don Harmon threw their hats in the ring. Lightfoot sent Harmon a conciliatory text message when he won. "Mr. President. Congrats on your election. Savor the moment. I look forward to working with you," she wrote. But their relationship soured over the coming months. In January 2021 Lightfoot texted Harmon to say her staff had brought her "comments that are concerning."

"If there is a personal issue that is of concern, let's put it on the table," Lightfoot texted.

Three days later, she messaged him again to complain about a firefighter pension bill that would boost costs for the city. "A courtesy call regarding the fire pension bill would have been helpful, particularly since there is no funding for it," Lightfoot said. "When that pension fund collapses, I will be talking a lot about this vote."

That April, State Senator Kimberly Lightford introduced a bill considered Lightfoot's counter. Longtime Springfield writer Rich Miller put it best: "Mayor Lightfoot said often during her campaign that she supported a 'fully elected' school board. This proposal is more like tokenism." That bill would've put the first school board election off until 2026 and then only had two out of seven members elected. In 2028 the mayor would get three more appointments, and the board would have one more elected, giving City Hall an eight to three majority. As a counter, it was bizarre and failed to stem the CTU bill's momentum.

That May, left-wing state senator Robert Peters saw Lightfoot at a Chicago Sky game and said hello. "First, she said to me was how 'we're gonna [fuck] her.' Then, how this 'would be a political problem for us.' I laughed and responded, 'what about the game?'" Peters tweeted.

As the months dragged on, Lightfoot needed help. Former Emanuel advisor Michael Sacks, a prominent business leader who opposed the elected school board bill, texted Lightfoot, encouraging her to take on a stalling strategy. "Thinking that the most important message and the most important thing is that you don't walk away and don't blow up. If you keep saying that you are willing to stay at the table and keep working and go over into veto and be the one willing to work, maybe they become unwilling and walk away and that helps you with Welch and helps Harmon and Welch to decide to let the clock run out," Sacks texted on May 29. "You just want to keep working and keep trying to make this work [for progress] and let them get [tired]."

"Agreed," Lightfoot responded.

A day later, she texted Sacks, "All I can say is 'oy vey!'"

Following up, Sacks texted Lightfoot to ask for marching orders. "1) Delay to veto 2) 24-28 not 26 3) smaller 4) financial report before not after. Those are my asks. Am I on target?"

"100 Percent on target," she responded.

Sacks gave Lightfoot his view on the dynamic in Springfield. "Feels like senate wants to pass something. My view is pass something that is solidly centrist," he said. "House won't pass and we keep working. As long as the senate members can say that they passed something."

That same day, Lightfoot texted Harmon: "It is important that we talk early. The direction things are going is totally inconsistent with what you committed to."

State Senator Sara Feigenholtz had privately opposed the bill and worked with Lightfoot to try to bring it down. But when it came time to vote, she cast her ballot in favor. That reality reflected a harsh truth for Lightfoot: legislators had a better relationship with the union or feared it more than the mayor's office, a real flip from the city's traditional power dynamics.

After the twenty-one-member elected school board bill passed the state senate, Feigenholtz texted Lightfoot, "Breath[e]. Don't react negatively. Look forward to working together for a trailer."

"I figured they were going to swing for the fences, and they did. Means very little," Lightfoot said. "We will get adults in the room."

That night, Sacks sent her a sad text. "Feel like a failure. Think it is terrible what they did. Sort of stunned so few would speak up. Going back and forth between sadness and anger/wanting to lash out. Fights not over. Have to regroup and settle on a strategy. Wish I could have been more help. Will talk soon."

Lightfoot's hope for a trailer bill that could help was misplaced. Legislation sometimes passes without full language around its implementation. That often comes later and is known as a *trailer*. It's not a measure that changes the original law but is a proposal that ensures it can be carried out smoothly. State Representative Kambium Buckner was baffled by the trailer talk. In mid-June Lightfoot criticized the elected school board plan as it barreled down the road and said she would continue fighting.

"I'm aware of the practical realities but as General MacArthur said, I've only just begun to fight," Lightfoot said. (It was actually Captain John Paul Jones who made the comment.) Two days later, it didn't matter who said what: Welch's House passed the legislation. The fight was effectively over, but Lightfoot made one last pitch to Illinois governor J. B. Pritzker, whom she called demanding that he veto the legislation. Like a lot of people in Springfield, Pritzker wasn't enamored with the law—he shared the concern that it was too big a board. But he didn't think it was his fight. He thought it was hers—and she lost.

Davis Gates later summed up Lightfoot's failure to gather allies: "She had offended everyone in the world."

Late in 2021 Chicago experienced the Omicron surge, with cases eventually rising to almost six thousand per day. What happened leading up to the 2021 return to school happened again: the teachers union started to raise concerns about safety, and Lightfoot dismissed it, this time as the "same old saber-rattling by teachers union leadership."

But the union wasn't bluffing. CTU officials asked teachers to vote on teaching remotely starting January 5, and Davis Gates was furious. "I am so pissed off that we have to continuously fight for the basic necessities, the basic mitigations," she said. They voted by a 73 percent margin to stay remote until January 18 or until COVID rates declined, setting off a pitched battle with CPS.

Lightfoot angrily denounced the "unlawful, unilateral strike" by the CTU. "Enough is enough," she said. "We are standing firm and we are going to fight to get our kids back to in-person learning. Period. Full stop."

Her previous encounters with the union were either failures or Pyrrhic victories. But this one led to a real change in her position and was angrier than previous clashes, and unlike earlier walkouts, where she somewhat impotently made final demands then continued negotiating or caved, she held a tough line. On January 6 Lightfoot said, "I will not allow them to take our children hostage."

By day three, both sides were filing unfair labor charges against each other. Lightfoot went on national television and said, "This is about politics. It's not about the pandemic."

For the teachers, it was insulting. They had members who were genuinely very afraid and worked up. Lightfoot kept pressing the offensive. She accused them of abandoning "kids and their families." Sharkey, who often tried to be diplomatic, accused her of being "relentlessly stubborn" and "relentlessly stupid." Lightfoot responded that it wasn't the first time a privileged white man had insulted her intelligence.

Unlike past encounters, however, it was the union that backed down. It ended up settling on pretty modest terms. My *Sun-Times* colleague Nader Issa got the best quote of the saga from a frustrated teacher, who noted the pay he lost and told him, "I just paid $3,200 for two KN95 masks." There wasn't a lot to show for the walkout but bad feelings.

In an internal document, which I obtained, Sharkey acknowledged the bad results. "We accomplished more than nothing, but less than we wanted," Sharkey said in a PowerPoint. He noted there were "plenty of reasons for dissatisfaction" and "some members will say, 'it wasn't worth it!' But we are grown ups. We realize—when we walk out, we don't get to know the outcome in advance. We also would have had nothing had we ducked this fight." He said they were "hurt by the things we couldn't control—MLL herself, and the national politics of return to school." His biggest worry, he said, "is the divisiveness of COVID in our union. I feel so strongly / this is so clear to me that it calls into question the integrity of people who disagree."

Lightfoot lost previous battles with the union, but this one was a national win. Coming nearly a year since the vaccine was widespread, it tested whether unions could force a school district to remain closed due to COVID cases. The answer was, essentially, no. But the standoff deepened the bad feelings between both sides. Sharkey was frustrated with Lightfoot, who he felt treated them as not having valid positions as she went on a "national speaking tour."

For her part, Lightfoot hammered the union for not caring about children as she braced herself for a reelection challenge from CTU that she expected to come. "We can never forget the impact on the lives of our children and their families. They must always be front and center. Every decision has to be made with them at the forefront."

.

20 | "NOT A GIMME"

IN JULY 2021 MAYOR Lori Lightfoot sat down for an interview with Kara Swisher at the *New York Times* in which she made waves. Asked about her reelection campaign, Lightfoot frankly acknowledged the job's toll and raised the possibility of not seeking a second term. "It's not a gimme," she said of the decision. "The toxicity of the debate, the physical and emotional toll that it's taking on all of us, those are serious issues. And we have to have a—my wife and I and my daughter and my close friends and my team, we have to have a serious conversation about why and what that would look like and what we believe that we would be able to accomplish. And could we even get it done, right? This is a tough time for mayors all across the country."

Although her statements indicated the contrary, Lightfoot was already gearing up and working hard to run for a second term. Not seeking reelection had some merit. Lightfoot could've bowed out and declared victory: *I led us through the toughest four years in a century. We kept the city strong against impossible odds. It's time for me to be with my family and pass the torch.* But that wasn't her style, even though she knew it would be an uphill battle. All her life, Lightfoot was considered an underdog, and she often beat the odds. The optics were also hard to swallow. In politics, people gauge one-termers as failures or misfits. Chicago particularly suffered from this unhealthy fixation on longevity due to its history of long-serving mayors. All of it weighed on her.

Alderperson Susan Sadlowski Garza, a popular labor leader who represented the working-class Tenth Ward on Chicago's Southeast Side, made clear how hard Lightfoot's race would be in an interview on the *Ben Joravsky Show*, a podcast by the veteran *Chicago Reader* columnist. Garza had been a close Lightfoot ally, exchanging friendly texts with her, including "I love you." But she grew frustrated by Lightfoot and her team's failure to engage and was angry that the administration broke its tentative commitment to allow a controversial scrap-shredder polluter to set up shop in her ward. When Joravsky asked if she would support Lightfoot, Garza vented, "I'm tired of being ignored. I'm tired of not getting phone calls returned. I'm tired of letting the inmates run the asylum. Yeah, no. Absolutely not. I have never met anybody who has managed to piss off every single person they come in contact with—police, fire, teachers, alderpersons, businesses, manufacturing, and that's it. I said it. That's it. I don't care."

Garza, who was in grief after a family member's recent murder, regretted making the comments publicly. But she stood by the truth of what she said. Days after the interview, Lightfoot texted Garza: "Sue, I love you. That has not changed." Garza did not text back.

Lightfoot was vulnerable, but you can't beat someone with no one, as the politicians say. The question quickly became, who will run against her? My least favorite part of the job is watching wannabes float their names. A lot of people just like attention or haven't thought the dynamics through, and fizzle—but not before getting a few headlines for themselves and wasting my time.

The first people to make loud inquiries about running against Lightfoot were white men, which also reflected dissatisfaction with Lightfoot from downtown business types. Arne Duncan, the former Obama White House education secretary and Chicago Public Schools head, had spent the past few years working in violence prevention. He had never run for a meaningful elected office but was occasionally mentioned as a potential contender due to his pedigree, decent looks, and media savvy brought by his close friend Peter Cunningham, a Daley administration loyalist. But those who spoke with Duncan almost universally came back with a clear takeaway: he didn't actually want to run. Duncan would couch his interest in reluctance. "I hoped she'd get better at the job. She hasn't," he would tell people.

Early in 2022 Duncan floated his interest in the run, but he quickly bowed out. Why was never clearly settled. People speculated about polls, but the truth is he didn't have the fire. That's one thing I always admire about Lightfoot: she does have the heart of a champion.

North Side US congressman Mike Quigley, a well-liked but bland moderate Democrat, also let it be known that he was thinking of running. Quigley made for an interesting potential candidate: he held Rahm Emanuel's former US House seat but had none of his charisma or drive. Quigley would sometimes jokingly compare himself to a twelve-year-old boy because he doesn't drink coffee or alcohol. At the same time Quigley was considering a run for mayor, he was eyeing the possibility of being on Adam Schiff's leadership team if he was able to replace Speaker Nancy Pelosi as the top House Democrat. Shortly after paying for a poll, Quigley dropped out of the race—claiming he wanted to help save Ukraine from the Russians as a member of the House Intelligence Committee. "After much consideration, I simply cannot walk away from my duty to safeguard democracy, fight for American values abroad, and stand up for the brave Ukrainian people in their time of maximum peril," he said. "Campaigning to serve as Mayor of Chicago would not allow me to fulfill this critical obligation." After Pelosi stepped down and Hakeem Jeffries became Democratic leader, Jeffries booted him from the committee.

Former Illinois governor Pat Quinn, who had lost his reelection in 2014, started to consider a run, even though he was widely considered past his prime. When I asked him how he would answer to folks who say he's washed up, the septuagenarian told me he had recently played basketball with a group of young men on the West Side who were impressed by his skills. Quinn ended up aborting his run, but not before calling a news conference to pontificate.

Downtown alderperson Brian Hopkins also declared his interest in the race, though people looked at his potential candidacy with skepticism. Since COVID, Hopkins had been vocal expressing long-term concern about the disease and criticism of government officials for not taking it more seriously. He tweeted about it so often that people thought he had a fixation. "Until we have a better understanding of this, we should stop describing some cases of Covid-19 as 'mild,'" he tweeted in summer 2020. "It's too soon to accurately predict the long-term effects that SARS-CoV2 infection will have on the vital organs." Later, in 2021, Hopkins tweeted, "'SARSCoV2 infection of brain tissue was confirmed . . .' this virus ultimately wants to kill us. Fortunately for humanity, it fails in 99% of attempts, at least in the short term. Key question, what about long term? What if we can't live with Covid, or future variants yet to evolve?" Some of his colleagues dismissed him as Darth Vader because they felt he overmasked.

Paul Vallas, who had been an also-ran in 2019, was watching closely as all of these men maneuvered. He had spent the past couple years criticizing the Chicago Teachers Union, Illinois governor J. B. Pritzker, and Lightfoot, including on rightwing talk-radio stations, which allies warned him would be a problem down the road, but he did it anyway. Campaign manager Brian Towne took Vallas's phone one day and blocked many right-wing Republicans in an effort to limit his exposure to far-right conservatives and muckrakers who could potentially cause embarrassment for a candidate running as a "lifelong Democrat" in a blue city. Vallas would explain it by saying he is willing to talk issues anywhere, a naive at best idea in today's political environment. He considered himself a problem solver and apolitical wonk interested in issues more than politics. He had unsuccessfully sought the Democratic gubernatorial nomination in 2002, losing to Rod Blagojevich, and had been Quinn's running mate when he lost reelection in 2014. Looking toward 2023, Vallas met with a variety of people considering a run and their backers and was frustrated by the lack of support. Once, I tried to get his comment on the various white candidates considering a run, and he sadly said, "What's wrong with me?" His campaign staff would be frustrated because they'd go to meetings and Vallas wouldn't make eye contact with potential donors.

Alderperson Raymond Lopez broke the seal by announcing a mayoral run in April 2022. He had been Lightfoot's most frequent critic and a lightning rod himself, due to his harsh stances against crime and gangs, including tough criticism of families and community members who he said were too sympathetic to criminals. His announcement had been long talked about but took people by surprise. How would he raise enough money to win? Lopez gave a brief speech announcing his candidacy where he focused solely on crime: "My No. 1 goal is safety. We must prioritize safety in our city or else nothing will happen." It was, by all accounts, the top issue, as residents remained concerned about violence. Lopez is one of the council's hardest workers and had a clear message on the top issue, which he hoped could build momentum, even though many of his peers considered him a shameless self-promoter. He later dropped out, but not before soaking in the attention.

Following Lopez, Willie Wilson announced he would again be running for mayor. He had recently given away $1.2 million in free gas as part of a chaotic promotion across the city that backed up traffic for many blocks, and he promised to keep giving. "Go out there and help those people who are homeless, that don't have food, that are still sick with COVID-19," he said to critics who suggested he was buying votes, as we reported in the *Tribune*. "Go out there with the people who can't get to work, who can't get to a babysitter. Go out there and tell those people you stopped giving because of some political season. I'm not that way."

Wilson had lost twice before but thought he could break through by spending more time with ethnic white voters on the Northwest and Southwest Sides who were drawn to his practical conservatism, while maintaining the strong base of support he had with Black residents. Around that time, Lightfoot visited a Black church in a skirt—the only time I've ever seen her in anything other than slacks. Wilson's potential appeal to the Black community seemed to have scared the pants off her, as she came in dressed more traditionally for the churchgoing community.

State Rep. Kambium Buckner announced his campaign in mid-May. A strong proponent of the elected school board bill and a broad series of criminal justice reforms known as the SAFE-T Act, Buckner was considered a future star in the party. He had a couple embarrassing DUIs in his background, which the Lightfoot campaign frequently talked about, but was an interesting potential dark horse if he could raise money. He criticized Lightfoot as too combative, saying "a mayor's job is not just to fight for the sake of fighting," and accused City Hall of failing on public safety. "If I thought we were doing a good job, I probably wouldn't be here right now talking to you," we quoted him saying.

As the campaign started taking shape, that May was an especially busy time for local government. First, Chicago alderpersons approved a remap. Every ten years, City Council is tasked with setting boundaries for wards, which the alderpersons often abuse to cut opponents out of their districts and make their reelection races easier. Northwest Side alderperson Jim Gardiner, for instance, cut small liberal parts of his district out in an effort to make his campaign easier as he faced an FBI investigation for potential bribery and bad headlines about his treatment of constituents. Lightfoot had been a proponent of redistricting reform long before running for office and as a candidate, but she abandoned it entirely, which reflected her lack of clout with alderpersons and her desire to avoid a fight with the powerful Black Caucus, which stood to lose seats due to population loss. It was another example of her giving up on the things she ran on.

Jason Ervin, the head of the Black Caucus who had been feuding with her, became a vocal supporter. "If Mayor Lightfoot runs for reelection, I will be supportive of her efforts," he told the *Sun-Times* in an interview that took his colleagues by surprise. "I do believe that she is running." When Lightfoot feuded with State's Attorney Kim Foxx, Ervin urged the top prosecutor and other alderpersons to make peace for the Black community. "When elephants fight, the grass gets trampled," Ervin said, in a private meeting.

For her part, Lightfoot used city government to help the Ervins as they made peace. In 2020, Treasurer Melissa Conyears-Ervin fired four staffers, including her chief of staff. I soon reported that the chief and another employee had alleged misconduct by the treasurer. Lightfoot blocked my attempts to receive records detailing Conyears-Ervin's misconduct and settled the whistle-blowers' complaint, but the *Tribune* eventually obtained the documents and reported Conyears-Ervin "used government workers to plan her daughter's birthday party and be her personal bodyguard while she also pressured public employees to hold events benefiting political allies and repeatedly misused taxpayer resources." The letter also alleged that Conyears-Ervin "tried to force BMO Harris—one of the banks where city money is deposited—to issue a mortgage tied to the building that houses the aldermanic office for" her husband, Jason. Lightfoot's attempt to hide the allegations was a vivid rebuke to her argument that she isn't a Chicago politician.

As she geared up to announce, Lightfoot dealt with an ugly tragedy when a teen was killed near the Bean in Millennium Park, the city's iconic backyard tourism destination. Her response was to ban unaccompanied youth from the park after 6:00 PM on weekends, drawing heated criticism. Lightfoot also picked Bally's to run the city's casino in River West, a move that drew anger from critics who felt that the city had gone out of its way to support its bid. Lightfoot also pushed a prepaid gas cards program through City Council, a clear response to Wilson's cash giveaways—one using taxpayer dollars.

Vallas entered the race following the Memorial Day holiday. "I'm running because the city is in crisis. The crisis is worsening," Vallas told me for a *Tribune* story on his announcement. "I believe I have the skills and the experience as well as the courage to provide the leadership the city desperately needs." Vallas was the first and only white candidate to enter the race, which gave him a real boost in a multicandidate contest, though he faced strong headwinds raising money due to his past electoral dysfunction. But there was a real sense of fatigue around his candidacy from some people who might've been considered natural supporters. One South Side alderperson would get calls from people urging him to support Vallas, but he couldn't fake enthusiasm. "If there's forty thousand people at a White Sox game and he's one of them, he might be the smartest man at the stadium. But he's a fucking idiot," the alderperson said, mocking his social skills and lack of common sense. "By the end of the game, no one's sitting by him. 'Hey, I'm trying to watch the game, stop talking.'"

Lightfoot finally made her reelection bid official in June, when she launched a video touting herself as a fighter for Chicago. "When we fight for change, confront a global pandemic, work to keep kids in school, take on guns and gangs, systemic inequality, and political corruption only to have powerful forces try and stop progress for Chicago—of course I take it personally, for our city," Lightfoot said in the video. "Change doesn't happen without a fight. It's hard. It takes time. And, I'll be the first to admit I'm just not the most patient person. I'm only human, and I guess sometimes it shows. But just because some may not always like my delivery doesn't mean we're not delivering." It was an attempt to take a weakness and make it a strength. As I wrote in the *Tribune*, "By embracing her image as a political pugilist, Lightfoot is betting that Chicago voters will see her as a righteous fighter rather than someone who throws unnecessary haymakers."

Her campaign also released a poster and button depicting her in a muscle car with the skyline hanging out of the car and the phrase "I'm ridin' with Lori." One consultant called it the sort of art a fifth-place also-ran uses.

Over the coming weeks, candidates kept piling into the clown car. Activist Ja'Mal Green announced a campaign. Alderperson Roderick Sawyer, whose father served as mayor after Harold Washington's death, announced a run—prematurely. Some allies wanted to launch a campaign after he had secured big-money donations, but he undercut their plans while sitting at the barber shop. *Sun-Times* ace Fran Spielman called and asked him if he was running. The guys at the barber shop egged him on, and he declared. It was the high point of his candidacy. Lightfoot, meanwhile, responded, "Another day, another man who thinks he can do this job better than me."

For Lightfoot, though, the large number of Black candidates was a concern. Although the city's African American residents aren't monolithic, it's impossible to separate race from political support in Chicago. Lightfoot's original base was white lakefront liberals, and with their disillusionment, she needed Black voters to fuel her campaign into a runoff. Sawyer criticized her for "trying to be super-Black." "White people have abandoned her. Lakefront has abandoned her. She needs a constituency that she can try to depend on," Sawyer told the *Sun-Times*. "So, she wants to be ultra-Black."

On the day she announced, Lightfoot held several events on the South and West Sides, then closed out her public schedule at Sidetrack, an iconic gay bar on the North Side that was largely empty for Lightfoot's gathering, a troubling sign for a candidate whose original base was on the north lakefront. That first day led to one of the most telling incidents of her time in office. Alderperson Derrick Curtis hosted an event for her on the day she launched her reelection, a packed breakfast staffed by city workers. Weeks later, Curtis accidentally shot himself in the hand and complained to the *Sun-Times* that Lightfoot hadn't called to check on him. What followed was a series of combative texts: "Tried to call you. Please call me," she texted, before following up: "I seriously do not understand you." The next day, she messaged him again. "Morning has broken and still no call. Gee wonder why." Her next messages took on a taunting air: "Will I see you tomorrow at the MLK breakfast?" "Missed you today." "Looking forward to seeing you today." After the City Council meeting, Lightfoot walked up to Curtis on the floor and said, "You say I don't talk to you. You say I don't reach out. I'm making sure there's a record." He unendorsed her.

In August Alderperson Sophia King launched a bid for mayor, creating a widely watched dynamic. A personal friend of the Obamas, King had served as alderperson for the prominent Fourth Ward. She knew a lot of rich people and was well-respected. Lightfoot's team worried that she could catch fire and strip Lightfoot of her gender advantage.

Several alderpersons attempted to recruit their Wrigleyville colleague Tom Tunney, a favorite of the business community and owner of the popular Ann Sather restaurant and the first openly gay member of City Council. Tunney, who had served as Lightfoot's Zoning Committee chair, called her to say he wouldn't seek reelection and let her know that he was thinking about running for mayor. The conversation didn't go well. "You're going to embarrass yourself," Lightfoot said, claiming, "I'm going to win the lakefront." She also lamented his lack of loyalty, since she had appointed him to the Zoning position. "I just think there are things that could be better in the city, and I think I can do it," Tunney said. (Tunney disputed this account. I heard about the exchange shortly after it happened from sources on both sides of the conversation.)

Over the coming weeks, Tunney vacillated so much behind the scenes that his colleagues started calling him Hamlet. In the end, Tunney didn't get into the race. Hopkins, meanwhile, told people he would've run for mayor—if only Tunney had dropped out a week sooner.

As the field started to settle, Lightfoot waited to see whom the Chicago Teachers Union would support, a challenge she had been anticipating from the beginning.

In the meantime, Lightfoot had a city to lead. That August, the administration began bracing for Texas governor Greg Abbott to begin busing migrants to Chicago in an attempt to embarrass the "Welcoming City." When the first buses arrived, Lightfoot rushed to greet them and assured the public it was under control. "We're ready. We are the village," Lightfoot said. "And we are going to make sure that whoever comes to Chicago, that we are going to take care of them, that they are going to find shelter here and that they are going to be welcomed. And we will do whatever it takes to make sure that their rights are respected."

In February 2022 CTU president Jesse Sharkey announced he wouldn't run for reelection. That left Stacy Davis Gates the obvious successor for his role. She had been bandied about as a potential mayoral candidate due to her dynamic persona and clashes with Lightfoot. But she decided to run for union president.

As the year unfolded, CTU brought in candidates for endorsement interviews, but they ultimately threw their support behind one of their own: Cook County commissioner Brandon Johnson. There was only one problem: he hadn't yet announced his candidacy.

Johnson and his supporters on the progressive left had been working to lay the groundwork for a campaign when Jesús "Chuy" García started making noise about running again. A longtime progressive leader, García had taken on Rahm Emanuel in 2015 before ending up in Congress. In March 2022 he'd basically ruled out a mayoral run during a *Sun-Times* interview in which he said, "I am not thinking about that whatsoever and I surely haven't talked with my wife about it. I've got to think that she'd be very reluctant for us to do it, and we do everything together. It's not on my radar right now," he said, alluding to his wife's struggles with multiple sclerosis. "The job is a huge bear and it will continue to be challenging and torturous on a daily basis, especially as funding dissipates and goes away. It will make it excruciatingly difficult to govern and provide good news to Chicagoans."

But as the coming weeks unfolded, García reconsidered, setting off alarm bells for unionists supporting Johnson who had previously backed García in 2015. As Lightfoot's weakness became clearer, García felt drawn to the idea of becoming Chicago's first Latino mayor. He also reflected on his forty-year journey as the elder statesman of the city's progressive movement—standing with Harold Washington against the machine, feuding with Richard M. Daley, and challenging Rahm Emanuel when others like Toni Preckwinkle were scared to take on the fight—and thought he could cap off his career with a milestone victory. Still, some people thought he was simply angling for some behind-the-scenes favor or enjoying the attention. Lightfoot showed up to the Southeast Side Labor Day Parade, and her team made a point of posting a photo of her and García to social media.

(In a separate encounter, Lightfoot walked around and asked staff if Alderperson Garza was present. When I asked Garza if she wanted to walk with Lightfoot, she said, "Fuck no!")

Days after the parade, García publicly acknowledged considering a run at a news conference where he announced his support for several aldermanic candidates. Lightfoot texted him days later: "We should sit down and chat, one on one. If you agree, let me know your availability." He did not text back, figuring they didn't have a relationship and it was too late. Days later, García wrote a letter to United Working Families (UWF), a political group closely aligned with CTU, asking it to hold off on endorsing a candidate until he made a decision:

> As many have inquired, I am putting a lot of thoughtful consideration into what the most important role would be for me this cycle. I am giving serious consideration to becoming a candidate. I am in consultation with family, allies, and leaders in different sectors to consider my responsibilities in DC to save our democracy from extremist attacks and to chart a better course for our city. Thus, I am respectfully requesting a deferral in making a final decision on endorsing any candidate until the field is more complete.

Again, 2023 presents us with the opportunity to draw attention to issues and create a vision to elect progressive candidates in our city and have an ally as our mayor. I want to make sure we do right by the residents of Chicago.

UWF blew off his letter and endorsed Johnson, setting off a potential confrontation between two progressive leaders. Delia Ramirez, who had won the Democratic primary for a newly created US congressional seat, told García that he needed to sit down with Johnson and figure it out. Both men shouldn't run, Ramirez said, noting concern about dividing the progressive movement and ending up with Lightfoot or Vallas. When Johnson and García met, however, it went poorly. Both sides have different accounts of their meetings, but they were acrimonious and it led to hurt feelings. García questioned whether Johnson would have the level of union support he thought he would get, with the exchange later recounted as him asking, "Why would they want to spend that much money on you?" Johnson, meanwhile, made a comment that García complained about later as calling him "old." They did make a pact not to attack each other.

While waiting for García, Johnson held off until October, when he made the decision official. His entry into the race brought new energy to the progressive movement, as Johnson, the son of a preacher, was a dynamic speaker who could address the thorniest subjects. At one forum, where candidates were asked how to make Black residents thrive in Chicago, Johnson responded, "Can we just be honest? They don't want Black people here. . . . And every administration has been willing to do that, whether it's calling for 'shoot to kill' or raising bridges. It's a wicked and unjust system."

García followed in November with an announcement coinciding with the fortieth anniversary of Harold Washington's candidacy in 1982. It was a nice day at Navy Pier, and he packed the space with supporters, including Stephanie Gadlin, a former spokeswoman for Karen Lewis. He started collecting endorsements from various trade unions and received a $1 million commitment from the powerful Operating Engineers Union. The future looked bright for García, whose team raised Lightfoot's ire by constantly promoting polls that showed him as the frontrunner.

Lightfoot assessed the landscape and knew she needed to address the city's crime problem. She frequently told residents that there was work to be done but they were seeing reductions in violence. *Plan* was the magic word her team singled out to help get her past the issue. Her first ads focused on crime and the pandemic. One featured two couch potatoes named after Oscar and Felix playing video games. "Lightfoot delivers? What about crime?" one asks. "People don't know. She's delivering record spending for violence reduction, getting guns off the street, and more money for police," the other responds. "You know we didn't get into this mess overnight. Getting out of it takes time, and Lightfoot has a plan. Right?" Lightfoot then appears and declares, "I couldn't have said it better myself." And she declines to play videogames with the weirdos, saying, "Love to, but I've got work to do for our city."

The problem with the ad is it wasn't serious enough for the issue. And Lightfoot never figured out how to talk about crime. At a North Side event reported on by Natasha Korecki, Lightfoot told the crowd, "I know for many of you, you're feeling a touch of violence, maybe for the very first time in your lives in Chicago." She bragged about suing out-of-state gun shops. "We warned them, we gave them the data, and they kept doing it. So this old litigator? We strapped it on, and we sued these fuckers—pardon my language." One resident shared this takeaway: "I feel worse. I still don't think she gets it." I remember reading Korecki's story and recalling Lightfoot's texts with Brendan Reilly about downtown being bad in the 1980s, which missed the point about the state of it now.

As she looked ahead to the February 28 runoff, where the top two vote-getters would make a runoff, Lightfoot felt good about the strategy she'd laid out. The goal was to defend her record and go after García, a candidate she and her team feared. *Chuy kills us, so let's kill him first* was the rationale. Although Lightfoot had her challenges, she started the new year strong, running an ad hitting García for connections to indicted House Speaker Michael Madigan and disgraced cryptocurrency fraudster Samuel Bankman-Fried. The ad was brutal and effective, and it sent García's numbers plunging. He mostly ignored it, hoarding his money instead for a later television blitz.

Vallas and Johnson followed Lightfoot on the air, running commercials focused on crime and Johnson's slogan "Brandon is better." They all marveled as the weeks ticked by and García remained off air.

Lightfoot's reelection bid was going better than expected, but some allies thought it was missing a key piece: an explicit apology for things that had gone wrong and a promise to be better. Candidates seeking reelection have an advantage over rivals in that they've previously earned the voters' support. That means voters are predisposed to vote for a candidate and want a good reason to do it again. They're forgiving when asked. She struggled with that piece, as Jonathan Martin reported for *Politico*:

> When I asked Lightfoot if she had regrets, she didn't hesitate. "Of course, you can't have lived through what we lived through and say I did everything perfect," she said, conceding: "We made mistakes."
>
> Yet she was quick to say she learned from those errors and, perhaps recognizing the voters she needs to mobilize, said she was judged more harshly as a Black woman.

Some folks thought the comments were hypocritical based on how harshly she judged others. In a text message complaining about Alderperson Ed Burke rallying his colleagues against her vaccine mandate, for instance, Lightfoot referred to an unnamed alderman as a dupe: "Burke, per usual, found a dumb, dumb person of color to do his bidding." She similarly made sexist remarks of her own. For instance, she referred to Alderperson Silvana Tabares as "a hand maiden of Mike Madigan." But even if Lightfoot had a point about how she was treated, it wasn't what the public wanted to hear. Black South Side alderperson Leslie Hairston summarized the mayor's dilemma to me: "You have to own stuff. You gotta own it. I think that she does not own all of the stuff that she should and it's—sometimes, it's because it was a bad decision, and not because you're a woman, or because you're African American, or because you're gay. You're an intelligent person with a lot of different skill sets that you could be using. We all make mistakes. So own up to them, and move on."

21 | "FALSE PROPHET"

POLITICIANS TRY TO AVOID getting on the debate stage with their rivals when they're in the lead (or are facing clowns, as Richard M. Daley did in 1995 when he was challenged by Spanky the Clown). But Mayor Lori Lightfoot couldn't afford to skip too many candidate forums this cycle. She was raising decent money thanks to Tom Bowen, a Rahm Emanuel alum, but it wasn't overwhelming. She was barely staying competitive with Brandon Johnson, Jesús "Chuy" García, and Paul Vallas, who had managed to defy his past failures by raising money from Republican donors and business leaders. But that fundraising weakness meant she had to make time for debates, where the other candidates ganged up on her.

Her first forum was the Access Living disability forum, an impossible venue for candidates to aim fireworks at each other. But Lightfoot addressed her broken promise to reopen Chicago's mental health clinics shuttered by Emanuel in a rare example of successfully taking a change of mind head-on. "When I entered office, there was a lot of conversation about reopening the mental health clinics. And I thought about that too, and argued for it. But then what I heard from the experts and what I heard from patients is that they didn't want clinician care that our clinics offer. What they wanted was to be able to go to culturally relevant services in their neighborhood and that's precisely what we've done," she said.

She got knocked off balance after her team emailed Chicago Public Schools teachers to recruit students for her campaign, a story broken by WTTW's Heather Cherone. At first, her team defended the ethical faux paus but quickly denounced it. Heading into more forums, Lightfoot faced a tough balance: Be tough, but not off-putting. Bloody up Vallas, but not too much because he's your favored runoff opponent. Ignore Johnson so he doesn't get too much oxygen. Kill García.

At a women's forum, Lightfoot attacked Vallas over abortion: "Remember how you felt when you heard about the draft [Dobbs] decision? It was like a punch in the gut," she said. "All of us took to social media except Paul Vallas, who's been silent on this for seven months until today. Shame on you!" Vallas had a long record of being pro-choice but had made a few clumsy comments about being personally opposed to abortion that his opponents used against him. He had been silent after Dobbs, perhaps to avoid alienating conservative supporters (he denied that), but tried to brush it off: "Lori likes to invent new facts to suit her narrative."

Willie Wilson filled his campaign appearances with folksy sayings. At a *Tribune* editorial board meeting, he declared, "I only have a seventh-grade education. I ran away from home at 13. Now all these guys, and you guys probably have more education than I have, but I probably can beat you making money because you work for somebody else." At another forum, Wilson said he would "take the handcuffs off the police and put them on the crook." During the first televised debate, Wilson roiled the field by declaring that fleeing suspects should be "hunted down like rabbits."

Sophia King tried a middle-of-the-road strategy. She called for balance. "We often deal with policy on the fringe: 'Defund the police,' 'Law and order.' Most people sit in the middle," she said at one forum. She would talk about the need to both uplift police and hold them accountable in hopes that others would be put off by the polarization of the field. She was never able to break through, in large part due to lack of fundraising. She could also be cagey with the media.

Johnson drew the sharpest contrast from his rivals, whom he criticized for relying too heavily on policing. He also took a hard shot at García, who had released a public-safety plan that Lightfoot's campaign said copied her ideas. "All due respect to Congressman García, he did not release a public safety plan," Johnson said. "He released Lori Lightfoot's public safety plan. As a teacher, I would call that plagiarism." Johnson also did an interview in which he criticized García for having "abandoned the progressive movement," infuriating the congressman. García's message was muddled at best. When we covered debates, I tried to give all nine candidates at least one mention, with more depending on the newsworthiness. Although García was a frontrunner, it was sometimes a struggle to fit him in because he spoke in vague platitudes. The political chattering class argued that he didn't want to be there or was taking it for granted that he'd make the runoff based on name value alone. Either way, the campaign wasn't connecting, and he was slow to adjust.

Slowly but surely, Johnson was building momentum, and the *Tribune* invited him to join Lightfoot and García for an editorial board session where she dissed the congressman for his relationship with Michael Madigan, the indicted Illinois House Speaker, whom Garcia reached a peace treaty with during the 2010s as their spheres of influence on the Southwest Side overlapped. "Clearly what he decided after losing in 2015 is, 'If you can't beat 'em, join 'em.' And he's made deal after deal after deal."

But the most memorable exchange of the session came when Lightfoot criticized Johnson over CTU's work stoppages, which she said hurt CPS by making the district unstable. "The fact of the matter is that we brought democracy to the city of Chicago," Johnson said, noting the elected school board. The two then engaged in a Bugs Bunny and Daffy Duck–like exchange during which he repeated, "We brought democracy," and she said, "Chaos."

Lightfoot privately complained that Johnson was a lightweight. During another forum, moderators asked the candidates to compliment the person next to him. Her idea of praising Johnson: "He spins a good story. You can tell that he was a preacher's son."

Soon, Lightfoot wasn't the only one going after Johnson. After Johnson criticized Vallas over the city's selective-enrollment high schools, the most successful academic campuses that require special admissions processes for students to get in, Vallas became angry and spun around in circles. "Shutting down the schools for 15 months had devastating consequences. And we are going to be paying the price for the next generation. So do not lecture me on schools." A frustrated Johnson shot back: "We were trying to save lives, and if saving lives from a 100-year pandemic is an inconvenience to you, then guess what, Paul, you don't deserve to be mayor."

Throughout it all, Vallas appeared to be weathering the storm, but his vulnerabilities were clear. I reported how his social media pages had liked racist, sexist, and homophobic comments, which the campaign explained by blaming unnamed associates, and then he made the claim that the pages had been hacked. Vallas also had a long history of running school districts with mixed results, which we reported on extensively. He was an intelligent, well-spoken man but hadn't held a real job in years and struggled to make connections. But nobody put serious money into attacking Vallas, and he had a clear path to the runoff with his conservative city base. In retrospect, it's clear to me that any other white candidate probably would've made the runoff in his stead.

Just a couple weeks out, Lightfoot came to a realization: she could lose out on the first round to Vallas and Johnson. The plan to kill García backfired, as white progressive voters were breaking for Johnson and García fell faster than expected. "We beat Chuy too fucking hard, and he didn't fight back," one Lightfoot aide recalled. Lightfoot started stepping up her attacks on Johnson during debates.

"I can't listen to Brandon Johnson talk about what he said, 'We need more public safety right now.' This is the man who said, 'Defunding is not a slogan; it's an actual political goal.' His goal is to destroy our police department by cutting our officers and making our communities less safe." Lightfoot's theory of the case was that she could use *defund* like a talisman that would kill Johnson instantly. Johnson had talked about defunding, but the criticism came off as ham-handed when he rebutted by talking about addressing root causes. Every few years, political consultants classify an issue as instant death and try to wrap it around their opponents' necks, but good candidates and campaigners can overcome unpopular positions.

Lightfoot, meanwhile, continued thrashing. Campaigning on Johnson's West Side, Lightfoot said, "It's Saturday and I'm not in church, but I'm going to talk to you about false prophets. He's got this airbrushed, West Sider, 'Oh, I'm a good guy, I'm a person of the people [persona].' But don't be fooled. Don't be fooled. Brandon Johnson wants to tax you out of the city. He said, 'I'm going to make all these investments,' but when somebody tells you that, you got to ask them, 'Well, how are you paying for it?'" She sharpened her argument from there: "Any vote for somebody not named Lightfoot is making sure that Chuy García or Paul Vallas runs this city, and you know what's going to happen with them in charge. They're never going to see the West Side." It was a naked and vicious appeal to racial politics.

Unfortunately for Lightfoot, she didn't have money left to light up Johnson the way she did García, so she had to work with word of mouth. She received another blow, however, in the days before the election, when Anjanette Young endorsed Johnson on the anniversary of the police raid on her home. "Brandon Johnson is someone I believe in because he supports things that matter to me as it relates to safety in our communities, police accountability and policies for more mental health services around the city," Young said. "And he is committed to making sure the trauma I endured at the hands of the police four years ago never happens to anyone again."

The hits kept coming. Alderperson Pat Dowell, Lightfoot's handpicked budget chair, dumped her and endorsed Johnson. It was a major surprise; Dowell is an influential Black leader who fits squarely into the mold of a traditional Chicago machine democrat, and she had not been particularly aligned with the teachers union's left-wing ethics. Her defection highlighted Lightfoot's total loss of control over local politics.

Illinois comptroller Susana Mendoza also held an emotional news conference days before the election criticizing the police pension board—staffed by Lightfoot appointees—for denying her cop brother full benefits after he was disabled by COVID on the job. Mendoza had been kind to Lightfoot after 2019, offering her help, but the mayor never took her up on it. In a *Sun-Times* story, Mendoza unleashed years of frustration on Lightfoot, dealing a big blow to the mayor's reelection campaign that her campaign still complains about. "I never thought the city of Chicago would betray our officers like that," Mendoza said. "I told her that not only did you not have my brother's back and any other police officers like him, you stabbed him in the back, and you twisted it into his heart. And you did the same to me."

The first couple batches of votes counted on election night put Vallas in first, Johnson in second, and Lightfoot third. There was no hope for a miracle. Lightfoot was quick to concede. At 8:14 PM, she texted Vallas: "Paul, trying to reach you."

When she came out to the crowd at her campaign party, Lightfoot put the best face on she could by addressing Black youth who saw her example in 2019. "I looked into the camera and spoke directly to young people of color who looked like me and to every kid who felt like I did when I grew up. And I'm going to do that again tonight. Obviously, we didn't win the election today, but I stand here with my head held high and a heart full of gratitude."

The mayor then spent the night at Moe's Cantina, a downtown bar, with staff. Some felt a sense of relief that it was all over. A longtime Lightfoot aide texted me the group's lessons the next morning: "You can't run on a platform and then completely abandon it. You can't run against the status quo, and then fill your administration with the status quo. And you can't be mean to everyone who tries to help you."

Beyond that, Lightfoot's time in office leaves one big lesson to me about leadership: being the boss means changing with the times and the moment. I'm not talking about people dropping core values for expediency. But Lightfoot never adapted from being a prosecutor and a hammer, traits and tools that are useful when you're putting away a criminal or banging in a nail or shaming Toni Preckwinkle and Bill Daley but that don't work for every problem. I remember being on a panel after the election and talking about contrasts between Lightfoot and Rahm Emanuel, who was not shy about yelling at people and kicking them in the shin. The difference was, he would follow up by kissing the boo-boo. Lightfoot would not kiss the boo-boo or acknowledge the boo-boo except to say the boo-boo was the boo-boo's own fault. That doesn't work.

EPILOGUE

BREAKING UP
WITH THE MAYOR

OVER THE NEXT FEW days, Lightfoot made clear she wouldn't be endorsing either of the candidates. Her positions on public safety and education were far closer to views held by Paul Vallas than Brandon Johnson, but there was too much bad blood. The lesson she shared with some allies was that this is what happens when you push the status quo too hard.

Vallas entered the runoff with a financial advantage but surrounded himself with hangers-on. At times, campaign staff would push back on decisions, and Vallas would shout, "I'm the candidate!" Former inspector general Joe Ferguson attended Vallas strategy calls, a move that puzzled campaign staff, as he is not a political professional. Vallas spent significant time with activist Ja'Mal Green, who won just 2 percent of the vote. Vallas tried to ingratiate himself with Black voters by seeking political endorsements from elected officials. He paid nearly $315,000 to alderpersons or their allies who endorsed him but lost in all those wards except two. Most critically, Vallas held off on launching negative television attacks against Johnson, giving his opponent crucial time to raise money and build a field operation without being defined negatively by his opponent. It was the major mistake for Vallas. Had Lightfoot made the runoff, she was ready to blast Vallas with a commercial on day one.

Seeking peace with former allies, Jesús "Chuy" García endorsed Johnson, giving him his support as the progressive movement transitioned from past to future. It wasn't a given: Some in García's circle thought he should stay out of the race. But he could not realistically avoid endorsing Johnson without doing significant damage to his progressive legacy, no matter how angry he was over the campaign. The endorsement was preceded by an uncomfortable meeting in which García lit into Johnson for his comments on the campaign trail. Johnson apologized.

To win over voters concerned with crime, Johnson promised not to cut the police budget and leaned into his affable personality. In the closing days of the campaign, the Vallas team dug up Johnson's delinquent water bills debt to the city, which would preclude him from serving if he didn't pay them off, and essentially called him a deadbeat. It backfired badly, galvanizing Johnson's supporters and emphasizing the working-class roots of a former teacher whose family used to run an extension cord out the window to borrow electricity from a neighbor's home. Johnson paid off his water bills and defeated Vallas in the runoff election by a close but comfortable margin on a platform promising to be the most progressive mayor in Chicago's history. The CTU took over City Hall, as Lightfoot long feared.

Lightfoot police superintendent David Brown almost immediately announced he would be returning to Texas as chief operating officer of a personal-injury law firm, a puzzling step down from leading the second-largest police department in America. When Lightfoot hosted Johnson at City Hall, she made sure the selection of a new top cop was the first issue she raised.

"We are going into a critical time period and I have been urging the senior leadership with the police department every single week, not to take their foot off the gas, making sure that they hold people accountable, that we continue to see the gains that started to come in, and eventually did come over the course of last year and have continued into this year," Lightfoot recalled in an interview with WBBM's Craig Dellimore. "But instability at the top of the police department is not a good thing, not only for the department and in leadership, but it's not a good thing for our city. And at this point, I think the mayor-elect is going to have to choose a new interim before he gets the final names provided to him later this summer or early in the fall. But it's also important that he takes some steps in the direction of the police department because he now will own responsibility for the day-to-day public safety of residents in the city. And he's got to work together with the police department. Absolutely he's got to hold them accountable. But he cannot afford to lose that department . . . and the officers over the course of this summer."

It was good advice but ironic. Lightfoot could've capped it off with: "Learn from my mistakes."

Lightfoot largely avoided local beat reporters on her way out. I was honestly disappointed in the mayor for refusing to speak with WTTW's Heather Cherone, *Sun-Times* reporter Fran Spielman, or me for farewell stories. It was a level of gutlessness I wouldn't have expected from the person I first covered. But she did do national press on the way out where she shared some of her thoughts. During a *Morning Joe* appearance, Lightfoot made some of her grievances known. "There's a reason why in 2020 part of Trump's national strategy was to go after cities and mayors like me by name, by city, not just me, but also Keisha Lance Bottoms in Atlanta, Muriel Bowser, in Washington, DC. And when the person with the biggest megaphone and biggest stage attacks you in a way that Trump attacked us, it unleashes a set of forces that are hard to control. Both dog whistles that were blown in 2020 are still resonating today. And it was fed by the uncertainty and the anger and then funded by right-wing forces that wanted to take down a big city mayor. Unfortunately," Lightfoot said, throwing in a diss on Vallas and Johnson, "the people who are jumping on the bandwagon of a Republican posing like a Democrat now got a Democratic socialist as the mayor. So, careful what you wish for."

Johnson inherited all the problems Lightfoot did, along with a new one: the migrant crisis. Lightfoot's first response, reiterating the city's welcoming status, was important for Chicago, but the administration badly mishandled the follow-through. As we reported in the *Tribune*, Lightfoot "failed for months to appoint someone to lead the mission, directed migrants to police stations and entered into costly contracts without a clear plan to transition new arrivals out of shelters." During early 2023, the buses slowed to a crawl and the city's urgency to build infrastructure stalled. But the buses began ramping up once Johnson took office, overwhelming his administration. In many ways, the migrant problem is harder to solve than COVID, because it affects fewer people directly. Because the coronavirus affected everyone, it was easier for all levels of government to mobilize and cut checks. Near the end of her administration, Lightfoot released a report called "The Welcoming City" that belied the problems to come: "Amid the confusion, we provided clarity. Amid the despair, we provided hope. We are Chicago—a Welcoming City. This report tells the story of how Chicago welcomed thousands of people with dignity and respect and provides a preview of our newest neighbors' next steps in their long journeys."

For his part, Johnson quickly moved to show he could be different from his predecessor. Before taking office, Johnson chose former chief of patrol Fred Waller to be his interim superintendent, a shrewd move aimed at reassuring cops that he wasn't as radical as they feared. During his inaugural address, Johnson looked to distinguish himself from Lightfoot by turning to face the alderpersons—and thanking them for their service. He spoke of unifying the city and hailed the "soul of Chicago." "It's alive and well in each and every one of us. We have so much in common, you all. We really do," Johnson said. "We know that we all suffer when these ills are allowed to fester and grow. These problems don't just affect particular neighborhoods, one community, or an ethnic group. It affects all of us." With his base of public workers (teachers), support on the West and South Sides, and positive persona, Johnson could be mayor for a long time. Or he could be eaten alive by the problems of Chicago and failures to adapt.

People wonder about Chicago's survival. It's a recurring topic, has been for decades. Can the city withstand its challenges with gun violence, segregation, and poverty? I tell them Chicago burned down in 1871 and rose from the ashes. It is the toughest city in America, built alongside one of the world's great lakes, a beautiful river flowing through its heart. That stays true no matter who works at City Hall.

ACKNOWLEDGMENTS

PEOPLE ASK ME WHERE I found the time to write a book. I tell them I half-assed my day job.*

The truth is, I feel tremendous gratitude to the *Chicago Tribune* for hiring me to cover City Hall and allowing me to pursue this project. It has been a great privilege to be the eyes and ears of nearly three million residents on their local government, and it wouldn't have been possible without support from Mitch Pugh, Peter Kendall, Phil Jurik, Jane Hirt, Colin McMahon, Chrissy Taylor, Robin Daughtridge, and Diana Wallace. But nobody did more for me than Bruce Dold.

Joe Biesk deserves his own line after editing me for years. He's kind of a big deal.

For two years I served as president of the Chicago Tribune Guild. In that time and since, our union won major victories against cruel odds, and I'm eternally grateful to our newsroom for supporting me as chair and the leadership team that helped keep the *Tribune* together. In particular, I'm grateful to Stacy St. Clair, Chris Boghossian, Christy Gutowski, Elise De Los Santos, Megan Crepeau, Jennifer Smith Richards, Sarah Freishtat, Steve Johnson, Madeline Buckley, Darcel Rockett, and Stacey Wescott.

I've been lucky to have shared bylines with dozens of colleagues. Everyone I've met in the newsroom has taught me something new about work and life.

I'm lucky to have received a great education with Chicago Public Schools and the University of Illinois at Chicago, where I learned everything I needed to make my way through the world. Maggie Malone gave me my first opportunity to practice newspapering at the *Flame*. Andy Van De Voorde hired me to my first real job. Mike Lacey inspired me with his credo, "As a journalist,

---

* To any corporate goons reading this and clutching dollars: it's a joke.

if you don't get up in the morning and say 'fuck you' to someone, why even do it?" Rick Barrs nurtured me as a young man who didn't know half as much as he thought. Kevin Hoffman was the worst boss I ever had but he taught me so much about writing. Alice Yin has been the best City Hall partner I can imagine. Joe Mahr took my love of FOIA and taught me how to really cook.

Thank you, John Conroy, for inspiring me to become a journalist. I'm still mad at you for that.

When I first started covering Chicago politics, Dan Mihalopoulos told me not to underestimate any of the alderpersons. Some of them might seem goofy, he said, but each of them was smart enough to reach City Council. For a decade, you've given me grounded advice and been a friend. Thanks to your family, too, for sharing.

It's an honor to work with and read the City Hall press corps, including folks who pop in and out: Mary Ann Ahern, Isis Almeida, Kelly Bauer, John Byrne, Bill Cameron, Elizabeth Campbell, Alma Campos, Heather Cherone, Jim Daley, Hal Dardick, Craig Dellimore, Monica Eng, Mariano Gielis, Tim Hecke, Erin Hegarty, Tonia Hill, Morgan Johnson, Shia Kapos, Dana Kozlov, Justin Laurence, Melody Mercado, Quinn Myers, A. D. Quig, Bill Ruthhart, Sarah Schulte, Paris Schutz, Shruti Singh, Mitch Smith, Sylvia Snowden, Fran Spielman, Becky Vevea, Mallory Vor Broker, Tiffany Walden, Craig Wall, and Mariah Woelfel.

Dear Lolly Bowean: I wish I were half the journalist you are.

Nina Ruvinsky is my rock. I love you. Also, shout-out to Sadie and Zooey.

My agent, Keely Boeving, was the first person to throw their support behind this idea. I'm sorry I subjected you to the grime of Chicago politics. Jerome Pohlen guided me through a daunting process with grace and patience. Kinsey Crowley helped with early research. Ben Joravsky and Jamie Kalven gave critical feedback. Alison Flowers reminded me to insert a favorite anecdote. Sergio Socite has been my best friend since college, and I wouldn't be anywhere without you.

My father, the original Gregory Royal Pratt, didn't leave me much except an interest in words, and that's enough. I'm lucky to know Grandma June, Aunts Toni and Rema, Uncle Dean, Cousins Anthony, Nicole, and Jamie, and Desiree.

My mother, Alicia Chavez, worked factory jobs to raise me under tough circumstances. There's no one I admire more. I inherited my interest in government and politics from Grandma Lides. Grandpa Salvador taught me mischief and love of hot dogs. Uncle Joel taught me responsibility and kindness, as he was effectively my dad. Much love to Uncles Chava, Arturo, Jose, and Luis and Aunt Maricella, as well as all my cousins, especially Andres and Baby Chava. Ratita, Greyback, and Lina have shown unconditional love—as long as they got their food and scritches.

Near the end of this writing journey, I woke up in a panic when I realized I had failed to mention Ja'Mal Green's bus. I regret the error.

I'm proud to have developed strong relationships with a wide array of public officials and scoundrels. Sometimes I get asked, why do people talk to you? And I say, obviously to be in a book. But in truth, there are a lot of dedicated public servants trying to make their city a better place who have been invaluable resources in my reporting and life. I won't embarrass you by naming you.

I appreciate Mayor Lori Lightfoot's willingness to serve, no matter how it ended.

NOTES

Prologue: Checkers

"Nailed it": Katherine Rosenberg-Douglas, "Mayor Lori Lightfoot Has Pizza Lunch with 4-Year-Old Boy Who Dressed as Her for Halloween," *Chicago Tribune*, November 5, 2019.

"They've endorsed Brandon Johnson": Dave Weigel, "Lightfoot scoffing at CTU's mayoral endorsement: 'They've endorsed Brandon Johnson. God bless. Brandon Johnson isn't going to be the mayor of this city,'" Twitter, January 21, 2023, https://twitter .com/daveweigel/status/1616891444580564993.

life-expectancy gap: Lisa Schencker, "Chicago's Lifespan Gap," *Chicago Tribune*, June 6, 2019.

1. The Breach

"100-yard stare": Quinn Ford, "Cops: Boy, 17, Fatally Shot by Officer After Refusing to Drop Knife," *Chicago Tribune*, October 21, 2014.

CHICAGO POLICE HAVE TOLD: Jamie Kalven, "Sixteen Shots," *Slate*, February 10, 2015, https://slate.com/news-and-politics/2015/02/laquan-mcdonald-shooting -a-recently-obtained-autopsy-report-on-the-dead-teen-complicates-the-chicago -police-departments-story.html.

"The plaintiffs contend very vehemently": Fran Spielman, "What Did Top City Lawyer Tell Aldermen About $5M Settlement for McDonald Family?," *Chicago Sun-Times*, December 6, 2015.

"I'm not worried about rioting": Fran Spielman, "Alderman Demands Release of Video of Police Officer Shooting Black Teenager," *Chicago Sun-Times*, April 15, 2015.

Calling herself a "girl scout": Maudlyne Ihejirika, "The Woman at the Center of Rahm Emanuel's Efforts to Reform the Police," *Chicago Sun-Times*, February 14, 2016.

"Get on the right foot": Dan Protess and Paris Schutz, "Before She Was Mayor: An In-Depth Profile of Lori Lightfoot," WTTW-TV, May 20, 2019, https://news.wttw .com/2019/05/20/profile-chicago-mayor-lori-lightfoot.

"very much afraid of failure": Gregory Pratt and Bill Ruthhart, "From Police Reform to the Chicago Question of Whether Ketchup Goes on a Hot Dog, Mayoral Candidates Debate," *Chicago Tribune*, February 19, 2019.

IMMENSE BLUNDER BY BIGGEST FIRM: James Warren, Maurice Possley, and Joseph Tybor, "Immense Blunder by Biggest Firm," *Chicago Tribune*, January 3, 1989.

"spelling out his philosophy": Cam Simpson, "Ald. Jones Convicted in Shovel Case," *Chicago Sun-Times*, January 29, 1999.

"The alderman is an unrepentant crook": Matt O'Connor, "Silver Shovel Target Jones Gets 41 Months," *Chicago Tribune*, June 12, 1999.

"had made a misleading statement": Natasha Korecki and Kristen East, "Why the U.S. Attorney Post Eluded Lori Lightfoot—Springfield Advances ERA—New Round of Gun Bills," *Politico*, May 31, 2018, https://www.politico.com/newsletters/illinois -playbook/2018/05/31/why-the-us-attorney-post-eluded-lori-lightfoot-springfield -advances-era-makes-history-new-round-of-gun-bills-274320.

"a junior lawyer following": John Byrne and Gregory Pratt, "Toni Preckwinkle's Top Adviser Fired After Online Post Invoking Nazis to Criticize Lori Lightfoot," *Chicago Tribune*, February 22, 2019.

"a good number": David Fogel, "Proposed Revamping of Office of Professional Standards" (memorandum), October 19, 1987, Police Torture Archive, https:// chicagopolicetorturearchive.com/.

"Lawyers who defend police-torture": John Conroy, "Blind Justices," *Chicago Reader*, November 30, 2006.

"window dressing": Ferman Mentrell Beckless, "OPS Head Pledges Not to be Part of 'Window Dressing,'" *Chicago Defender*, June 10, 2002.

"I realize that accepting this job": Beckless, "OPS Head Pledges."

"As a citizen": Frank Main, "'Tenacious' New Cop Watchdog," *Chicago Sun-Times*, June 7, 2002.

"to complete the investigation": Art Golab, "Hillard 'Upset' by Cops' Conduct," *Chicago Sun-Times*, April 26, 2003.

"We will not turn this": Carlos Sadovi, "Activist's Death Sparking Questions," *Chicago Tribune*, May 30, 2004.

argued *"that Molina's death"*: Jason Meisner, "Jury Awards $1M in '04 Lockup Death," *Chicago Tribune*, November 5, 2023.

"walking a difficult line": Stephen Sonneveld, "Lesbian Lawyer Lives Her Passion," *Windy City Times*, April 24, 2013.

"that it created an environment": Steve Warmbir, "U.S. Jury Fines City $1 Million," *Chicago Sun-Times*, May 3, 2003.

"in a high crime neighborhood": David Heinzmann, "U.S. Attorney Candidate Added to Legal Team in High-Stakes Police Neglect Case," *Chicago Tribune*, December 6, 2012.

2. "Sixteen Shots and a Cover Up"

"Why were those shots necessary?": Bloomberg, "Ferguson Cop Testified That He Feared for His Life," *Daily Herald* (Chicago), November 25, 2014, https://www.dailyherald .com/article/20141125/business/141129002/.

"It's very demoralizing to police": Cynthia Hubert, "DA: Lodi Police Officers Justified in Killing Mentally Ill Army Vet," *Sacramento Bee*, December 30, 2014.

"We have allowed our police": Aaron C. Davis, "'YouTube Effect' Has Left Police Officers Under Siege, Law Enforcement Leaders Say," *Washington Post*, October 8, 2015.

Of the eighteen who kept their jobs: Fran Spielman, "Emanuel Continues Shakeup of Chicago Police Board," *Chicago Sun-Times*, July 5, 2015.

"We've seen with what's happening": Fran Spielman, "Former Federal Prosecutor Picked to Run Chicago Police Board," *Chicago Sun-Times*, May 31, 2015.

"Many of our communities": Fran Spielman, "New Police Board President Walks a Tightrope at Confirmation Hearing," *Chicago Sun-Times*, July 21, 2015.

"opened an investigation into the shooting": Dan Hinkel and Matthew Walberg, "Long Inquiry Before Charges in Laquan McDonald Shooting Prompts Scrutiny," *Chicago Tribune*, November 25, 2015.

"a federal law that bans": Timothy M. Phelps, Annie Sweeney, and Steve Mills, "Feds to Conduct Civil Rights Probe of Chicago Police," *Chicago Tribune*, December 7, 2015.

"The shooting of Laquan McDonald": Mary Wisniewski, "Chicago Creates Police Task Force After Officer Charged with Murder," Reuters, https://www.reuters.com /article/us-usa-race-taskforce-idUSKBN0TK45K20151201.

"On one hand, ending up": Bill Ruthhart and Annie Sweeney, "Emanuel Now Open to Justice Department Review of Chicago Police," *Chicago Tribune*, December 3, 2015.

"accountability in the context": Fran Spielman, "Police Board Launches Search for New Chicago Police Superintendent," *Chicago Sun-Times*, December 10, 2015.

"He is a different kind": Fran Spielman, "Emanuel in Political No-Win Situation with Top-Cop Pick," *Chicago Sun-Times*, March 18, 2016.

A March 22 Tribune story: Bill Ruthhart, "Emanuel Says He Won't Be Rushed on Top Cop Choice," *Chicago Tribune*, March 22, 2016.

"on one word": Bill Ruthhart and John Byrne, "Emanuel: New Top Cop Johnson Will 'Restore Trust and Restore Pride' in CPD," *Chicago Tribune*, March 28, 2016.

"no regard for the sanctity": Monica Davey and Mitch Smith, "Chicago Police Dept. Plagued by Systemic Racism, Task Force Finds," *New York Times*, April 13, 2016.

"We made it very hard for people": Andy Grimm and Fran Spielman, "Racism, Lack of Accountability Plague Chicago Police Department," *Chicago Sun-Times*, April 13, 2016.

"I don't really think": Bill Ruthhart, "Emanuel Acknowledges Racism in Chicago Police Department," *Chicago Tribune*, April 13, 2016.

"I do share your concern": Andrew Kaczynski, "Attorney General Jeff Sessions: Consent Decrees 'Can Reduce Morale of the Police Officers,'" CNN, April 14, 2017, https://www.cnn.com/2017/04/14/politics/kfile-sessions-consent-decrees/index.html.

"fundamentally flawed" and *"will not advance the cause"*: Fran Spielman, "Police Board Prez Lightfoot Says Reform Memo 'Fundamentally Flawed,'" *Chicago Sun-Times*, June 30, 2017.

"indulging in fantasy": Bill Ruthhart, "Emanuel Police Board Chair Says Mayor's Reform Approach Is 'Set Up for Failure,'" *Chicago Tribune*, June 29, 2017.

"The mayor and his people": Ruthhart, "Emanuel Police Board Chair."

3. Slaying Goliath

"People across the city": Erika Wozniak and Jen Sabella, "The Lori Lightfoot and Amara Enyia Show," August 23, 2016, in *The Girl Talk*, podcast, 69:38, https://www.spreaker.com/user/yeahbutstill/the-girl-talk-the-lori-lightfoot-and-ama.

"totally mischaracterized my comments": Kim Janssen, "First 'Flattered,' Police Board Boss Lightfoot Later Slams Door on Mayoral Run," *Chicago Tribune*, August 24, 2016.

"He [expanded] full-day kindergarten": Bill Ruthhart, "Chicago Mayor Rahm Emanuel Explains the Surprise That Shook the City and Why He Won't Seek Re-Election," *Chicago Tribune*, September 5, 2018.

"I'm going to look through it": Brandis Friedman, "Mayor Declines to Say Whether He'll Reappoint Police Board President," WTTW-TV, July 31, 2017, https://news.wttw.com/2017/07/31/mayor-declines-say-whether-he-ll-reappoint-police-board-president.

"It's all about the next election": Bill Ruthhart and John Byrne, "'People Don't Like the Mayor,' Vallas Says in Unsparing Campaign Kickoff Against Emanuel," *Chicago Tribune*, May 2, 2018.

a glowing profile in the Wall Street Journal: Dorothy J. Gaiter, "He Swept Floors and Later Mopped Up in the Gospel Biz," *Wall Street Journal*, October 15, 1996.

"My money that I worked hard for": Gregory Pratt, "Mayoral Hopeful Who Gave Thousands in Cash, Checks: 'I'm Just Tired of White People Telling Me What to Do,'" *Chicago Tribune*, August 9, 2018.

"Buying votes on the West Side": Pratt, "Mayoral Hopeful."

"I'm just tired of": Pratt, "Mayoral Hopeful."

"Between the taxes, our economy" to *"While I am very emotional"*: Bill Ruthhart, "Garry McCarthy, Former Top Cop Fired by Rahm Emanuel, Details Why He's Challenging Him for Chicago Mayor," *Chicago Tribune*, March 21, 2018.

"If I were to make that decision": John Byrne, "Police Board Boss Lori Lightfoot Says She's Considering Mayoral Run, But Is 'Not There Yet,'" *Chicago Tribune*, April 10, 2018.

"Thank God they're making progress": Mary Ann Ahern, "Lori Lightfoot Considers Run for Chicago Mayor," NBC Chicago, April 10, 2018, article and video, 1:24, https://www.nbcchicago.com/news/local/lori-lightfoot-considers-run-for-chicago-mayor/43708/.

"He supposedly once said": David Marchese, "Lori Lightfoot, Mayor of Chicago, on Who's Hurt by Defunding Police," *New York Times*, June 22, 2020.

"I'm here to talk about": Liz Baudler, "Lightfoot Formally Announces Mayoral Candidacy," *Windy City Times*, May 10, 2018.

She did not come close: Bill Ruthhart, "Lightfoot Reports $243K in Campaign Cash, Tops Among Emanuel Challengers," *Chicago Tribune*, May 17, 2018.

"There is a wave of women" to *"not an incredibly well-run system"*: Addy Baird, "Lori Lightfoot Claims She's the Next Progressive Darling, Democratic Socialists Say Otherwise," ThinkProgress, July 12, 2018, https://thinkprogress.org/lori-lightfoot-a-oc-1c3435db6232/.

"that we also don't shy away": Barnini Chakraborty, "Rahm Emanuel Under Increasing Fire for Linking Chicago Violence and Morals in Minority Neighborhoods," Fox News, August 18, 2018, https://www.foxnews.com/us/rahm-emanuel-under-increasing-fire-for-linking-chicago-violence-and-morals-in-minority-neighborhoods.

"He doesn't see us": Bill Ruthhart, "Chicago's Mayoral Race on Display as Emanuel, Opponents Politick at Bud Billiken Parade," *Chicago Tribune*, August 11, 2018.

LIKE GOD, YOU KNOW: Jacqueline Heard, "Like God, You Know He's There," *Chicago Tribune*, May 26, 1996.

"My children are my children": Nicole Cardos, "Chicago Attorney Jerry Joyce Talks About His Bid for Mayor," WTTW-TV, January 10, 2019, article and video, 10:39, https://news.wttw.com/2019/01/10/chicago-attorney-jerry-joyce-talks-about-his-bid-mayor.

"This has been the job": Ruthhart, "Chicago Mayor Rahm Emanuel Explains."

"This is undeniably big news": Ruthhart, "Chicago Mayor Rahm Emanual Explains."

"No," Emanuel responded: John Byrne, "Mayor Rahm Emanuel Says Chicago's Next Leader Isn't in the Race Yet," *Chicago Tribune*, September 5, 2018.

4. Pirate Booty

"We need to find a worthy": Mike Riopell, "Comptroller Susana Mendoza Demurs on Mayoral Run Speculation, Doesn't Rule Out a Candidacy," *Chicago Tribune*, September 5, 2018.

"Say cheese!": John Kass, "Comptroller Mendoza Confronts Chicago Tough Guy Leaving Crash Scene with 2 Magic Words: Say Cheese!," *Chicago Tribune*, September 16, 2017.

"Take your fucking tampon out": Lisa Donovan, "Mendoza's Chicago: The City Has a New Clerk, and She's Not a 'Go-Along, Get-Along' Politician," NPR Illinois, February 1, 2018, https://www.nprillinois.org/statehouse/2012-02-01/mendozas-chicago-the-city-has-a-new-clerk-and-shes-not-a-go-along-get-along-politician.

"I'm not going to change my name": Bill Ruthhart, "'I'm Not Going to Change My Name': Bill Daley on Why He's Seeking to Become Family's Third Chicago Mayor," *Chicago Tribune*, September 17, 2018.

"I want to work with somebody": Bill Ruthhart, "Chance the Rapper Brings His Star Power to a Long-Shot Campaign, Backing Amara Enyia for Chicago Mayor," *Chicago Tribune*, October 16, 2018.

"Amara doesn't have anything": *City So Real*, episode 2, "Blood Sport," directed by Steve James, aired on National Geographic, October 29, 2020, https://films.nationalgeographic.com/citysoreal.

"He said he was thinking": Jose Martinez, "Amara Enyia Recalls Meeting with Kanye West: 'He Told Me He Doesn't Support Trump's Views,'" Complex, February 25, 2019, https://www.complex.com/music/a/jose-martinez/chicago-mayoral-candidate-amara-enyia-on-kanye-west-he-told-me-he-doesnt-support-trumps-views.

"This notion that city government": John Kass, "Emanuel Still Pulling Strings in the City of Tribes," *Chicago Tribune*, September 6, 2018.

"The insulting part of that": John Byrne, "Lori Lightfoot Says She's Not Leaving Chicago Mayoral Race, Accuses Toni Preckwinkle of 'Machine-Style Bullying,'" *Chicago Tribune*, October 23, 2018.

Later, the Tribune reported Preckwinkle: Ray Long and Hal Dardick, "Toni Preckwinkle Fired Her Chief of Staff This Fall. But an Adviser Warned Her Months Earlier About His Treatment of Women," *Chicago Tribune*, November 8, 2018.

"mother figure": Gregory Pratt, "Toni Preckwinkle's Former Security Chief Alleges She Fired Him to Save Her Mayoral Campaign," *Chicago Tribune*, December 7, 2018.

"I can't stand these Mexicans": Gregory Pratt, "Cook County Promoted Former Chicago Alderman Once Recommended for Firing After Allegedly Saying, 'I Can't Stand These Mexicans,'" *Chicago Tribune*, October 31, 2018.

"I am disappointed that": David Jackson and Ray Long, "Obama's First Campaign Seen as Clouding Image," *Chicago Tribune*, April 8, 2007.

"As city employees": Alexandra Arriaga, "Lightfoot: Give Preckwinkle a 'Bag of Coal' for Bad-Faith Petition Challenges," *Chicago Sun-Times*, December 17, 2018.

"This is a rigged game": *City So Real*, "Blood Sport."

"I will be the first and only": Craig Wall, "Chicago Mayor's Race: Toni Preckwinkle Withdraws Petition Challenge to Lori Lightfoot," ABC Chicago, December 24, 2018, article and video, 1:47, https://abc7chicago.com/toni-preckwinkle-lori-lightfoot-chicago-mayors-race-politics/4960748/.

5. Butcher Paper

"Mount Henry": Robin Amer, Season 1, 2018, in *The City*, podcast, https://www.thecitypodcast.com/season-1/.

Medrano pleaded guilty to extortion: John W. Fountain, "Ex-Alderman with a Past Puts Hopes in the Voters," *New York Times*, December 21, 2002.

"presided over a heated three-hour hearing": David Kidwell, Patrick Judge, and Dan Mihalopoulos, "The King of Recusals: How Ald. Ed Burke's Private Law Business Intersects with His Public Power," WBEZ Chicago, December 26, 2018, article and audio, 7:49, https://www.wbez.org/stories/the-king-of-recusals-how-ald-ed-burkes-private-law-business-intersects-with-his-public-power/66a3a501-4b73-4ccd-b676-d794854c1554.

Despite the baggage: Paris Schutz, "Why Aldermen Who Need Extra Help Call Ed Burke," WTTW-TV, March 14, 2019, article and video, 3:30, https://news.wttw.com/2019/03/14/why-aldermen-who-need-extra-help-call-ed-burke.

"I think Ald. Burke should reconsider": Nicole Cardos, "After 23 Years on City Council, Ald. Solis Not Seeking Re-Election," WTTW-TV, November 26, 2018, article and video, 7:51, https://news.wttw.com/2018/11/26/after-23-years-city-council-ald-solis-not-seeking-re-election.

"I've been in office": Louis Casiano, "Chicago Alderman Expects to be Vindicated After Federal Agents Raid His Offices," Fox News, November 30, 2018, https://www.foxnews.com/politics/federal-agents-raid-office-of-chicago-alderman-who-formally-represented-trump-on-tax-dispuites.

"political silence": Bill Ruthhart, Gregory Pratt, and John Byrne, "Political Silence: Why the Federal Raid on Powerful Ald. Ed Burke Has Left Chicago Mayoral Candidates Quiet," *Chicago Tribune*, December 3, 2018.

"I like Gery Chico": Fran Spielman, "Ald. Ed Burke Endorses Old Friend, Former Employee Gery Chico in Race for Mayor," *Chicago Sun-Times*, October 22, 2018.

"It seems all these other folks": Ruthhart, Pratt, and Byrne, "Political Silence."

"another politician": Bill Ruthhart and Jason Meisner, "Campaign Money Tied to Ald. Edward Burke's Alleged Extortion Scheme Was Intended for County Board President Toni Preckwinkle," *Chicago Tribune*, January 3, 2019.

"Are the written timesheets": Gregory Pratt, "Toni Preckwinkle's Administration Hired Ald. Edward Burke's Son to Nearly $100K-a-Year County Job," *Chicago Tribune*, January 4, 2019.

"an employee of the county": Bill Ruthhart, "At *Tribune* Meeting, Five Chicago Mayoral Candidates Duck Specifics on How to Fill Pension Hole," *Chicago Tribune*, January 15, 2019.

"I'm leaving, going to watch": Gregory Pratt, "Ald. Edward Burke's Son Was Under Investigation for Misconduct Allegations When Toni Preckwinkle's Administration Hired Him," *Chicago Tribune*, January 23, 2019.

"I had a meeting with Ed Burke": Gregory Pratt, "Preckwinkle, Burke Met Before Son's Job," *Chicago Tribune*, January 24, 2019.

"I want to get a good massage": Jon Seidel et al., "Viagra, Sex Acts, Use of a Luxury Farm: Feds Detail Investigation of Ald. Solis," *Chicago Sun-Times*, January 29, 2019.

"How about anything?": Fran Spielman, "Aldermen Named in Secretly Recorded Chat Admit Sending Business to Reyes' Firm," *Chicago Sun-Times*, February 4, 2019.

"The political machine": Lori Lightfoot, "The political machine is crumbling . . . ," Twitter, January 23, 2019, https://twitter.com/LoriLightfoot/status/1088076538787057667.

"Voters don't want a candidate": Amanda Vinicky, "Speaker Madigan the Latest Snared in Solis Wiretap," WTTW-TV, January 29, 2019, article and video, 9:55, https://news.wttw.com/2019/01/29/danny-solis-fbi-recording-michael-madigan.

"challenge with these forums": Bill Ruthhart, "How a Federal City Hall Corruption Investigation Is Dominating Chicago's Crowded Race for Mayor," *Chicago Tribune*, February 1, 2019.

"Bill Daley has barely been out here": Ruthhart, "How a Federal City Hall Corruption Investigation."

"Some of these people in this group": Ruthhart, "How a Federal City Hall Corruption Investigation."

"Never to rarely do I get asked": Ruthhart, "How a Federal City Hall Corruption Investigation."

Lightfoot reported making an average: Bill Ruthhart, "Financial Secrecy," *Chicago Tribune*, December 13, 2019.

"I was asleep and Amy woke me": City So Real, episode 4, "If You Want to Break the Machine," directed by Steve James, aired on National Geographic, October 29, 2020, https://films.nationalgeographic.com/citysoreal.

"This sort of Trump-style": John Byrne, "Lori Lightfoot Gets in Shouting Match with Preckwinkle Ally over Proposal to Appoint County Assessor," *Chicago Tribune*, February 18, 2019.

"It was good business for": Bill Ruthhart and Gregory Pratt, "Mendoza on Offensive in Mayoral TV Debate," *Chicago Tribune*, February 18, 2019.

"So what do you think of us now?": Julie Bosman, Mitch Smith, and Monica Davey, "Two African-American Women Are Headed for Runoff in Chicago's Mayor Race," *New York Times*, February 26, 2019, https://www.nytimes.com/2019/02/26/us/chicago-election.html.

6. Bring in the Light

"I am an independent reform candidate": Bill Ruthhart and John Byrne, "Hours After Historic Election, Lori Lightfoot and Toni Preckwinkle Each Argue They're More Progressive Than the Other," *Chicago Tribune*, February 27, 2019.

"I think I have the strongest": Ruthhart and Byrne, "Hours After Historic Election."

"We're making strategic decisions": Juan Perez Jr., "With 2 Weeks Before Mayoral Election, Toni Preckwinkle Not Airing TV Ads: 'We're Making Strategic Decisions,'" *Chicago Tribune*, March 19, 2019.

"I would never use VIP Limo": Lori L., review of VIP Limousine, Yelp, August 20, 2017, https://www.yelp.com/biz/vip-limousine-chicago-4?hrid=kujg2NNrI90eN57e4J4_ZA.

I watched Lightfoot argue with a woman: Gregory Pratt, "How Chicago Mayoral Candidate Lori Lightfoot Shakes 'Wealthy Corporate Lawyer' Label on the Campaign Trail," *Chicago Tribune*, March 29, 2019.

"It's important to remember": Gregory Pratt and Juan Perez, "Toni Preckwinkle and Lori Lightfoot Clash over 'Blood on Hands' Comment During Debate," *Chicago Tribune*, March 26, 2019.

"You've made the hallmark": Juan Perez and Gregory Pratt, "In Final TV Debate, Lori Lightfoot Conjures Ronald Reagan in Countering Toni Preckwinkle: 'There She Goes Again,'" *Chicago Tribune*, March 27, 2019.

"This is a person who is complaining": Perez and Pratt, "In Final TV Debate."

"This election is really about": Bill Ruthhart and Gregory Pratt, "Racial Politics Heat Up in Chicago Mayor's Race with Lori Lightfoot Under Attack at Toni Preckwinkle Rally," *Chicago Tribune*, March 23, 2019.

"racist bully boy": Kim Janssen, "Preckwinkle Calls Former Top Cop Garry McCarthy a 'Racist Bully Boy,'" *Chicago Tribune*, November 2, 2016.

7. "I Support Bozo"

"I don't believe what we need": Ben Joravsky, "Rahm Decrees: No Elected School Board Vote for You!," *Chicago Reader*, October 14, 2014.

"stand shoulder to shoulder" and *"She will need your support"*: Gregory Pratt, "Aldermen Pay Tribute to Chicago Mayor Rahm Emanuel in His Final City Council Meeting. Ald. Walter Burnett: 'You a Hustler, Man. In a Good Way!,'" *Chicago Tribune*, April 10, 2019.

"slow down": Lightfoot for Chicago, Lincoln Yards press release, 2018, https://lightfootforchicago.com/press-release-lightfoot-slow-down-lincoln-yards-to-allow-for-transparency-collaboration/ (site discontinued).

"Enjoy this moment in the sun": Fran Spielman and Tina Sfondeles, "Lightfoot to Developers of 'The 78,' Lincoln Yards: 'Enjoy Your Day in the Sun,'" *Chicago Sun-Times*, April 11, 2019.

"The machine was built to last": Julie Bosman and Mitch Smith, "Lori Lightfoot, Chicago's Mayor-Elect, in Her Own Words: 'I'm Ready to Fight,'" *New York Times*, April 8, 2019.

"People think you can't": Jseattle, "Another Hill Candidate for City Council: Classen's Hope for the 'Capitol Hill Model,'" *Capitol Hill Seattle Blog*, April 14, 2011, https://www.capitolhillseattle.com/2011/04/another-hill-candidate-for-city-council-classens-hope-for-the-capitol-hill-model/.

"The short version is": Gregory Pratt, "Chicago Mayor-Elect Lori Lightfoot Takes Part in Back of the Yards Peace March: 'We Want the Violence to End,'" *Chicago Tribune*, May 18, 2019.

8. "Trained Seals"

"Chicago ain't ready for reform": June Sawyers, "Chicago Politics in the Grand Style of 'Paddy' Bauler," *Chicago Tribune*, September 11, 1988.

"If you're not doing anything wrong": John Byrne and Gregory Pratt, "Chicago Aldermen React to Mayor Lori Lightfoot's Inaugural Address," *Chicago Tribune*, May 20, 2019.

"take it outside 'cause": Maya Dukmasova, "Black Caucus Members Eject Protesters from Fund-Raiser, Call Themselves 'Gangsters,'" *Chicago Reader*, July 27, 2019.

"Anything further, alderman?": Fran Spielman, "Lightfoot Bests Burke in Early City Council Skirmish," *Chicago Sun-Times*, May 29, 2019.

"we were interrupted by Ald. Burke's soliloquy": John Byrne, Juan Perez, and Gregory Pratt, "In First Test, Lightfoot Bests Burke as She Pushes Agenda," *Chicago Tribune*, May 30, 2019.

It led to an embarrassing story: Fran Spielman, "Ald. John Arena Under Fire for Demanding Parking Perk Before Cubs-Sox Game," *Chicago Sun-Times*, May 21, 2018.

He later resigned his post: Fran Spielman, "Former Alderman Resigning from City Planning Job," *Chicago Sun-Times*, January 3, 2020.

"If we start a precedent": John Byrne and Gregory Pratt, "Mayor Lightfoot Tells Alderman Who Opposed Her Hiring His Predecessor to a $123,996-a-Year Job to Worry About 'What Matters to His Ward,'" *Chicago Tribune*, October 2, 2019.

"People truly associate me": Gregory Pratt, "Chicago Treasurer Melissa Conyears-Ervin Hired Private Security Using Taxpayer Funds After CPD Found There Was No Threat. She Disagreed, Saying People Call Her 'The Money Lady,'" *Chicago Tribune*, November 25, 2019.

"I think about that movie": John Byrne and Gregory Pratt, "Mayor Lori Lightfoot Blasts Aldermen over Their Debate of Possible Study of Whether LGBTQ Businesses Face Discrimination in Getting Government Contracts: 'Our Children Are Watching,'" *Chicago Tribune*, January 15, 2020.

"You should still have aldermanic": Fran Spielman, "Lightfoot's Most Powerful City Council Ally Urges Her to Abandon Threat to Abolish Aldermanic Prerogative over Zoning," *Chicago Sun-Times*, January 24, 2020.

9. Early Successes

"They offered up Black ministers": Paris Schutz, "Lightfoot Claims Uber Paid Off African American Ministers," WTTW-TV, November 13, 2019, article and video, 5:07, https://news.wttw.com/2019/11/13/lightfoot-claims-uber-paid-african-american-ministers.

"Most aldermen, most politicians, are hos": Jeff Coen and Dan Mihalopoulos, "Former Alderman Pleads Guilty to Fraud," *Chicago Tribune*, August 7, 2008.

"Some of the largest investments": Gregory Pratt, "Mayor Lori Lightfoot's Signature Invest South/West Program Is 3 Years Old. But Some of Its Big Projects Were Already Planned When She Took Office," *Chicago Tribune*, January 13, 2023.

"Here's my new practice for memos": John Byrne and Gregory Pratt, "As Chicago Mayor Lori Lightfoot's Two-Year Anniversary Approaches, Top-Level Vacancies Are

Mounting: 'This Has Been a Very Tough Year, I Think, on a Lot of People,'" *Chicago Tribune*, May 13, 2021.

"We are surrounded by impropriety": Todd Feurer, "Aldermen Back Crackdown on Lobbying by Elected Officials; 'This BS Is Over With,'" CBS Chicago, December 4, 2019, https://www.cbsnews.com/chicago/news/aldermen-city-council-lobbying -ban/.

10. Accountability Mondays

"have to set the example": Gregory Pratt and Jeremy Gorner, "Mayor Lori Lightfoot Says No Summer Vacations for Chicago Police Brass, but One Leader Still Took a Trip," *Chicago Tribune*, June 14, 2019.

Despite being wealthy men: Gregory Pratt and Jeremy Gorner, "Chicago Police Still Providing Former Mayors Richard M. Daley and Rahm Emanuel Taxpayer-Funded Security Details," *Chicago Tribune*, November 5, 2019.

"This is a guy who has sacrificed": Gregory Pratt, "Chicago Mayor Lori Lightfoot Defends Police Superintendent Eddie Johnson's Tenure as He Faces Investigation," *Chicago Tribune*, October 24, 2019.

"We're happy to take your questions": Mark Konkol, "Please Pretend Retiring Chicago Top Cop Isn't Under Investigation," *Patch*, November 7, 2019, https://patch.com /illinois/chicago/please-pretend-retiring-chicago-top-cop-isnt-under-investigation.

"no question whether the shooting": Jeremy Gorner, Dan Hinkel, and Todd Lighty, "Top Police Brass Defended Laquan McDonald Shooting After Seeing Video, Records Show," *Chicago Tribune*, December 23, 2016.

"While at some point the IG's report": Jeremy Gorner, Gregory Pratt, and John Byrne, "Mayor Lori Lightfoot Fires Chicago's Police Superintendent Weeks Before His Retirement: 'Eddie Johnson Intentionally Lied to Me,'" *Chicago Tribune*, December 3, 2019.

"While I recognize this news": Gorner, Pratt, and Byrne, "Mayor Lori Lightfoot Fires."

11. "All Is Not Forgotten"

"All is not forgotten": Fran Spielman, "All 7 Members of the Chicago Board of Education Step Down," *Chicago Sun-Times*, May 22, 2019.

"issued billions of dollars": Jason Grotto, Alex Richards, and Heather Gillers, "Despite Borrowing $10 Billion to Fund School Construction, Chicago Still Has an Overcrowding Problem. Millions Also Went to Schools That Now Stand Empty," *Chicago Tribune*, December 7, 2013.

"Dartmouth was a really bad experience": Lisa Furlong, "Karen (Jennings) Lewis," *Dartmouth Alumni Magazine*, May/June 2011, https://dartmouthalumnimagazine.com/articles/karen-jennings-lewis-%E2%80%9974.

"the real cause of the achievement gap": Furlong, "Karen (Jennings) Lewis."

"That was the moment I was radicalized": Heidi Stevens, "Stacy Davis Gates Won't Back Down," *Chicago*, April 9, 2022, https://www.chicagomag.com/chicago-magazine/may-2022/stacy-davis-gates-wont-back-down/.

"Fuck you, Lewis": Ben Joravsky, "Mayor Rahm to Karen Lewis: Won't You Be My Friend?," *Chicago Reader*, September 12, 2013.

"I know bad words too": Kim Janssen, "On Eve of Battle, CTU Boss Karen Lewis Offers Olive Branch to Rahm," *Chicago Tribune*, September 28, 2016.

"the strike that brought teachers unions": Dylan Scott, "The Strike That Brought Teachers Unions Back from the Dead," *Vox*, last modified July 5, 2019, https://www.vox.com/the-highlight/2019/6/28/18662706/chicago-teachers-unions-strike-labor-movement.

"We planted seeds in 2015": Gregory Pratt, "Amid Departures and Upheaval, Progressive Candidates See Path to Chicago City Council," *Chicago Tribune*, January 19, 2019.

12. La La Land

"We have a governor who has": Juan Perez, "'Where Will the Money Come From? Rich People,' Chicago Teachers Union Says as It Seeks Increased Pay, Staffing in Contract," *Chicago Tribune*, January 15, 2019.

"We are committed to negotiating": Gregory Pratt, "As Chicago Teacher Contract Issues Remain Unsettled, CPS and CTU Ramp Up Rhetoric Looking for a Deal," *Chicago Tribune*, September 15, 2019.

"Every problem in society": Hannah Leone and Gregory Pratt, "Bernie Sanders, John Cusack Rally with Chicago Teachers as Strike Vote Begins," *Chicago Tribune*, September 25, 2019.

"since CTU has given CPS": Gregory Pratt and Hannah Leone, "Mayor Lori Lightfoot 'Concerned' CPS Contract Deal with Teachers Remains Elusive as Deadline Nears: 'We Can't Bargain Against Ourselves,'" *Chicago Tribune*, October 7, 2019.

"You'd think if that was": Hannah Leone et al., "CPS Strike Watch: Chances of Averting a Walkout Over Next 3 Days Is Getting 'More Remote,' Teachers Union President Says," *Chicago Tribune*, October 14, 2019.

"I believe there's more": Leone et al., "CPS Strike Watch."

"You're at it again": Jeff Schuhrke, "Karen Lewis is addressing the IFT convention . . . ," Twitter, October 19, 2019, https://twitter.com/JeffSchuhrke/status/1185586658781093889.

"Everyone in America should": Bill Ruthhart and Juan Perez, "U.S. Sen. Elizabeth Warren on the Picket Line with Chicago Teachers: 'Everyone in America Should Support You in This Strike,'" *Chicago Tribune*, October 22, 2019.

"They haven't reached out": Lynn Sweet, "Lightfoot Presidential Endorsement: Likely Not Sanders, Warren or Biden," *Chicago Sun-Times*, January 23, 2020.

13. "Stay Home, Save Lives"

"I talked to the superintendent": Jeremy Gorner and John Byrne, "Chicago Violence Rises in January, Raising Mayor Lori Lightfoot's Concern," *Chicago Tribune*, January 31, 2020.

"Chinatown, as you can see": Gregory Pratt, "Mayor Lori Lightfoot Says US Cities Need Federal Guidance and Financial Help to Deal with Coronavirus Outbreak," *Chicago Tribune*, February 2, 2020.

"So far in Chicago": Angie Leventis Lourgos, Lisa Schencker, and Karen Ann Cullotta, "Following CDC Coronavirus Warning, Lightfoot Urges: 'Let's Not Get Ahead of Ourselves.' Local Health Officials Say 'All Preventable Steps' Being Taken," *Chicago Tribune*, February 26, 2020.

"The city and state have done": Greg Hinz, "Coronavirus Poses a Dire Threat to City and State Budgets," *Crain's Chicago Business*, March 3, 2020, https://www.chicagobusiness.com/greg-hinz-politics/coronavirus-poses-dire-threat-city-and-state-budgets.

"needs a wartime financial plan": Paul Vallas, "Commentary: Chicago Needs a Wartime Financial Plan, Now," *Chicago Tribune*, April 1, 2020.

"Over the course of this crisis": Lisa Donovan, "The Spin," *Chicago Tribune*, April 1, 2020.

"drink a lot of Paddy's Irish whiskey": Dan Petrella, Gregory Pratt, and John Byrne, "Gov. J. B. Pritzker Questions Whether Chicago's St. Patrick's Day Parades Should Go On," *Chicago Tribune*, March 10, 2020.

"You will never look at": Fran Spielman, "Lightfoot's 'Authenticity' to Be Center of Plan to Re-Brand Chicago," *Chicago Sun-Times*, October 15, 2020.

"limit ticketing, towing, and impounding": Kelly Bauer, "Chicago to Reduce Parking Tickets, Stop Debt Collection Until April 30 as Coronavirus Hits Residents Hard," Block Club Chicago, March 18, 2020, https://blockclubchicago.org/2020/03/18/chicago-to-stop-all-debt-collection-parking-tickets-until-april-30-as-coronavirus-hits-residents-hard-financially/.

City Hall tried to gently walk it back later: Stacy St. Clair, Jennifer Smith Richards, and Gregory Pratt, "Despite Mayor Lori Lightfoot's Announcement of Ticketing Relief During the Pandemic, Thousands Received Parking Citations Anyway: 'It's a Betrayal, Just Absolutely Ridiculous,'" *Chicago Tribune*, September 21, 2020.

She responded by demanding: Justin Laurence, "Lightfoot Canceled Her *Chicago Tribune* Subscription over Reporting She Didn't Like, Leaked Emails Show," Block Club Chicago, May 13, 2021, https://blockclubchicago.org/2021/05/13/lightfoot-canceled-her-chicago-tribune-subscription-over-reporting-she-didnt-like-leaked-emails-show/.

"You can't let expediency": Heather Cherone, "Aldermen OK Measure Giving Lightfoot Emergency Powers Ordinance," WTTW-TV, April 21, 2020, https://news.wttw.com/2020/04/21/aldermen-ok-measure-giving-lightfoot-emergency-powers-ordinance.

"We had a very frank": Dan Petrella et al., "Lightfoot Drops Opposition to Pritzker's Order for Tighter Restrictions in Chicago," *Chicago Tribune*, October 28, 2020.

"If we do not reverse this trend": Gregory Pratt and John Byrne, "Mayor Lori Lightfoot Unveils Plan to Send More COVID-19 Vaccines to Black and Latino Neighborhoods," *Chicago Tribune*, January 25, 2021.

14. Pop the Weasel

"I led it four years ago": Fran Spielman, "Lightfoot 'Got My Man' in David Brown, But Did She Subvert Process for Choosing Top Cop?," *Chicago Sun-Times*, April 3, 2020.

"I've never been mayor before": Spielman, "Lightfoot 'Got My Man.'"

"We have to do better": Fran Spielman and Mitch Dudek, "Lightfoot: Memorial Day Weekend's Violent 'Bloodbath' Was a 'Fail' by City's New Top Cop," *Chicago Sun-Times*, May 26, 2020.

"I just try not to do stuff": Frank Main and Manny Ramos, "CPD Supt. David Brown Says Predecessor's Violence-Reduction Strategy Didn't Work—But His Does," *Chicago Sun-Times*, April 22, 2021.

"a more militaristic, shock-and-awe style": Fran Spielman, "Top Cops Try to Clear the Air After Brown Rips Predecessor's Strategies, Dedication to Police Reform," *Chicago Sun-Times*, April 23, 2021.

15. "The City Is Up for Grabs"

That Sunday, Lightfoot held a painful: Heather Cherone and Paris Schutz, "'What Are We Going to Have Left in Our Community?' Aldermen React with Panic, Sorrow to Unrest," WTTW-TV, June 5, 2020, article and audio, 1:18:42, https://news.wttw.com/2020/06/05/what-are-we-going-have-left-our-community-aldermen-react-panic-sorrow-unrest.

"Everywhere I went I asked": Fran Spielman, "Lightfoot: 'We Will Reopen Tomorrow,'" *Chicago Sun-Times*, June 2, 2020.

Later, Alice Yin and I dug: Gregory Pratt and Alice Yin, "Mayor Lori Lightfoot Pledged $10 Million to Businesses Damaged by Looting. The City Paid Out Far Less, Records Show," *Chicago Tribune*, August 24, 2020.

"blockade on wheels": Gregory Pratt and Alice Yin, "Chicago Has Spent at Least $222 Million in Overtime So Far in 2020, Already over Budget for the Year," *Chicago Tribune*, October 6, 2020.

"psychopaths with guns": Fran Spielman, "Police Union Slams Co-Chair of New Panel Reviewing CPD Use-of-Force Policy," *Chicago Sun-Times*, June 15, 2020.

16. Bigger than the Italians

"I absolutely have no plans": ABC Chicago, "Mayor Lori Lightfoot Doesn't Plan to Eliminate Columbus Day City Holiday Despite CPS Decision to Only Honor Indigenous People's Day," ABC Chicago, February 28, 2020, article and video, 0:41, https://abc7chicago.com/columbus-day-indigenous-peoples-chicago-public-schools-cps/5974187/.

"I have been watching with great interest": Shelby Bremer, "Lightfoot Doesn't Support Removing Chicago's Columbus Statues," NBC Chicago, June 19, 2020, https://www.nbcchicago.com/news/local/lightfoot-doesnt-support-removing-chicagos-columbus-statues/2292422/.

"swarmed the Christopher Columbus statue": Alice Yin, "Attempt to Topple Christopher Columbus Statue in Chicago's Grant Park Prompts Standoff with Police, Arrests and Rebuke of Mayor," *Chicago Tribune*, July 18, 2020.

Lightfoot released a Twitter thread: Lori E. Lightfoot, "Hundreds took to the streets yesterday . . . ," Twitter, July 18, 2020, https://twitter.com/mayorlightfoot/status/1284535742136385537.

"She got a big dick, all right": Mack Liederman, "Mayor Lightfoot Gets Roasted at the Wieners Circle," Block Club Chicago, April 11, 2022, https://blockclubchicago.org/2022/04/11/mayor-lightfoot-gets-roasted-at-the-wieners-circle/.

"Don't come to me for shit": Gregory Pratt and John Byrne, "Mayor Lori Lightfoot Has Delivered a Warning to Chicago Aldermen Who Might Vote Against Her Budget: Sources," *Chicago Tribune*, November 12, 2020.

"I don't consent to being recorded": Gregory Pratt, "Lightfoot Doubles Down on Property Tax Hike in Private Meeting, Tells Aldermen Not to Record Her," *Chicago Tribune*, November 15, 2020.

17. "My Name Is Anjanette Young"

"What is going on?!": Dave Savini, Samah Assad, and Michele Youngerman, "'You Have the Wrong Place': Body Camera Video Shows Moments Police Handcuff Innocent, Naked Woman During Wrong Raid," CBS Chicago, December 17, 2020, article and video, 8:20, https://www.cbsnews.com/chicago/news/you-have-the-wrong-place-body-camera-video-shows-moments-police-handcuff-innocent-naked-woman-during-wrong-raid/.

INNOCENT WOMAN: CHICAGO POLICE HANDCUFFED ME: Dave Savini, Samah Assad, and Michele Youngerman, "Innocent Woman: Chicago Police Handcuffed Me While I Was Naked During Wrong Raid," CBS Chicago, November 12, 2020, article and video, 6:48, https://www.cbsnews.com/chicago/news/innocent-woman-chicago-police-handcuffed-me-while-i-was-naked-during-wrong-raid/.

"Just a 'heads up' FYI that": Gregory Pratt, "Chicago's Top Lawyer, Mark Flessner, Resigns Amid Uproar over Anjanette Young Raid, Video," *Chicago Tribune*, December 20, 2020.

tweeted a link to the report: Gregory Pratt, "Wow: Mayor Lori Lightfoot's law department . . . ," Twitter, December 14, 2020, https://twitter.com/royalpratt/status/1338714706752790528.

"What video?": Gregory Pratt, "Mayor Lori Lightfoot Apologized, but Her Administration Takes Hard Line with Anjanette Young in High-Stakes Lawsuit over Botched Raid," *Chicago Tribune*, July 2, 2021.

After receiving Flessner's email: Gregory Pratt, "Lightfoot's Former Top Attorney, Who Resigned over Anjanette Young Raid Scandal, in Dispute with Mayor over Whether She Later OK'd More City Work for Him," *Chicago Tribune*, September 27, 2021.

"Why would I have sought": Pratt, "Lightfoot's Former Top Attorney."

18. A City in Crisis

"I think we all know": Gregory Pratt, "As Another Violent Summer Ends in Chicago, Mayor Lori Lightfoot Vows to Fight Crime. But Critics Say the City Is in Crisis," *Chicago Tribune*, September 10, 2021.

It backfired on Lightfoot, too: Bella BAHHS, "An Abolitionist's Midterm Conversation with Mayor Lori Lightfoot," The Revolutionary Column, The TriiBE (website), May 21, 2021, https://thetriibe.com/2021/05/the-revolutionary-column-an-abolitionists-midterm-conversation-with-mayor-lori-lightfoot/.

"This was not about this": John Byrne and Gregory Pratt, "No Vote on Renaming Lake Shore Drive for DuSable as City Council Adjourns amid Fight over Mayor Lori Lightfoot's New Law Department Nominee," *Chicago Tribune*, June 23, 2021.

"Like most Bears fans": Lori E. Lightfoot, "On the Bears bid to buy Arlington Racecourse . . . ," Twitter, June 17, 2021, https://twitter.com/mayorlightfoot/status/1405645431648907264.

Ferguson's departure left Lightfoot: Gregory Pratt, "Mayor Lori Lightfoot Slow to Hire a New Permanent City Inspector General," *Chicago Tribune*, February 21, 2022.

"I learned to drive in Boston": Fran Spielman, "Chicago's New Inspector General Has No Intention of 'Staying in Her Lane,'" *Chicago Sun-Times*, April 28, 2022.

"Unfortunately, my disappointment": Gregory Pratt and Madeline Buckley, "Chicago Police Leader Resigned over 'Inability' of Department Brass 'to Even Feign Interest' in Reform, Then Accused Officials of Retaliation," *Chicago Tribune*, November 11, 2021.

"As I leave these streams": Gregory Pratt, "Top Lightfoot Public Safety Adviser Resigned amid Concerns About City's Ability to 'Keep Moving . . . Forward' on Crime Prevention and Consent Decree," *Chicago Tribune*, November 12, 2021.

Lightfoot arrived at the hospital: Michael Sneed, "Chicago Cops Give Cold Shoulder to Mayor Lightfoot at Hospital After Two Officers Shot," *Chicago Sun-Times*, August 9, 2021.

"We don't have twenty minutes for this shit": Fran Spielman and Frank Main, "Grieving Chicago Police Officers Direct Their Anger at CPD's Second-in-Command," *Chicago Sun-Times*, August 10, 2021.

"wasn't part of the friends-and-family program": Fran Spielman, "Lightfoot Defends First Deputy for Trying to Speed Up Ritual at Morgue for Officer Ella French," *Chicago Tribune*, August 11, 2021.

"a city in crisis": Matt O'Shea and Susan Lee, "Chicago's Public Safety Crisis Threatens Our Whole City," *Chicago Sun-Times*, September 3, 2021.

"Dear Alderman O'Shea": Gregory Pratt, "With City Budget Vote Looming and Crime Top of Mind, Mayor Lori Lightfoot Clashes with Aldermen over Police Spending," *Chicago Tribune*, November 4, 2022.

calling him an "idiot": "Days After $1 Million Smash-and-Grab, Lightfoot Walked Out of Meeting with 'Idiot' Luxury Car Dealer—Then a City Inspector Showed Up with a Ticket Book," *CWBChicago* (blog), January 12, 2022, https://cwbchicago.com/2022/01/days-after-1-million-smash-and-grab-lightfoot-walked-out-of-meeting-with-idiot-luxury-car-dealer-then-a-city-inspector-showed-up-with-a-ticket-book.html.

"Mayor Lori Lightfoot's plan": Rex Huppke, "Mayor Lori Lightfoot's Plan to Seize Property from Gang Members Is Great If You Like Terrible Ideas," *Chicago Tribune*, January 21, 2022.

19. "Adults in the Room"

"Well, that's not really for me to say": Bill Ruthhart and John Byrne, "How Michael Madigan's Departure Accelerates a Shift in Chicago Politics from Old-School Machine to New-Era Progressives," *Chicago Tribune*, March 5, 2021.

"They don't stop to listen": Gregory Pratt and John Byrne, "The Standoff over Chicago Schools Is Over for Now. What's Next for Mayor Lori Lightfoot and CTU?," *Chicago Tribune*, February 13, 2020.

"They took a strike for the contract": Hannah Leone et al., "As CPS Schools Reopen, District Vows to 'Hold Employees Accountable Who Are Not Reporting to Work' and Will Begin Docking Pay Tuesday," *Chicago Tribune*, January 12, 2021.

"Tomorrow will be the fourth": Hannah Leone et al., "School District and Union Talks Fall Apart as Lightfoot Pushes Reopening to Tuesday," *Chicago Tribune*, January 31, 2021.

"cooling off period": Hannah Leone et al., "CPS Calls for 2 Days of 'Cooling Off' as It Reports Progress in Averting a CTU Strike; Remote Learning Continues Tuesday and Wednesday," *Chicago Tribune*, February 1, 2021.

"My patience with delays": Hannah Leone and Gregory Pratt, "CPS Proposes Slower Phase-In for School Reopening but CTU Says Any New Lockouts Would Spur a Strike: 'We Don't Leave People Behind,'" *Chicago Tribune*, February 5, 2021.

"literally trying to pit us": Leone and Pratt, "CPS Proposes Slower Phase-In."

"think, ultimately, they'd like to take over": Dana Goldstein, "Chicago Mayor Lori Lightfoot on What She Learned from Battling the Teachers' Union," *New York Times*, February 14, 2021.

"Mayor Lightfoot said often during her campaign": Rich Miller, "Legislators Face Tough Negotiations to Craft a Bill for an Elected Chicago School Board," *Chicago Sun-Times*, April 16, 2021.

"First, she said to me": Robert Peters, "Last Sunday I was chilling . . . ," Twitter, June 2, 2021, https://twitter.com/RobertJPeters/status/1400172957952004100.

"same old saber-rattling": Tracy Swartz, "CPS Reopens amid Another COVID-19 Surge, but Chicago Teachers Union Eyes Vote on Whether to Refuse to Work In-Person if District Doesn't Meet Safety Demands," *Chicago Tribune*, January 3, 2022.

"I am so pissed off that we": Swartz, "CPS Reopens."

"Enough is enough": Tracy Swartz and Gregory Pratt, "Chicago Public Schools Cancels Classes Again for Thursday as Deadlock with Union Continues; Trump, Biden Press Secretary Each Comment on Impasse," *Chicago Tribune*, January 5, 2022.

"This is about politics": David Rutz, "Chicago Mayor Lightfoot Blasts Teachers Union over School Closings: Trying to 'Politicize the Pandemic,'" Fox News, January 6,

2022, https://www.foxnews.com/media/chicago-mayor-lightfoot-blasts-teachers
-union-pandemic.

"kids and their families": Stefano Esposito, "CTU Union Head Accuses Mayor of Being
'Relentlessly Stupid' in Her Position on Reopening Schools," *Chicago Sun-Times*,
January 10, 2022.

"I just paid $3,200 for two KN95 masks": Nader Issa, "Even though the labor
action is suspended . . . ," Twitter, January 10, 2022, https://twitter.com/i/web
/status/1480730350070423553.

20. "Not a Gimme"

"It's not a gimme": Kara Swisher, "'It's a Tough Time to Be Mayor': Lori Lightfoot
Responds to Her Critics," *New York Times*, July 26, 2021.

"I'm tired of being ignored": Gregory Pratt, "Onetime Lightfoot Ally Says She Will
'Absolutely Not' Support Mayor's Reelection Bid: 'I'm Tired of Being Ignored,'"
Chicago Tribune, February 28, 2022.

"After much consideration": "US Rep Mike Quigley Will Not Run for Chicago Mayor
in 2023," NBC Chicago, April 28, 2022, https://www.nbcchicago.com/news/local
/us-rep-mike-quigley-will-not-run-for-chicago-mayor-in-2023/2819079/.

tweeted about it so often: Brian Hopkins, "until we have a better understanding . . . ,"
Twitter, August 21, 2020, https://twitter.com/AldermanHopkins/status
/1296929426807107588; Brian Hopkins, "SARSCoV2 infection of brain tissue . . . ,"
Twitter, December 12, 2021, https://twitter.com/AldermanHopkins/status
/1470162491183411204.

"My No. 1 goal is safety": Gregory Pratt, "Ald. Ray Lopez Announces Run for Chicago
Mayor in 2023; Cites Public Safety as No. 1 Issue," *Chicago Tribune*, April 6, 2022.

"Go out there and help those people": Gregory Pratt and Shanzeh Ahmad, "Willie Wilson
Is Promising Another $1 Million in Free Gas But His Giveaways Raise Campaign
Questions," *Chicago Tribune*, April 19, 2022.

"a mayor's job is not just": John Byrne, "State Rep. Kam Buckner Joins Race for Chicago
Mayor: 'A Mayor's Job Is Not Just to Fight for the Sake of Fighting,'" *Chicago
Tribune*, May 12, 2022.

Northwest Side alderperson Jim Gardiner: Heather Cherone and Paris Schutz, "Feds
Probe Gardiner for Bribery, Pay-to-Play: Sources," WTTW-TV, September 14,
2021, article and video, 2:36, https://news.wttw.com/2021/09/14/feds-probe
-gardiner-bribery-pay-play-sources.

"If Mayor Lightfoot runs for reelection": Fran Spielman, "Black Caucus Chairman Jason
Ervin Delivers Early Endorsement of Lightfoot Reelection," *Chicago Sun-Times*,
September 17, 2021.

"used government workers to plan": Gregory Royal Pratt, "Chicago Treasurer Accused of Misconduct and Ethical Violations in Letter City Kept Secret for Years," *Chicago Tribune*, September 5, 2023.

"I'm running because the city is in crisis": Gregory Pratt, "Paul Vallas Enters Chicago Mayor's Race; Former CPS Head Says Lightfoot 'Has Proven Incapable of Dealing with These Crises,'" *Chicago Tribune*, June 1, 2022.

"By embracing her image": Gregory Pratt, "Chicago Mayor Lori Lightfoot Releases Video Announcing Bid for Second Term," *Chicago Tribune*, June 7, 2022.

"White people have abandoned her": Fran Spielman, "Sawyer Cut as Speaker at Ribbon-Cutting in His Ward After Spat with Lightfoot, He Says," *Chicago Sun-Times*, September 2, 2022.

Curtis accidentally shot himself: Fran Spielman, "Lightfoot's 'No. 1 Cheerleader' in City Council Rethinking Support over Mayor's Failure to Call After He Accidentally Shot Himself," *Chicago Sun-Times*, January 10, 2023.

"Tried to call you": Sam Charles, "'Nothing Happened,' Ald. Derrick Curtis Says of Shooting That Left Daughter Wounded," WGN-TV, January 18, 2023, article and video, 2:51, https://wgntv.com/news/chicago-news/nothing-happened-ald-derrick -curtis-says-of-shooting-that-left-daughter-wounded/.

"We're ready": Elvia Malagón, Tina Sfondeles, and Fran Spielman, "Chicago Welcomes Immigrants Bused Out of Texas with Open Arms," *Chicago Sun-Times*, September 1, 2022.

"I am not thinking about that whatsoever": Fran Spielman, "Garcia Says Lightfoot Faces Toughest Re-Election Challenge of Any Mayor in 40 Years," *Chicago Sun-Times*, March 2, 2022.

"Can we just be honest?": Gregory Pratt, Alice Yin, and A. D. Quig, "Brandon Johnson, Mayor Lightfoot's Newest Progressive Challenger, Contends She's 'Disconnected . . . with Working People,'" *Chicago Tribune*, October 27, 2022.

"I know for many of you" to *"I feel worse"*: Natasha Korecki, "Chicago Mayor Lori Lightfoot Is in Danger of an Early Re-Election Knockout," NBC News, February 19, 2023, https://www.nbcnews.com/politics/elections/chicago-mayor-lori-lightfoot -risks-early-re-election-knockout-rcna66785.

"When I asked Lightfoot": Jonathan Martin, "Calling the Police: Lightfoot Needs a Lifeline," *Politico*, February 28, 2023, https://www.politico.com/news/magazine/2023/02/28 /lightfoot-chicago-mayoral-election-on-politics-00084669.

21. "False Prophet"

"When I entered office": Alice Yin and Gregory Pratt, "Lightfoot, García Make First Appearances at Mayoral Candidate Forum," *Chicago Tribune*, January 9, 2023.

At first, her team defended: Heather Cherone, "Lightfoot Campaign Asks CPS Teachers to Encourage Students to Help Her Win Reelection in Return for Credit," WTTW-TV, January 11, 2023, article and video, 10:19, https://news.wttw.com/2023/01/11/lightfoot-campaign-asks-cps-teachers-encourage-students-help-her-win-reelection-return.

"Remember how you felt": Gregory Pratt and Alice Yin, "Mayor Lori Lightfoot Pounces on Challenger Paul Vallas During Punchy Women's Forum," *Chicago Tribune*, January 14, 2023.

"I only have a seventh-grade education": Alice Yin, A. D. Quig, and Gregory Pratt, "Chicago Mayoral Candidates Share Ideas on City Investment, Schools and Crime," *Chicago Tribune*, January 17, 2023.

"hunted down like rabbits": Alice Yin, A. D. Quig, and Gregory Pratt, "In First Chicago Mayoral Debate, Challengers Attack Lori Lightfoot's Record While She Aims to 'Finish the Job We Have Started,'" *Chicago Tribune*, January 20, 2023.

"We often deal with policy": Gregory Pratt, "Candidates Ja'Mal Green and Sophia King Take Aim at Mayor Lightfoot's Leadership Style," *Chicago Tribune*, January 19, 2023.

"All due respect to Congressman García": Yin, Quig, and Pratt, "In First Chicago Mayoral Debate, Challengers Attack."

"abandoned the progressive movement": Fran Spielman, "Brandon Johnson Accuses Chuy Garcia of 'Abandoning the Progressive Movement,'" *Chicago Sun-Times*, January 19, 2023.

"Clearly what he decided": Alice Yin and Gregory Pratt, "'You Brought Chaos': Mayor Lightfoot Defends Record Against Challengers 'Chuy' García and Brandon Johnson," *Chicago Tribune*, January 23, 2023.

"The fact of the matter is": Yin and Pratt, "'You Brought Chaos.'"

"He spins a good story": Alice Yin, Gregory Pratt, and A. D. Quig, "Crime Takes Center Stage at Forum as Mayor Lori Lightfoot Interrupts Opponents and Moderator to Defend Record," *Chicago Tribune*, January 26, 2023.

"Shutting down the schools": Alice Yin and Gregory Pratt, "Mayoral Candidates Clash at Forum: 'Don't Lecture Me About Schools,'" *Chicago Tribune*, February 3, 2023.

"I can't listen to Brandon Johnson": Alice Yin, Gregory Pratt, and A. D. Quig, "Mayor Lori Lightfoot Defends CPS Students During Mayoral Forum, Criticizes Moderator: 'You're Describing Them as If They're Dumb,'" *Chicago Tribune*, February 9, 2023.

"It's Saturday and I'm not": Alice Yin and Gregory Pratt, "Lori Lightfoot Takes Aim at Brandon Johnson as Mayoral Race Enters Final Two Weeks: 'Do Not Be Taken In by the False Prophets,'" *Chicago Tribune*, February 13, 2023.

"Any vote for somebody": Alice Yin et al., "With Chicago's Mayoral Election Just Days Away, Candidates Focus on Turning Out Their Bases, and Making the Runoff Cutoff," *Chicago Tribune*, February 25, 2023.

"Brandon Johnson is someone": Gregory Pratt, "Anjanette Young Endorses Brandon Johnson for Chicago Mayor on Anniversary of Botched Police Raid on Her Home," *Chicago Tribune*, February 21, 2023.

"I never thought the city of Chicago": Frank Main, "Susana Mendoza: Lightfoot Betrayed Chicago Cops Disabled by COVID-19, Including Mendoza's Brother," *Chicago Sun-Times*, February 21, 2023.

"I looked into the camera": Gregory Pratt and Alice Yin, "Mayor Lori Lightfoot Concedes Defeat, Setting Stage for Chicago's Mayoral Race to Be Between Brandon Johnson and Paul Vallas," *Chicago Tribune*, February 28, 2023.

Epilogue: Breaking Up with the Mayor

He paid nearly $315,000: A. D. Quig and Gregory Pratt, "Paul Vallas Outspent Brandon Johnson Nearly 2-to-1 in Losing Mayoral Bid," *Chicago Tribune*, April 19, 2023.

"We are going into": Lori Lightfoot, "Mayor Lori Lightfoot—Final Interview," by Craig Dellimore, *At Issue*, WBBM radio, April 30, 2023, audio, 28:20, https://omny.fm/shows/at-issue-on-wbbm-newsradio/mayor-lori-lightfoot-final-interview#description.

"There's a reason why": Lori Lightfoot, "Outgoing Chicago Mayor: I Leave Office with My Head Held High," *Morning Joe*, MSNBC, May 8, 2023, video, 9:14, https://www.msnbc.com/morning-joe/watch/outgoing-chicago-mayor-lori-lightfoot-i-leave-office-with-my-head-held-high-173422149609.

"failed for months": Gregory Royal Pratt, Nell Salzman, Alice Yin, and Dan Petrella, "A Year in, Chicago's Migrant Crisis Exacerbated by City Hall and State Delays, Hefty Contracts and Questionable Decisions," *Chicago Tribune*, September 2, 2023.

"Amid the confusion, we provided clarity": *The Welcoming City: The Lightfoot Administration's Response to the Asylum Seeker Mission* (City of Chicago, 2023), https://www.chicago.gov/content/dam/city/sites/texas-new-arrivals/pdfs/The-Welcoming-City.pdf.

INDEX

Abbott, Greg, 191

abortion, 198

Access Living disability forum, 197

Accountability Monday meetings, 94–95

activists, 87

Aguayo, Berto, 74

Ahern, Mary Ann, 96

AL Media, 39

alderpersons, 69–71, 76, 81, 187

Alexander, Cedric, 19

Alvarez, Anita, 17

Amer, Robin, 47

American Federation of Teachers, 115

antiviolence march, 73–74

Arena, John, 57, 79

Arwady, Allison, 126–127, 172

Assad, Samah, 150

Austin, Carrie, 76, 79

Axelrod, David, 141

Back of the Yards neighborhood, ix,
    72–74

Bailey, Darren, x

Baird, Callie, 7

Baker McKenzie law firm, 4–5

Balanoff, Tom, 37

ballot challenges, 44–45

Bankman-Fried, Samuel, 194

Barrera, Leticia, 72

Bauler, Paddy, 75–76

Beacon Media, 55, 60

Beale, Anthony, 70, 163

Bears, 164–165

Beaudet, Matthew, 79

Beck, Charlie, 98, 101–102, 129, 133,
    165–166

Bennett, William, 104

Berlin, Steve, 90

Berrington, Marques, 151–153

Berrios, Joe, 55–56

biographical sketch of Lightfoot, 4–5

Bird Box, xiii–xiv

Black Caucus, 80–81, 127, 147,
    187–188

Black community
    COVID-19 pandemic and, 128
    declining population, xiii
    support from, 66, 162, 187, 189–190

Blagojevich, Rod, 185–186

Board of Ethics, 90–91, 156

body-worn camera footage, 151

Boik, Bob
    career of, 98, 165
    leadership of, 94, 131
    protests and, 135–136

Bottoms, Keisha Lance, 205

Bowen, Tom, 197

Bowser, Muriel, 205

Boyd, Miracle, 144

Boyd, Rekia, 1, 41

Boyle, John "Quarters," 38

Bradley, William, 95

Bratton, Bill, 101

bridges, 135–137

Bronzeville, 9

Brookins, Howard, 3, 163

Brooks, Anita, 90

Brown, David
confidence in, 169
hiring of, xiv–xv, 129–133
organizational chart proposal,
165–166
protests and, 142
resignation of, 204

Brown, Dorothy, 28, 45, 153, 162

Brown, Michael, 3, 15

Buckner, Kambium, 179, 187

Bud Billiken Parade, 42

budget plans, 84–86, 147–148

Burge, Jon, 3

Burger King, 50

Burke, Ed, Jr., 49–52

Burke, Edward
blaming, 161
City Council position, 77–78
conflict with, 195
FBI raid on, xii, 48–49
Finance Committee and, 32
Mendoza and, 38
political attacks and, ix
protests and, 139
security detail of, 96

Burke, Joseph P., 48

Burnett, Walter, 70, 81

Bush, George H. W., 67

Byrne, John, 48–49, 96, 124

Caldero, Roberto, 53

Called to Rise (Brown), 130

Calloway, Will, 1, 3

Camden, Pat, 1

campaign websites, 28

Cannon, Ashley, 90

Cardona, Felix, 162

Carlson, Tucker, 162

Carter, Eric, 131, 167

casino development, 84, 188

Catanzara, John, 145

Cato, Ernest, 95, 129–130

Caucus of Rank and File Educators, 104

CBAs (Community Benefits
Agreements), 86

CBS, 151–154

Centers for Disease Control (CDC), 122,
124

Ceres Cafe, 97

Chance the Rapper, 40

Cherone, Heather, 138, 197, 205

Chicago Bears, 164–165

Chicago Defender, 7

Chicago Federation of Labor, 83, 174

Chicago Police Board, 6, 16, 129, 165

Chicago Police Department (CPD)
Accountability Monday meetings,
94–95
body-worn camera footage, 151
Civilian Office of Police
Accountability, 18, 21
CompStat meetings, 94–95
consent decrees, 21–22, 93, 166–167
criticism of, 93–94
Ferguson Effect and, 15
Independent Police Review Authority
(IPRA), 12, 16–17, 18, 21
McDonald case and, 1–3, 16

misconduct, 1, 3, 7
morale of, 15–16, 20
Office of Constitutional Policing and
    Reform, 101
Office of Professional Standards
    (OPS), 6–8, 10–12, 18
Police Accountability Task Force, 4,
    17, 19–21
relationship with, 159
saturation policing by, 132
search warrants, 149–157
superintendent of, xiv–xv, 129–133
vacation time for, 95–96
Young case and, 149–157
Chicago Public Schools (CPS)
COVID-19 pandemic and, 172–176,
    179–181
resources of, 111
Chicago Teachers Union (CTU)
contract proposal and, 111–115
COVID-19 pandemic and, 128,
    172–176, 179–181
Emanuel and, 67
endorsement by, 191
history of, 103–107, 112
Johnson and, xi
"Keeping the Promise" rally, 103
Preckwinkle and, 43–44
strike by, 116–118
teachers' walkout, 106
Chico, Gery, 49, 52, 54
Christopher, John, 47
City Club of Chicago, 30, 38
City Council, 69–71, 76, 81, 187
City So Real (documentary series), 40, 55
civil rights violations, 10–11
Civilian Office of Police Accountability,
    18, 21, 150

Civilian Police Accountability Council
    proposal, 63
Classen, Maurice
    on Brown, 132, 133, 166
    on Carter, 131
    Columbus statue and, 145
    CTU contract proposal and, 116
    departure of, 165
    Flessner hire and, 156
    hiring of, 72
    interactions with Lightfoot, 89
    Johnson scandal and, 97
    leadership of, 94
    McDonald case and, 99
    protests and, 141–142
    Young case and, 153
Clinton, Bill, 67
Clinton, Hillary, 18
Cochran, Steve, 34
Cochran, Willie, 86
"code of silence" speech, 18–19
Cole, Marcelyn, 63
Colom, Vilma, 43
Columbus statue, 143–145
ComEd, 171
Committee on Committees and Rules, 163
Community Benefits Agreements
    (CBAs), 86
CompStat meetings, 94–95
Conroy, John, 7
consent decrees, 21–22, 93, 166–167
conspiracy theories, 137
Conyears-Ervin, Melissa, 80, 188
Cork and Kerry, 146
corruption, 75–76, 91
"cover up by investigation" theory, 17
COVID-19 pandemic, 121–128, 172–
    176, 179–181, 185

CPD (Chicago Police Department). *See* Chicago Police Department (CPD)
CPS (Chicago Public Schools). *See* Chicago Public Schools (CPS)
crime statistics, xiv, 121, 131, 159, 162
criticism, 89
Cross, Jennell, 93
CTU (Chicago Teachers Union). *See* Chicago Teachers Union (CTU)
Cullerton, John, 68, 177
Cunningham, Peter, 184
curfew, 136–138
Curtis, Derrick, 190

Daley, Bill
  ballot challenges and, 44
  Burke scandal and, 49
  mayoral campaign of, xii, 53–54
  political attacks on, 57
  political record of, 39–40, 65, 78–79
Daley, Richard J., xi
Daley, Richard M.
  CTU and, 104, 112
  political record of, xi, 12–13, 29
  rivals, 197
  security detail of, 96
damage control, 154
Darlin, Randy, 132, 136
Davis Gates, Stacy
  COVID-19 pandemic and, 173
  CTU contract proposal and, 111–118
  CTU president role and, 191
  leadership of, 105–110
  on Lightfoot, 43
  support of Johnson, xi
De Blasio, Bill, 32
Deal, Joe, 68
"defer and publish" maneuver, 163

Dellimore, Craig, 204
demonstrations, 135–142
Department of Homeland Security, 141
dick comments, 89, 144–145
Dobbs decision, 198
Donald, Cynthia, 98, 100–101
Donovan, Lisa, 38
Douglass, Frederick, 105
Dow, Robert, Jr., 93
Dowell, Pat, 84, 138, 201
drawbridges, 135–137
Dumke, Mick, 25, 52
Duncan, Arne, 161, 184
DuSable, Jean Baptiste Point, 162–163

Egan, Lynn, 64
Eilman, Christina, 13
elected school board, 68, 105, 176–179
election of Lightfoot, xii–xiii
Emanuel, Rahm
  "code of silence" speech, 18–19
  CTU and, 67, 105–106
  decision not to seek reelection, 34
  Eilman case, 13
  McDonald case, 1–4, 16, 18
  on the next mayor, 176–177
  police reform and, 15–22
  political opinions of, 67, 69
  political record of, 78–79, 86
  reputation of, xv, 38, 79, 105–106, 202
  security detail of, 96
  transition for Lightfoot, 67–68
  2011 election, xi–xii
  2015 election, x, 27
  Young case and, 153
Emergency Powers Ordinance, 127
endorsements, 55, 65, 203

Enyia, Amara, 33, 40–41, 65
Equality Illinois, 55
Ervin, Jason, 80, 123, 127, 188
Escamilla, Anthony, 101
Eshleman, Amy, 26, 52, 55
ethics issues, 90–91, 156
excessive force, 10–11

Fair Workweek legislation, 83
Fardon, Zach, 13
Fassnacht, Michael, 125–126
FBI raid on Burke's office, 49–50
Feigenholtz, Sara, 84, 178–179
Ferguson, Joseph, 17, 90, 99–101, 165
Ferguson Effect, 15
Fight Back for a Better Tomorrow, 57
fines and fees reform, 86, 126–127, 148
First Tuesdays at the Hideout, 25, 107
Fitzgerald, Patrick, 6, 13
Flessner, Mark, 13, 26, 99, 152–156
Floyd, George, viii, 135
Fogel, David, 7
Fojtik, Rob, 54–55
Ford, Nick, 7
Foreman, Ghian, 129
Foxx, Kim
    on Brown, 132
    conflict with, 101, 110, 142
    election of, 37
    Ervin and, 188
    interactions with Lightfoot, 12, 30,
        32, 42
    Young case and, 154, 156–157
Franczek, Jim, 112–115
Fraternal Order of Police, 141, 145, 169
Freedom of Information Act (FOIA)
    requests, 3, 32, 151
French, Ella, 167

Frey, Jacob, 135, 141
Frisch, Michael, 72, 113–116
Fronczak, Caroline, 152–153
fundraising, 30, 31, 49–50, 54, 197

Gadlen, Delwin, 42
Gadlin, Stephanie, 193
gambling expansion, 84
Garcia, George, 9–10, 12
García, Jesús "Chuy"
    CTU and, 44, 116
    endorsement of Johnson, 203–204
    endorsement of Lightfoot, 65
    mayoral campaign of, ix, x–xi,
        191–194, 197–200
    political record of, 27, 48, 192
Gardiner, Jim, 57, 79–80, 187
Garza, Susan Sadlowski, xv, 83, 139,
        183–184, 192
Gates, Davis, 179, 180
gender-neutral pronouns, 77
Girl Talk interview, 25–26, 52
Goodrich, Paul, 71
Gordon-Booth, Jehan, 172
Gorner, Jeremy, 96, 99, 141
Grant Park, 143–145
Grassroots Alliance for Police Account-
        ability (GAPA) proposal, 63, 97
Grau, Hiram, 98
Green, Ja'Mal, 44, 161, 189, 203
Griffin, Ken, 40
Grisko, Carolyn, 149
Guevara, Reynaldo, 12
Guglielmi, Anthony, 98
Guide, Bill, 146
Guidice, Rich, 136
gun violence, 16
Gutierrez, Luis, 71

Hadden, Maria, 144
Hairston, Leslie, 195
Hampton, Alaina, 171
Hanford, Elizabeth Kathryn, 151
Harmon, Don, 177, 178
Harris, Michelle, 77, 87, 138, 161
Hendon, Rickey, 29–30, 44
Hendricks, John, 145
Hickey, Maggie, 140
Hideout, 25, 52, 107
homicide statistics, xiv, 121, 131, 159
Hopkins, Brian, 142, 185, 191
Huppke, Rex, 169–170
Hynes, Dan, 71–72, 84

I Now Pronounce You Chuck & Larry, 81
identity politics, 32
Illinois Federation of Teachers, 117
inaugural address, 75–76
Independent Police Review Authority (IPRA), 12, 16–17, 18, 21
Indigenous Peoples' Day, 143
International Housewares Association, 122
Invest South/West project, 88
Issa, Nader, 180
Italian Americans, 145

Jackson, Janice, 173, 176
Jacobs, Caryn, 152
Janssen, Kim, 26
Jeffries, Hakeem, 185
Johnson, Brandon
    CTU and, xi, 44, 191–194
    election of, 203–204
    endorsements, 191, 203–204
    leadership of, 206

mayoral campaign of, xi, xii, xv, 197–201
Johnson, Eddie, 20, 30, 93–101
Joint Civic Committee of Italian Americans, 145
Jones, John Paul, 179
Jones, Virgil, 5
Joravsky, Ben, 25, 52, 107–108, 184
Joy, Ra, 107
Joyce, Jeremiah, 33
Joyce, Jerry, 33, 40, 44
Judge, Patrick, 48
Jungle, The (Sinclair), 72

Kaegi, Fritz, 55
Kalven, Jamie, 2, 3, 17, 60
Kambhampati, Sandhya, 86
Kaplan, Jacob, 38
Kass, John, 41
"Keeping the Promise" rally, 103
Keller, John, 42
Kelley, Clifford, 86
Kelly, Robin, viii
Kidwell, David, 48
Kimmons, Gyata, 91
King, Sophia, 162, 190, 198
Kirkpatrick, Anne, 21
Klonsky, Joanna
    advice of, 54, 70
    Arena and, 79
    Foxx and, 142
    Joravsky and, 107–108
    mayoral campaign and, 57
    Young case and, 152
Kocoras, Charles P., 6
Korecki, Natasha, 194
Koschman, David, 99
Ku Klux Klan, 4

Lake Shore Drive, 162–163
Landon, Emily, 124
Latin Kings gang, 9
Latino Caucus, 148
leadership, 202
Lee, Susan, 98, 131, 150, 165, 167–168
LeFurgy, Kate, xv, 148, 153
legalized marijuana, 80
Lewis, Karen, 43, 104–106, 108, 117–118, 193
Lewis, Taylor, 159
LGBTQ community, 55, 80–81
license plate readers, 168
Lightford, Kimberly, 177
Lincoln Yards, 68
Little Italy, 145
lobbyists, 91
Loevy, Jon, 9–12
Long, Ray, 171
looting, 138–142
Lopez, Raymond, 71, 73–74, 139, 163, 186
Lurie, Dan, 72
Luurs, Gaby, 87
Lynch, Loretta, 15

MacArthur, Douglas, 179
Madigan, Lisa, 18
Madigan, Michael, 38, 68, 171–172, 194–195, 199
Madison, Sybil, 165, 167
Maldonado, Roberto, 53
Malinowski, Sean, 98, 129–130
marijuana, 80
Marin, Carol, 48
Martin, Jonathan, 195
Martin, Matt, 85
Martwick, Robert, 55–56, 78

Mason, Roswell B., viii
Mayer Brown law firm, 4, 12
mayoral campaign
    announcement of, 31
    Burke scandal and, 49–50
    denial of, 28
    endorsements, 55, 65
    fundraising, 30, 31, 54
    Girl Talk interview, 25–26
    rivals, 29–45, 56–57
    runoff election, 57–58
    stump speech, 50
    themes of, 31–32
    TV commercials, 60
    victory speech, 66
    websites, 28
McCarthy, Garry
    Emanuel and, 27
    firing of, 17, 94
    interactions with Lightfoot, 66
    leadership of, 16
    mayoral campaign of, 30
McCulloch, Robert, 15
McDonald, Laquan
    Emanuel and, xii, 18–19
    murder investigation of, 16
    murder of, 1–2, 73, 99
    Preckwinkle and, 60
McGrath, Jason, 142
media
    blaming, viii
    mayoral campaign and, 54
    TV commercials, 54–55
Medrano, Ambrosio, 47
Meigs Field, 145
Mellet, Dave, 57–58
Memorial Day weekend violence, 132
memos, 89

Mendoza, Susana
  ballot challenges and, 45
  Burke scandal and, 49
  endorsements, 55
  on Lightfoot, 201
  mayoral campaign of, xii, 38–39
  political attacks and, 52, 57
mental health clinics, 197
Meza, Celia, 89–90, 153, 156, 163, 167
migrant crisis, 205
Mihalopoulos, Dan, 48
Millennium Park, 188
Miller, Rich, 177
Milstein, Michael, 140
minimum wage, 85
Mitchell, Greg, 138
Molina, May, 8
monuments, 143–145
Moore, David, 162, 163
Moreno, Joe, 53
Munoz, Ricardo, 53
Musk, Elon, 27

Napolitano, Anthony, 140
Nulph, Kelsey, 73

Obama, Barack, xii, 27, 44
Obama Presidential Center, 86–88
Ocasio-Cortez, Alexandria, 31–32
Office of Constitutional Policing and
  Reform, 101
Office of Emergency Management and
  Communications (OEMC), 136
Office of Professional Standards (OPS),
  6–8, 10–12, 18
"office time," 159–161
O'Hare International Airport, xi, 27
O'Kane, Harry, 4

O'Malley, John, 165, 167, 168
Operating Engineers Union, 193
Operation Silver Shovel, 47
Oshana, Zamir, 9
O'Shea, Matt
  conflict with, 144, 146, 168
  on corruption, 76, 91
  endorsement of Lightfoot, 65–66
  op-ed by, 167–168
  St. Patrick's Day parade and,
    123–124
O'Toole, Kathleen, 98

Palmer, Alice, 44
pandemic, 121–128
parliamentary maneuvers, 163
pattern-or-practice investigations, 17
Patterson, Aaron, 8
Patton, Stephen, 2, 3, 13
Pelosi, Nancy, 185
pension funds, 83–84
Perez, Manny, ix, 63, 68, 72
Perillo, Joe, 169
Perl, Nadia, 54
Peters, Robert, 178
phallic comments, 89, 144–145
Police Accountability Task Force, 4, 17,
  19–21
pop tax, 42
Posner, Richard, 5
power, 68, 164
Pratt, Greg
  conflict with, 147, 154
  coverage of Lightfoot, 162, 205
  interactions with Lightfoot, xiii–xiv,
    xv
Precious Blood Ministry of
  Reconciliation, 72–74

Preckwinkle, Toni
  Burke scandal and, 49–52
  CTU and, 43–44
  mayoral campaign of, xii, 37–38,
    41–45
  political attacks and, 64–65
  political record of, 59
  TV commercials, 60
Presence Health, 48
Pritzker, J. B.
  COVID-19 pandemic and, 123–125,
    127–128
  elected school board bill and, 179
  election of, 71–72
  political record of, ix, 80, 117
  political strategy of, x
Progressive Caucus, 85
property taxes, 147
prosecutor position, 5
protests, 135–142, 144
public monuments, 143–145

Quigley, Mike, 184–185
Quinn, Kevin, 171
Quinn, Marty, 171
Quinn, Pat, 84, 185, 186

race and racism
  Colom on, 43
  Emanuel on, 21
  force of, 79
Ramirez, Delia, 193
Ramirez-Rosa, Carlos, 57, 71
Ramsey, Chuck, 98
Rauner, Bruce, 38, 57
real estate transfer tax, 78
Reboyras, Ariel, 71, 76
redistricting, 187

reelection bid, x–xi, 183, 189–191,
    193–195, 197–201
Reifman, David, 68
Reilly, Brendan
  advice of, 70–71
  Beale and, 163
  conflict with, 169
  interactions with Lightfoot, 78, 127,
    139, 194
Reiter, Bob, 83, 174–175
reparations, 80
respect, 78
Reyes, Norma, 6
Reyes, Victor, 53
Riccio, Anthony, 95, 98
ride-share companies, 85
riots, 138–142, 144
rivals, 29–45, 56–57
Rivera, Arnie, 117
Rodriguez Sanchez, Rossana, 71, 85,
    137–138
Rountree, Janey, 16
Ruiz, Anel, 87, 89
Rule 14, 8
runoff elections, 57–58, 203–206
Rush, Bobby, 65–66, 140
Ruthhart, Bill, 48–49
Ryan, George, 8

Sabella, Jen, 25
Sacks, Michael, 178–179
SAFE-T Act, 187
Sainvilus, Marielle, 89
Sanchez, Melissa, 86
Sanders, Bernie, 113–114
saturation policing, 132
Saulter, Keenan, 150–152, 155
Savini, Dave, 150

Sawyer, Roderick, 70, 80, 189–190
schedule, 159–161
Schiff, Adam, 185
Schneider Fabes, Lisa, 32, 71, 91
school board, 68, 105, 176–179
Schutz, Paris, 138
Scott, Michael, 76
search warrants, 149–157
Sears Tower, xi
security details, 96
Service Employees International Union
    (SEIU), 37
Servin, Dante, 41
Sessions, Jeff, 21–22
sexism, 195
Shakman-exempt positions, 51
Sharkey, Jesse
    COVID-19 pandemic and, 172,
        174–175, 180–181
    CTU and, 105–106, 113–115,
        117–119
    interactions with Lightfoot, 43,
        108–109, 176
    leadership of, 191
    on Lightfoot, 176
shutdowns, 123–128
Sidetrack, 190
Sigcho-Lopez, Byron, 154
Sinclair, Upton, 72
Smith, Brandon, 3
Smith, Jim, 87, 96, 118, 123, 146–147
Smith, Michele, 91
Smyrniotis, George, 145
Solis, Danny, 47–48, 53
South by Southwest, 122
South Side Irish Parade, 123–124
Southeast Side Labor Day Parade,
    192

Spanky the Clown, 197
Spielfogel, David, 32
Spielman, Fran, 81, 189, 205
Sposato, Nick, 140
St. Patrick's Day parade, 123–124
statues, 143–145
Stewart, Marilyn, 104
Stone, Geoffrey R., 5
Streeterville, xiv
stump speech, 50
Suffredin, Larry, 13
Sutton, Martinez, 1
Swisher, Kara, 183

Tabares, Silvana, 195
Taliaferro, Chris, 137
Taylor, Jeanette, 86–87, 163–164
teachers' strikes, 106, 116–118
Tharp, John, 151
Timothy King, 145
Tirado, Jose, 95
Towne, Brian, 185–186
trade-show industry, 122
trailer bills, 179
transition of power, 67–68
TRiiBE interview, 162
Troutman, Arenda, 86
Trump, Donald
    Burke and, 48
    congratulations from, 66
    COVID-19 pandemic and, 121
    election of, 21
    political strategy of, 205
    protests and, 141
    transition of power and, 67
    West and, 41
Trump, Ivanka, 70
Tunney, Tom, vii, 70, 132, 190–191

TV commercials, 54–55
2020 Census, xiii

Uber, 85
United Working Families (UWF), 106,
    192–193
University of Chicago, 4–5
US Attorney's Office (USAO), 5–6
US Seventh Circuit Court of Appeals, 5

vaccines, 128
Valderrama, Franklin, 1–2
Valencia, Anna, 86, 148
Vallas, Paul
    on the COVID-19 pandemic, 122
    endorsement of Lightfoot, 65
    mayoral campaign of, x, xi, xv,
        185–186, 188–189, 194, 197–200
    political record of, 27–29
    runoff election, 203–204
Van Dyke, Jason, 1, 3, 16–17, 73, 99
Vasquez, Andre, viii, 124
Veysey, John Thomas, III, 5
Viagra, 53
victory speech, 66
Villagomez, Jessica, 137
Villegas, Gilbert, 71, 78–79, 146, 161–162

Waguespack, Scott
    budget vote and, 85
    endorsement of Lightfoot, 56–57
    interactions with Lightfoot, 81
    leadership of, 70
    Preckwinkle and, 52
    protests and, 137

Waller, Fred, 94, 98, 206
Warren, Elizabeth, 117
Washington, Harold, 7, 27, 48, 77
Watson, Cleopatra, 70
Watts, Ronald, 52
Weingarten, Randi, 115
Welch, Emanuel "Chris," 172
"Welcoming City" report, 205–206
West, Kanye, 41
White, Jesse, 70
White, Rodney, 6
Williams, Chad, 166–167
Williams, Tony, 39
Willie's Hideaway Lounge shooting, 9
Wilson, Darren, 15
Wilson, Willie
    endorsement of Lightfoot, 66
    interactions with Lightfoot, 70
    mayoral campaigns of, 29–30, 44,
        186–187, 198
    reparations plan and, 80
Winters, Arewa, 140
Witzburg, Deborah, 165
World Business Chicago, 91
Wozniak, Erika, 25

Yanez, Carlos, 167
Yelp review, 61
Yin, Alice, 140
Young, Anjanette, 149–157, 163–164,
    200–201
Youngerman, Michele, 150

Ziman, Kristen, 129–130